RESPECT YOURSELF, PROTECT YOURSELF

INTERSECTION: TRANSDISCIPLINARY PERSPECTIVES
ON GENDERS AND SEXUALITIES
General Editors: Michael Kimmel and Suzanna Walters

*Sperm Counts: Overcome by Man's Most
Precious Fluid*
Lisa Jean Moore

*The Sexuality of Migration: Border
Crossings and Mexican Immigrant Men*
Lionel Cantú, Jr.
Edited by Nancy A. Naples and Salvador
Vidal-Ortiz

*Moral Panics, Sex Panics: Fear and
the Fight over Sexual Rights*
Edited by Gilbert Herdt

*Out in the Country: Youth, Media, and
Queer Visibility in Rural America*
Mary L. Gray

*Sapphistries: A Global History of Love
between Women*
Leila J. Rupp

Strip Club: Gender, Power, and Sex Work
Kim Price-Glynn

*Sex for Life: From Virginity to Viagra, How
Sexuality Changes throughout Our Lives*
Edited by Laura M. Carpenter and John
DeLamater

*The Bully Society: School Shootings and the
Crisis of Bullying in America's Schools*
Jessie Klein

*One Marriage Under God: The Campaign
to Promote Marriage in America*
Melanie Heath

*Respect Yourself, Protect Yourself:
Latina Girls and Sexual Identity*
Lorena Garcia

Respect Yourself, Protect Yourself

Latina Girls and Sexual Identity

Lorena Garcia

NEW YORK UNIVERSITY PRESS
New York and London

NEW YORK UNIVERSITY PRESS
New York and London
www.nyupress.org

References to Internet websites (URLs) were accurate at the time of writing.
Neither the author nor New York University Press is responsible
for URLs that may have expired or changed since the manuscript was prepared.

LIBRARY OF CONGRESS CATALOGING-IN-PUBLICATION DATA
Garcia, Lorena.
Respect yourself, protect yourself : Latina girls and sexual identity / Lorena Garcia.
p. cm. — (Intersections)
Includes bibliographical references and index.
ISBN 978-0-8147-3316-5 (cl : alk. paper)
ISBN 978-0-8147-3317-2 (pb : alk. paper)
ISBN 978-0-8147-3318-9 (ebook)
ISBN 978-0-8147-6991-1 (ebook)
1. Hispanic American teenage girls—United States—Psychology. 2. Self-perception in adolescence—United States. 3. Gender identity—United States. 4. Sex instruction for girls—United States. I. Title.
HQ798.G37 2012
155.2—dc23
2012016649

New York University Press books are printed on acid-free paper,
and their binding materials are chosen for strength and durability.
We strive to use environmentally responsible suppliers and materials
to the greatest extent possible in publishing our books.

Manufactured in the United States of America
c 10 9 8 7 6 5 4 3 2 1
p 10 9 8 7 6 5 4 3 2 1

I dedicate this book with love
to my parents, Aurelio and Mercedes;
to Noe, my partner in this life;
and to our amazing sons, Nicolas and Leonardo.

CONTENTS

ACKNOWLEDGMENTS

I am deeply grateful to the young Latinas and mothers who participated in this study. This book would not have been possible without their willingness to share very personal aspects of their lives. I hope that I have done some justice to their words and experiences. I am also very appreciative of the Chicago community organizations that opened their doors to me.

I thank the following institutions for their instrumental support in the form of financial resources or time off from teaching at various stages of this project: the Center for Chicano Studies at the University of California at Santa Barbara (Chicano/Latino Working Poor Research Grant); the Social Science Research Council (Sexuality Research Dissertation Fellowship); the Woodrow Wilson National Fellowship Foundation (Dissertation Grant in Women's Studies); the UCSB Graduate Division (Fletcher Jones Dissertation Fellowship and Graduate Opportunity Fellowship); and the Institute for Research on Race and Public Policy Fellowship at the University of Illinois at Chicago.

I also want to thank New York University Press, especially executive editor Ilene Kalish; her editorial assistant, Aiden Amos; editing and production assistant Alexia Traganas; and copyeditor Jerilyn Famighetti, as well the anonymous reviewers for all of their hard work helping me to get this book ready for publication.

I was blessed to have the opportunity to work with and learn from my advisor, Denise Segura, in the department of sociology at the University of California, Santa Barbara (UCSB). I am indebted to her for her investment in me, for her guidance, and for her confidence in the significance of this project from the very start. Her mentorship and friendship have been invaluable to me. I have also benefited tremendously from my interactions with other UCSB faculty who have provided me with important advice and feedback. A special thank-you to Beth Schneider, Sarah Fenstermaker, and Avery Gordon for contributing to my development as a sociologist. I also received encouragement, nurturance, friendship, and mentoring from my graduate school peers. Much gratitude to these folks, especially Lorena Torres, Light Carruyo, Susana Peña, Peter Chua, Carlos Alamo-Pastrana, Sylvanna Falcon,

Karl Bryant, Darcie Vandegrift, Molly Talcott, Dana Collins, Socorro Casta-ñeda-Liles, Meika Loe, and Elida Bautista.

This book was written at the University of Illinois at Chicago (UIC), where I have immensely benefited from the wholehearted support of a rich network of colleagues and friends, particularly in the department of sociol-ogy and in the Gender and Women's Studies and Latin American and Latino Studies programs. I especially thank my mentoring team, Laurie Schaffner and Stephen Warner. Steve has closely read my work, enthusiastically offer-ing substantial feedback, and Laurie has shared instrumental insights. She consistently reminded me to focus on completing this book, especially at moments when I was tempted to take on other professional responsibilities. I am so glad I listened to her. I am grateful to Barbara Risman for connect-ing me with my fabulous mentoring team and also for the mentoring she has offered me. On numerous occasions, she provided me with generous feed-back on drafts of manuscripts, including some chapters of this book. Thanks also to Nilda Flores-González for being so giving in countless ways, from providing me with strategic professional advice to sharing her lunch with me, I have learned much from her. I am also appreciative of Anna Guevarra. We both worked together many late nights in our department offices and it really made the writing of this book less lonely on those evenings.

I would also like to thank other colleagues and friends at UIC and else-where: Badia Ahad, Frances Aparicio, Jennifer Brier, Michelle Boyd, Cory Capers, Andy Clarno, Cathy Cohen, Sharon Collins, Claire Decoteau, Maria de los Angeles Torres, Tyrone Forman, Francesca Gaiba, Myrna García, Judith Gardiner, Elena Gutiérrez, Ayesha Hardison, Marisha Humphries, Helen Jun, Maria Krysan, *Las Profes* Online Writing Group (Mari Castañeda, Martha Fuentes-Bautista, Amanda Lewis, and Mérida Rúa), Zitlali Morales, Amalia Pallares, Chavella Pittman, Isaura Pulido, Barbara Ransby, Gayatri Reddy, Beth Richie, Kerry Ann Rockquemore, David Stovall, Arlene Torres, and Lourdes Torres for saying or doing something at just the right time, no matter how small, to keep me moving forward. I also want to thank Lillian Gorman for her detailed editing of the Spanish language in the manuscript. And I thank my research assistants: Alexandrina Almazan, Priya Bhatnager, Amy Brainer, and Jeniffer De La Rosa.

A special note of thanks to Mérida Rúa for being there for me when I needed to vent or just have a good laugh. She has been an encouraging and constructive sounding board every step of the way. Importantly, she has always made sure that I celebrate every single milestone in this process.

My deepest appreciation to my parents, Aurelio and Mercedes, as well as my siblings, Orlando, Yesenia, and Nora, for their unconditional love and support. My parents have always reminded of the importance of faith and of being grateful for all of my blessings, big and small. My sincerest gratitude to you for teaching me to see the extraordinary in the ordinary—a lesson that has always served me well.

Finally, I want to especially acknowledge my loving partner, Noe, and our sons, Nicolas and Leonardo, for all that they do for me. They have lovingly and so very patiently cheered me on to the finish line, especially when I felt I could not take another step. They always gave me space and time to write when I needed them without a single complaint. Noe, *mil gracias*, for going above and beyond the call of duty so often to make my life easier when I was completely overwhelmed with this project. You and our sons have profoundly enriched my life, and I thank you both for the constant reminder to slow down and be in the moment. Thank you for keeping me grounded and for helping me keep it all in perspective.

1

Introduction

Studying the "Other" Girls

I walked eighteen-year-old Alicia to the reception area of the Chi-Town Health Teen Center after we wrapped up our first interview. I had met the high school senior two weeks earlier when she came in for an appointment to obtain birth control pills. We chatted about our weekend plans as we made our way toward the door, the previously busy waiting room, with its colorful flyers and posters, now empty. One hot-pink flyer shouted, "Come join our teen group!" Another bright-green flyer simply read, "Please ask for your brown bag at the front counter" (each bag contained twelve condoms). A large poster featuring a smiling brown-skinned Latino baby asked, "Have you immunized your child?" In less than thirty minutes, the center would close for the day; the rusted steel folding gate on the outside entrance was already extended at four in the afternoon. Alicia paused in front of the door to cautiously pull back the curtains on the windows of the double doors. Nervously surveying the street, she explained that she did not want to be "busted" by her parents or other relatives as she left the center. She had told her parents that she was going to attend a yearbook club meeting after school on that Friday. Satisfied that she would not be discovered at the Chi-Town Health Teen Center, the confident young Mexican woman quickly said good-bye and stepped outside. I stood in the doorway and watched her briskly walk away as she tightly clutched her backpack straps; I kept an eye on her until she turned a corner a block away.

More than a month after our initial interview, Alicia and a couple of her friends were in the "teen computer lab" at Hogar del Pueblo, another community organization in her Chicago West Town neighborhood on the city's Near Northwest Side. Alicia participated in a youth program there. On that unseasonably warm October afternoon, the three young women had the computer lab to themselves, since the rest of their peers were hanging out in the gym or in the youth lounge, where typically they listened to hip hop or reggaeton music, played pool, or just sat on couches or tables to talk. Despite having access to at least ten unused computers that afternoon, Alicia and her friends were tightly gathered around her computer monitor, concentrating on a Planned Parenthood website. They were doing homework, so they said, for a class project on health; I was already in the computer lab editing a "youth program" flyer as part of my volunteer service at Hogar del Pueblo. "Well, it says that the pill is like almost 99 percent effective," one of Alicia's friends said as she pointed to the screen. "But," without looking away from the screen, Alicia quickly responded, "you gotta be able to take it every day." Clicking onto other links, she furrowed her brow and tightened her lips as she and her friends continued to discuss the effectiveness of different birth control options for the next forty minutes. At one point, Alicia seemed to hold back tears as her lips slightly trembled. Immediately, one of her friends gave her a reassuring hug and squeezed her arm. Witnessing this exchange, I felt my stomach drop slightly as I wondered if Alicia had forgotten to take a birth control pill and now worried that she was pregnant. She left before I had a chance to ask her if she was all right.

I found out why Alicia was upset a week later when we sat down for our second interview. With anger in her voice, she said that her fourteen-year-old sister and she had been fighting over whose turn it was to wash the dishes when her sister suddenly told their parents that Alicia had a boyfriend. "They started trippin' and yellin' at me because they don't let us have boyfriends," she told me tearfully. "My dad is always like, 'You can't have a boyfriend until you're like thirty,' which is really stupid!" The next day, Alicia came home from school to find the bedroom she shared with her sister turned inside out. Her mother, having just scoured the bedroom, sat on Alicia's bed. "She was like, 'I'm only gonna ask you this once and you better tell me the truth, have you had sexual relations with your boyfriend?' I was like, 'Nope,' and acted like I didn't know what she was talking about." Relieved that her mother had not discovered her birth control pills or condoms hidden between some books, Alicia told me, "She probably would've sent me to Mexico or something crazy like that if she found them!" In the wake of that confrontation, Alicia opted to use the Depo-Provera shot after researching birth control methods with her friends. This was the "class project on health" they were doing the day I saw them together in the Hogar del Pueblo computer lab. Picking at a loose thread on the wrist of her worn sweater, Alicia confided, "To tell you the truth, I really don't want to be using the shot 'cause some of the stuff I read about it freaks me out. . . . But at least my mom can't find out. Like with the pills, there's always a chance. And I keep my condoms in my school locker now, she can't be all up in my business there." She continued, "I know that people think that girls my age shouldn't be bothering with sex right now because of this or that." Pausing, she then insisted, "But that's like saying that we have no sexual feelings, which ain't true! I thought a lot about it [sex] before doing anything and made sure I knew how to take care myself. No one made me do anything." Alicia's experiences in making choices about and gaining access to safe-sex resources highlight just some of the challenges Latina girls face in their efforts to practice safe sex.[1]

The Latina girls I came to know, like Alicia, told me about their efforts to sexually "take care" of themselves or "handle" their business and the challenges they encounter in doing so, exhibiting behaviors and perspectives that do not quite fit into the prevailing idea that the sexuality of young women, particularly that of girls of color, is a social problem. Many may resist picturing what this entails for a teenage girl, especially for a young woman of color, because of the firmly held expectation and belief that they should abstain from sexual activities until marriage or at least until they are more mature and responsible. Others may acknowledge that young women are sexual beings and assert that if they are going to engage in sexual activities, they should practice safe sex, but without any real consideration of exactly what this demands of girls.[2] For instance, the simple act of opening the door to a health center requires girls to negotiate their own understanding of their sexuality, as well as to reckon with what others expect of them or think of their sexuality. The conversations and exchanges I had with Latina girls and some of their mothers during two years of fieldwork for this book reveal that there is an untold story about Latina youth and sexuality, one that goes beyond their pregnancy, birth, and STD rates.

This book evolved out of my experiences working with pregnant and parenting teenage girls at a Chicago-area teen health center from the mid- to late 1990s. This was my first job after graduating from college, and I was eager to roll up my sleeves and to put my sociology degree to use in my community. I came to know and learn from a tremendous group of women at the center—midwives, nurses, medical assistants, licensed clinical social workers, case managers, health educators, and intake receptionists—who were all committed to providing quality, affordable, and accessible health care and social services to young people. As at many other nonprofit organizations that serve poor and low-income communities, the staff had to be flexible in terms of the tasks individuals took on to meet the needs of the young people, predominantly Latina/o youth, who walked through our doors. Thus, in addition to my case manager duties for the pregnant and parenting teen program, I sometimes worked with girls at the center who were not pregnant or parenting but who were there for any of a variety of other services. They were brave young women seeking safe-sex resources, HIV testing, or information about their sexual and reproductive health care rights or just looking for someone to listen to them and reassure them of their right to dream about and pursue promising futures.

These girls are doing some of the very things that we often say we want young people to do when concerns about their ability to make informed sexual choices are raised. But these are not the young women we usually talk to in our development of research, policy, and program efforts to address the negative sexual outcomes that disproportionately impact young women of color. Instead, we tend to focus on identifying and correcting the "problematic" sexual behavior of girls of color. We want to know answers to the following types of questions: Why do they get pregnant? Why do they have sex so young? Why do they get STDs? And why do they not practice safe sex? These questions, of course, are important and deserve our attention, but not all of it. My interactions with Latina youth at the health center made me realize that we know very little about other dimensions of their sexual lives, such as their understandings of and approaches to safe sex. My questions and concerns about these "other" girls followed me to graduate school and informed what would become the topic of *Respect Yourself, Protect Yourself*.

The Crisis in Youth Sexuality Research

The sexuality of young people, particularly girls' sexual behavior, has generally been approached as a crisis. The dominant stance in our society on the sexuality of teenage girls is that of a problem: "sexually active" girls are promiscuous, engage in unprotected sex, get pregnant, have children, and thus find themselves socially, economically, and educationally deprived and disadvantaged.[3] Undeniably, these are serious consequences that should not be taken lightly. Nevertheless, this approach to studying girls' sexuality is problematic and limiting in several ways. First, research on the sexuality of young people predominantly fixates on girls, thereby continuing to place the burden of the "problem" of pregnancy and STDs onto young women. Second, because the focus on girls is encoded in a racial scheme, sexually active young women of color become, in effect, the problem itself.[4] If we look closely at the "crisis" framing of girls' sexuality, it becomes clear that we are talking about not all groups of girls but African American and Latina girls specifically. Third, quite often this research conflates sexuality and pregnancy.[5] This narrow perspective has led to an overpowering emphasis on pregnancy prevention, with inadequate attention paid to the meanings that youth assign to their sexuality.[6] And, yet, as the sociologist Janice M. Irvine argues, it is precisely these meanings that can allow us to unpack the myriad ways in which youth negotiate their sexuality and sexual experiences.[7]

This book explores the meaning and practice of sexuality in the lives of Latina girls. Through a focus on their sexual agency, it explains the processes by which some Latina girls engage ideas about safe sex and choose to enact self-protective sexual practices and, more important, how this relates to their understanding and negotiation of their emerging sexuality. This book shows that Latina girls' sexual lives are complicated and involve a confrontation with racism, patriarchal and heterosexual privilege, and socioeconomic marginality. Drawing on twenty-four months of ethnographic research and interviews with second-generation Mexican and Puerto Rican young women and their mothers, *Respect Yourself, Protect Yourself* highlights the challenges that emerge for Latina girls when they seek to practice safe sex while still maintaining their claim to a respectable femininity in a larger sociocultural context in which they are not recognized as sexual actors. I found that central to their strategies for negotiating the contradictions and dilemmas they faced as sexual actors who are young, working class, and Latina was the notion of sexual respectability.

Women of color have historically been sexually stereotyped in the United States. For instance, African American women have been depicted as sexually aggressive and uncontrollable, Latinas as sexually provocative and hypersexual, and Asian women as sexually submissive, "dragon ladies," or a combination of the two. Despite the differences in the stereotypes associated with each group, these constructions have all rested upon the idea of the moral superiority of white women, specifically middle- and upper-class white women. Scholars who have focused on the connections among gender, sexuality, and race/ethnicity have documented how racialized communities elaborate on ideas about morality to challenge negative depictions of women of color.[8] These scholars have demonstrated how some of these communities articulate and present a "politics of respectability" that is especially anchored in the sexual integrity of women of color as a way to either reflect the community's sexual values as similar to those of white middle- and upper-class culture or to claim superiority over the dominant society. Importantly, this work has highlighted the ways in which this strategy to counter racism has also exacerbated the inequalities that women and LGBTQ-identified individuals experience both within and outside their communities, pointing to a need to better understand how different members of the same community may experience a politics of respectability. This book expands on and contributes to this scholarship by accounting for the ways in which second-generation Mexican and Puerto Rican girls engage a politics of respectability in their formation of sexual identities, particularly their sexual subjectivities.

Gender and Sexuality as Social Constructs

Sexual subjectivity is a productive point of entry through which to investigate girls' meanings of sexuality and safe sex, as well as the strategies they develop in relation to these meanings.[9] The developmental psychologist Deborah L. Tolman posits sexual subjectivity as a "person's experience of herself as a sexual being, who feels entitled to sexual pleasure and sexual safety, who makes active sexual choices, and who has an identity as a sexual being."[10] Attending to how girls form their sense of themselves as sexual beings brings to the foreground their sexual agency, which refers to the ability to make choices about one's own body and to control and modify one's sexual practices. It includes deciding whether and how to act on sexual feelings.[11] Research has consistently shown that girls across various groups often have a difficult time acknowledging themselves as sexual subjects and enacting their sexual agency in empowering ways.[12] In general, girls' descriptions of their sexual experiences and feelings reflect a perception of themselves as sexual objects, rather than as sexual subjects. That is, they tend to see sex as something that just happens to them, rather than something that they decide on or desire. Previous studies have identified some of the mechanisms that contribute to girls' limited sexual subjectivity, such as mother-daughter communication about sex, age at sexual initiation, sexual double standards, and a culture and ideology of love and romance, providing further evidence that the gender patterns we often observe in relation to sexuality, far from simply reflecting biologically rooted "drives," are produced by social practices.

I analyze the social processes that shape Latina girls' sexual experiences and relevant identity formations. A social constructionism theoretical framework informs my investigation of Latina girls' gender and sexuality. This perspective on both gender and sexuality has proved to be fruitful in advancing new knowledge and questions. Research guided by this theoretical position has challenged the assumption that gender and sexuality are naturally occurring categories by exposing the ways particular meanings are assigned to these categories and how they are utilized to organize our social world in ways that privilege some groups and disadvantage others. The "doing gender" approach is one such social constructionist theorization that has shed light on how gender is understood to be something that women and men accomplish in social interaction. Rather than attending to gender as traits and behaviors that individuals possess, this approach analyzes gender as a situated accomplishment that is influenced by accountability. That is, it views social interactions as involving judgments about how individuals meet expectations of appropriate feminity and masculinity, so that the people involved in a given exchange within a certain context are aware that they are being evaluated on their adherence to gender prescriptions.[13] By attending to how men and women "do gender" and, more recently, how they "undo gender" in social interactions, as well as by exploring the social construction of gender at the level of identities and institutions and the integration of all of these approaches, feminist sociologists have been able to convincingly argue that it is gender inequality that creates gender differences, not the other way around.[14]

Sexuality scholars in disciplines such as sociology and history and in interdisciplinary fields such as queer studies and race/ethnic studies have also demonstrated that sexuality, far from being just an aspect of one's identity, is given shape and meaning by larger social, political, and historical forces that are marked by struggles for power.[15] For instance, critiquing heterosexuality as a phenomenon that is often taken for granted in theoretical and empirical work on sexuality, several scholars have interrogated heterosexuality and made evident some of the ways in which heterosexuality is organized, maintained, and reproduced in our society.[16] Thus, a key insight of a social construction framework has been an explication of how gender and sexuality constitute modes of inequality that structure experiences and opportunities. Some scholarship grounded in this theoretical stance has also challenged the assumption of a natural relationship between gender and sexuality in which gender is perceived as automatically dictating the expression of sexuality or sexual identity. The poststructuralist philosopher, Judith Butler, for example, conceptualizes gender as a performance that is limited by the rules of normative heterosexuality.[17] According to Butler, the repetition of heteronormative gender performances serves to reinforce our understanding and acceptance of gender as a neat, dichotomous category. This theorization of gender also invites us to consider sexuality (along with sex) as performative. As the anthropologist Gayle Rubin asserts, while gender and sexuality do seem to influence one another, sexuality should not be and cannot be explained by gender alone.[18] Instead, care should be taken to explore analytically their specific dynamics and how they inform one another.

In this book, I consider the relationship between gender and sexuality in the lives of working-class Latinas. But, in doing so, I bring into analytic view the relevance of race and ethnicity and generational status. My approach to the study of Mexican and Puerto Rican girls' construction and experience of sexuality, safe sex, and identities is centrally grounded in the broader framework of intersectionality.[19] This theoretical perspective underscores the need to account for the intersecting or interlocking relationships that link social formations, such as race/ethnicity, class, gender, sexuality, and age. Categories such as gender, sexuality, and race/ethnicity are therefore understood to constitute one other to produce differential experiences and opportunities for groups.[20] Intersectionality has been a powerful analytical tool for the study of Latina sexualities, especially in that it has provided Chicana and Latina feminist scholars a means by which to challenge the tendency to rely on stereotypes about Latina/o sexualities in the formulation of research agendas and explanations.[21] Until quite recently, research on Latinas/os sexual lives has primarily focused on describing "Latina/o culture," often in very problematic ways. Culture is too often taken for granted in studies of Latinas/os, approached as an unchanging factor that heavily influences Latina/o sexual and reproductive attitudes and behaviors. I strongly agree with other sociologists who study Latina/o sexualities about the need to move beyond and to complicate cultural frameworks.[22] One way to develop more sophisticated analyses of sexualities that do not overemphasize culture at the expense of structure is to develop our sociological inquiry into meaning-making, which necessitates that we expand our analysis beyond the standard categories associated with culture: values, norms, and behaviors.[23] I follow the sociologist Ann Swidler's assertion that a culture is not a unified system pushing action in a consistent direction but, rather, a "tool kit" or repertoire of skills, habits, and styles (rather than values or preferences) that provides the resources from which individuals and groups select to develop strategies of action.[24] *Respect Yourself, Protect Yourself* privileges the sexual agency of young Latinas to uncover and understand how the interplay between structure and culture shapes their sexual lives.

Methods

My investigation of how Latina girls experience their emerging sexuality and their approaches to safe sex entails in-depth interviews with Mexican and Puerto Rican young women, as well as with a subset of mothers, and ethnographic fieldwork conducted in Chicago between September 2002 and November 2004.[25] Home to the one of largest Mexican and Puerto Rican communities in the United States[26] and with an extensive history of inter-Latina/o exchanges,[27] Chicago is a rich site from which to continue to develop knowledge of U.S. Latina/o sexual identities, practices, and cultures. At the time of this study, the second largest Mexican and Puerto Rican communities in the United States resided in Chicago. The sample of Latina youth includes twenty Mexican-origin girls and twenty Puerto Rican girls. Of those, eight self-identified as lesbian and the rest as heterosexual. The average age of young women was sixteen. With the exception of one girl,[28] all are second generation, the U.S.-born children of immigrants and/or migrants, meaning that at least one parent was born in Mexico or Puerto Rico. All lived with their working-class families, their parents generally employed in the service sector or in factories. The sample of eighteen mothers included ten Mexican women and eight Puerto Rican women; four of the mothers had daughters who identified as lesbian. Appendix A provides more demographic information about the study participants.

To maintain confidentiality, I have assigned pseudonyms to study participants, the people they reference in their interviews, and the organizations they accessed. And, with the exception of their self-identified racial/ethnic identities and ages, I have also altered the physical descriptions for all the girls and mothers, for example, changing the hair length and/or height of one study participant, while altering the weight and/or hair color of another study participant. I felt that this was necessary to safeguard the anonymity of the girls and their mothers.

I recruited participants through four Chicago community organizations, all of which offered services for youth at the time of my fieldwork (I offer more information about each of the organizations in Appendix B). I established access to the agencies through my previous employment at one of the community organizations, where I worked with pregnant and parenting teens. Three of the organizations were concentrated in the West Town area when I conducted this study, which is composed of neighborhoods located just west and northwest of the Loop (Downtown Chicago area). At the time of the study, Mexicans constituted 53.1 percent of the Latina/o population in West Town, and Puerto Ricans made up 35.6 percent of that population. In

2000, the median income for Latina/o households in this area was $28,157. Low-income Latina/o families in this area have been steadily experiencing displacement as a result of the gentrification process that gathered momentum in the 1990s; while 62 percent of the West Town population was Latina/o in 1990, in 2000 Latinas/os fell to 46.9 percent of West Town residents.[29] The other agency is located in the Pilsen neighborhood (Chicago's Lower West Side), located just south and west of the Loop. Latinas/os in Pilsen have remained a majority, holding steady at 88 percent of the Pilsen population between 1990 and 2000; during my fieldwork, Mexicans constituted 91.7 percent of the Pilsen Latina/o population, and Puerto Ricans made up 1.9 percent of that population. In 2000, the median income for Latina/o households in Pilsen was $27,610.[30] Pilsen has been more successful than West Town in challenging gentrification; however, the mid-1990s southward expansion of the University of Illinois at Chicago has heightened developer interest in the area, threatening to continue to displace community residents.

I interviewed young women who met the following criteria: (a) self-identified as Mexican or Puerto Rican, (b) self-defined as sexually active, (c) between the ages of thirteen and eighteen, (d) self-defined as practicing safe sex and, (e) had no children. I provide consent process details in Appendix B. Rather than define the term "sexually active" for research participants, I asked them to share their understandings of the term to better comprehend Latina girls' constructions of sexuality. I also sought to capture Latina girls' conceptualizations of safe sex. Young people have been a target audience for safe-sex education campaigns, and it is important to consider how youth translate them and fuse them into their own meaning system. Thus, I did not impose a definition of the term "safe sex" in my recruitment or exclude girls from the study if they did not report consistent condom, dental dam, or finger cot use (behavior most typically associated with safe sex). Instead, I asked participants what "safe sex" meant to them. The requirement for participants to self-define as practicing safe sex provided insight into how girls come to see themselves as practicing safe sex, the processes that inform their definitions of safe sex and enactment of safe sex, and what this means for their formation of sexual identities. Using focused but open-ended questions, I asked girls about their lives at home, in their communities, and at school, especially asking that they share with me their views about their sexuality and gender, their understandings of safe sex, and the meanings they assign to their sexual experiences. I conducted two to three in-depth interviews with each participant and transcribed all interviews. With the exception of interviews with five girls that took place in their homes, all interviews with young women occurred at the community centers in private rooms.

I gained access to mothers through their daughters. At the conclusion of our first interview, I asked young women if their mothers might be willing to participate in this study. I asked this only of young women who had obtained parental consent, since their mothers were already aware that their daughters were participants in a study on Latina youth and sexuality. If girls indicated that their mothers would be interested in being interviewed, I then asked them to provide my contact information to their mothers. Thus, the mothers in this sample initiated contact with me about their participation in the project. Using focused but open-ended questions, I asked the mothers about their current lives, the gender and sexual scripts they teach their daughters, their perceptions of their own sexuality and that of their daughters, and their understanding of safe sex. I conducted one to two interviews with each mother and transcribed all of these interviews, as well. Upon their invitation, I usually interviewed mothers in their homes.

At the onset of interviews, I asked participants what language they preferred for their interview. The interviews with young women were carried out primarily in English, although girls code-switched into Spanish on occasion throughout their conversations. Focusing on a Puerto Rican community in New York City, the anthropolitical linguist Ana Celia Zentella writes about the value of code-switching for Latinas/os, noting that "switching serves many significant social and discourse functions beyond that of filling in forgotten words or phrases [Duran 1981] . . . code-switching allows Puerto Ricans to make a graphic statement about the way they live with a foot in each of 'Dos Worlds/Two Mundos.'"[31] The young women I spoke with occasionally utilized the Spanish language to communicate their negotiations of experiences and meanings of such an intimate subject as sexuality. In terms of the mothers, fourteen mothers requested Spanish as the language for their interviews. I have translated the Spanish-language interviews into English. However, in using quotations, I have kept some of their Spanish phrases and words. Of the four mothers who did not request Spanish-language interviews, two of them stated that they did not have a language preference for their interview. However, these four mothers did code-switch frequently throughout their interviews, weaving English and Spanish together within their narratives.

I supplemented formal interviews with participant observation and informal interviews with Latina girls. This component of my fieldwork allowed me to complement and clarify some of the information I had collected during interviews with study participants. This strategy also permitted me to gain further insight into contexts and interactions within which young Latinas negotiate and express their sexual subjectivity, particularly moments they shared with their peers.

On Being Both an Insider and an Outsider

As the U.S.-born daughter of Mexican immigrants who was raised in a work-ing-class Latina/o neighborhood in the West Town community of Chicago, I entered the field anticipating that my shared identity with the young women and their mothers would shape my rapport and interactions with them and also have certain implications for how my presence as a researcher would be interpreted by them. Feminist scholars' analyses of a researcher's multiple identities have highlighted the significance of insider and outsider identi-ties in the field.[32] In her assessment of what she terms the "insider/outsider debate," the sociologist Nancy Naples points out that the fixed distinction often made between insider and outsider positioning obscures the dynam-ics of power and difference between researchers and study participants, rather than shedding light on them. She argues, "The bipolar construction of insider/outsider also sets up a false separation that neglects the interactive processes through which 'insiderness' and 'outsiderness' is constructed. . . . Rather, they are ever-shifting and permeable social locations that are dif-ferentially experienced and expressed by community members."[33] Guided by such insight on researcher positionality, I entered into the study with an understanding of my identity as fluid rather fixed, permitting me to be more sensitive to how it was constructed by the research participants and by myself and the implications of this for our interactions, as well as the data I was able to collect.

It was in our interviews that Latina youth and mothers interrogated aspects of my identity in greater depth. Before we began our first "formal" interview, study participants interviewed me on topics such as my age, educational experiences, ethnicity, and marital status, in addition to the intended purpose and use of the project itself. Girls were usually much more direct in their questioning, asking me how old I was or where I lived and with whom. In her self-reflexive account of her study on urban working-class households in Turkey, the sociologist Hale C. Bolak also found that one key way in which research participants developed their perceptions of her as an insider and/or outsider was by asking her questions related to her gender identity, class background, and relationship status.[34] Similarly, the sociologist Naheed Islam experienced informants' "pre-interviews" of her in her research on race in an Asian community in Los Angeles.[35] She under-stood these "pre-interviews" as a means for study participants to evaluate her relationship to members of the community and her specific gendered constructions of community. The topic that Latinas girls and their moth-ers were most curious about in our "pre-interviews" was my educational experiences. They wanted to know about living in a dorm as an undergraduate student, how my parents felt about my leaving home to go to college and, later, graduate school, and how I convinced them to "let me" go. They were also interested in the college application process and how I paid for school. Many of them asked for advice on these educational issues. I regarded all of their questions and concerns, including personal questions, as important to the research.[36]

I also negotiated my positionality in the field by making certain decisions about my clothing choices. I was in my late twenties when I conducted my fieldwork but appeared to be younger. I opted to dress casually when at the community organizations unless there was a special event, such as an awards ceremony. Generally, I wore jeans, a t-shirt or sweater, including sweatshirts, and athletic shoes or sneakers. This decision was informed by my observation of the attire worn by the majority of the youth program staff at the organizations where I most regularly interacted with groups of young people. Though the youth program staff introduced me to the young people and explained that I was a graduate student working on a research project, I believe that most of the youth perceived me to be a social work intern or college student there to volunteer. I decided early on to volunteer at the agencies as way to establish trust with interview respondents and as part of my reciprocation efforts. My work as a volunteer at all but one of the organizations did permit the young women to become familiar with me prior to their first interviews. During these first interviews, in which young women asked me questions about myself, all of them learned that I was from Chicago; some discovered that I had grown up in the same neighborhood as they had, and a handful came to realize that we were graduates of the same elementary school. After the initial interview, they each seemed more relaxed with me, suggested by their lengthier conversations with me, their willingness to confide in me, or their occasional inclusion of me in some of their interactions with peers while hanging out at the organizations.

I chose to modify my clothing selections for my interactions with mothers. Given my youthful appearance when I conducted my fieldwork, I made it a point to "dress up" more in preparing to interview them, opting to wear dress pants or jeans and a career-type blouse or sweater, along with dress shoes, such as flats or boots. This decision was also informed by my desire to help mothers feel as comfortable as possible, given the sensitive nature of the interview topic. I thought this would be facilitated by my adoption of a more professional appearance in their presence, allowing them to feel more at ease about the legitimacy of my researcher training and knowledge about sexuality. Furthermore, I hoped to communicate my respect for them as adults and for their time. An important lesson that was communicated early on to my siblings and me by our parents and by other family members was that we needed to present ourselves as being "bien educada or educado." This referred to the importance of seeming well educated to others, not in a traditional school sense but, rather, by reflecting that one was raised properly. Importantly, this meant that you knew how to be well mannered and show others the proper respect they deserved, especially adults. I was concerned that if I dressed "too" casually, the mothers might read this as an indication that I did not think they were important enough for me take care with my appearance. This "outfit strategy" might have been different if the main focus of the study were not sexuality, particularly daughters' sexuality, and if I had more opportunities to interact with mothers outside of interviews.

It is undeniable that my status as a cultural "insider" mattered in critical ways for how my fieldwork experiences unfolded; for instance, it facilitated my ability to gain access to study participants, shaped the framing of some of the questions I posed to them, and permitted me to be attuned to the nuances in their meanings and practices of sexuality, including safe sex. The ability for my informants and me to relate to each other became apparent in some of the stories they shared with me, with which I could identify because of my own experiences growing up in circumstances similar to those in which they now lived— educational inequalities in Chicago Public Schools, the significance of particular family formations, such as that of *compadrazgo* (co-parenthood with extended family members and/or friends), and struggles with certain neighborhood-related issues, such as gang violence, poverty, and gentrification.

Nonetheless, I learned from the self-reflexive analyses of researchers who also shared similarities with those they studied that I could not assume ready access to informants or expect them to automatically feel a certain level of comfort with me just because of our shared identities. Equally as important, I knew that I had to be careful not to take my "insider" status and knowledge for granted.[37] This meant that I had to be willing to delve deeper and ask questions to which they expected me to know the answer as a cultural "insider," though some of their stories and experiences might resonate with my own or those of other women I knew. When I probed and asked them to explain a perspective or experience they shared with me, it was not uncommon for some of them to give me a perplexed look or even tell me, "Don't you know this?" This helped me become cognizant of the need to simultaneously negotiate my "insider" status and my identity as a feminist researcher. It was in those instances that some of the important differences between my informants and myself became apparent to both of us.

Re-Thinking "At Risk" Youth

As of 2009, Latinas/os were the largest and youngest nonwhite racial/ethnic group in the United States, accounting for 18 percent of all young people in the United States between the ages of sixteen and twenty-five.[38] Because of the size and age of this population, along with the number of births to Latina teens, Latina youth have recently emerged as the central subjects of concern and objects of intervention efforts related to sexual and reproductive outcomes. Much of the literature on the sexuality of Latina girls is encapsulated within a discourse of risk. Research on pregnancy and sexually transmitted diseases treats Latina girls as an "at risk" population. Empirically, there is some reason to do so. For example, despite celebratory announcements of a decrease in over-all U.S. teen births between 1991 and 2002, the decline in pregnancy rates was less steep among Latina girls. Since 1995, they have had the highest teen birth rate among all other major racial/ethnic groups in the United States.[39] In addition, the Centers for Disease Control considers Latina/o youth to be at increasing risk for contracting sexually transmitted infections. While I do not dispute such data, I suggest that they paint a one-dimensional picture of Latina girls' sexual lives. My research findings show that the reality is far more complex.

Some research has strategically homed in on the experiences of certain youth we often fail to take notice of in our quest to document and explain the various risks and failures besetting young people living in disadvantaged communities.[40] This body of scholarship presents young men and women as active agents, focusing on how they navigate the multiple inequalities shaping their lives to construct more positive realities, outcomes, and futures than what is predicted for them. For instance, the sociologist Frank F. Furstenberg Jr. and his colleagues have shed new light on the lives and outcomes of young people growing up in poverty by exploring how success unfolds for youth living in poor socioeconomic circumstances.[41] Similarly, some education research has contributed to our understanding of pathways to academic achievement for marginalized youth, especially for students of color.[42] The sociologist Prudence L. Carter, for instance, contributes new understandings of how African American and Latina/o students' formation of racial and ethnic identities can positively inform their ability to be successful in school.[43]

Alongside this intellectual orientation, there have also been groundbreaking edited volumes that highlight the agency, strengths, and positive development of young women of color. Some key works falling into this category include *Urban Girls: Resisting Stereotypes, Creating Identities*, edited by Bonnie J. Ross Leadbeater and Niobe Way; *Sugar in the Raw*, by Rebecca Carroll; *My Sisters' Voices: Teenage Girls of Color Speak Out*, edited by Iris Jacob; *Colonize This!*, edited by Daisy Hernández and Bushra Rehman; and *Urban Girls Revisited*, edited by Bonnie J. Ross Leadbeater and Niobe Way. Together, these texts demonstrate that there is variation among girls living under adverse conditions in terms of their responses to the hardships that define their day-to-day experiences and in other ways. Research and texts such as these permit us to understand not only the unequal contexts in which different groups of young people make their way into adulthood, but also how marginalized youth persevere to expand their life chances. Importantly, they challenge us to reconsider how we set out to understand and address the inequality in their lives.

In Respect Yourself, Protect Yourself, I want to reorient the study of Latina girls to better understand their sexual lives. Almost no previous research examines how Latina youth themselves understand their sexuality, particularly how they conceptualize and approach sexual safety and pleasure. This book, empirically and theoretically, advances this line of inquiry by focusing on a unique sample of Latina girls. My sampling procedure required potential research participants to meet specific criteria that included self-identification as sexually active and practicing safe sex. Thus, I deliberately sought out a theoretically driven sample of girls that would allow for an exploration of the meanings and mechanisms through which Latinas attempt to create positive sexual experiences for themselves. Conclusions from this study cannot be generalized to the Latina population at large given the extent to which study participants were self-selected. For instance, since the young women were recruited from community organizations, the findings may be limited to girls who may have it "more together" than some of their peers who are not accessing community organizations. Additionally, since study participants were self-selected, they may have also been more concerned about and/or knowledgeable about safe sex. But this study does provide insight into the ways in which a group of Latina girls, living under a particular set of circumstances shaped by the intersection of race/ethnicity, gender, sexuality, class, and generational status, approach and negotiate their sexual identities and safe sex. A study such as this may not be able to establish generalizations, but it can uncover the limits of generalization and, as the sociologist Schulamit Reinharz writes, "invalidate one [generalization] and suggest new research directions."[44] In this book, I draw attention to the experiences of second-generation Mexican and Puerto Rican girls who are not pregnant or mothers, but who are growing up in circumstances similar to those familiar to many of the Latina girls represented in negative sexual-outcome statistics.

It is not enough to understand why young women become pregnant or are at risk for contracting sexually transmitted diseases. Equally, if not more interesting, is an exploration of why they do not get pregnant or contract sexually transmitted diseases and instead seek ways to honor their sexual selves. Thus, while some of their peers are being asked why they are not practicing safe sex, I am turning the question around. I ask questions such as these: What exactly does safe sex mean to Latina girls who seek to practice it? How do they understand safe sex in relation to their emerging sexuality? Whom do they talk to about safe sex, pleasure, and their sexual experiences? And how do they do this? In asking these questions, I do not mark this group of Latina girls as exceptional or as having "overcome the odds."[45] Such an approach would only rely upon and reproduce dichotomous ways of interpreting the sexuality of young women, as, for example, virgins or nonvirgins, sexually innocent or sexually promiscuous, and good girls or bad girls, binaries that obstruct our ability to consider and acknowledge the diversity among them. Instead of trying to determine whether they are "successful" in their sexual self-protective efforts or whether they "truly" possess an empowered sexual subjectivity, I present their experiences to direct attention to how Latina girls seek to develop and enact their sexual subjectivity and sexual agency and the constraints under which they do this for themselves.

Organization of this Book

In chapter 2, I analyze the ways in which Latina mothers and their daughters communicate with each other about safe sex and sexuality by focusing on how mothers respond to the discovery of their daughters' sexual behaviors and their daughters' interpretations of the sex education lessons they provide to them. I consider the specific strategies that Latina mothers adopt to simultaneously address their daughters' emerging sexuality and the gender, sexual, and racial/ethnic inequalities they and their daughters face. I highlight the centrality of notions of respectable femininity in these mother-daughter interactions surrounding sexuality and for their identities as Latina women, and more specifically, as Mexican and Puerto Rican women.

In chapter 3, I consider the classroom as another context in which Latina girls encounter lessons about sexuality and respectable femininity. I begin by examining how sexism, racism, and the presumption that all girls are heterosexual structure the content and delivery of school-based sex education for Latina girls. I specifically focus on their middle school experiences, particularly their interactions with teachers and sex educators. I show that Latina youth encounter racialized gendered stereotypes that limit their access to useful sex education and reinforce their disadvantages. I then turn to why it was important to this group of girls that they be able to learn about safe sex in the classroom by drawing attention to how they situated their respectability in relation to their future educational and career possibilities.

Chapter 4 looks at the meanings Latina girls assign to safe sex and how these meanings fit into their formation of their femininity. I explore the processes by which this group of Latinas, as young women who engage in partnered sexual behavior, maintain their claim to a respectable femininity. I consider how this plays out in the social world of their peers. This chapter illustrates that sexual respectability operates as a gendered sexual and racial/ethnic boundary formation that they utilized to set themselves apart from other Latina girls and white young women and that enabled and constrained their sense of themselves as sexual subjects.

In chapter 5, I explore how Latina girls negotiate sexual safety and sexual pleasure with their sexual partners by focusing on the strategies that they employ to obtain their partners' cooperation with their self-protective efforts. I illustrate how young women draw on respectability to challenge and yet appeal to accepted notions of masculinity and femininity in their safe-sex strategies. I suggest that their approaches to masculinity and femininity enhance their ability to practice safe sex but also limit their efforts to interrupt the gender and sexual inequality they encounter as girls. In the concluding chapter, I briefly summarize major points and show the broad implications of this study for social policy. I recommend practical ways in which those working directly with girls and policymakers can develop best practices for sex education that will facilitate positive and healthy sexual experiences and outcomes for all youth.

2

"She's Old School Like That"

Mother and Daughter Sex Talks

I was wrapping up my first interview with Carmen, the mother of seventeen-year-old Minerva, when Carmen's sister unexpectedly stopped by for a visit on her way home from running errands. Carmen introduced us, reminding her sister that I was doing interviews with Latina girls and their mothers. Taking off her winter hat and gloves as she shook off the powdery snow from her boots on a welcome mat, the sister dismissively commented to Carmen, "*¿Qué se gana uno con hablar de eso? Minerva ya hizo lo que hizo* [What does one gain from talking about that? Minerva already did what she did]."

Then, turning to me, she matter-of-factly told me, "*Yo le dije que Minerva se le iba a echar a perder si no la controlaba más* [I told her that Minerva would become ruined if she did not place more restrictions on her]." I did not know how to respond to her as I noticed that Carmen was blushing and averting her gaze when her sister made these remarks. After a brief, awkward silence, Carmen straightened her shoulders, looked me right in the eye, and assertively stated, "I've always taken care of her, but, as you see, *hace lo que le da la gana* [she does whatever she wants]. . . . And, even so, Minerva still needs my advice." In our next interview, a couple of weeks later, Carmen brought up her sister's comments: "I was so mad at her. It bothers me that she thinks like that . . . *como que si mi hija ya no vale la pena* [as if my daughter is no longer worth it (the effort)]."

Like Carmen, other mothers struggled with the judgments they encountered about their daughters' sexual behavior and, by extension, their parenting skills. Mothers frequently told me they initially felt quite embarrassed about what they understood to be their personal shortcomings and those of their daughters. For this reason, I assumed it would be difficult to find mothers who would be willing to talk to me about their interactions with their daughters on the topic of sexuality, especially those that unfolded upon their discovery of daughters' sexual activities. But mothers contacted me and expressed interest in the study, often making comments such as, "We need to talk about this topic more" and "This is something we should not be embarrassed about." Despite such assertions, most mothers were still very self-conscious at the onset of interviews, seeming almost apologetic about their parenting and about their daughters' behavior. As Betina, a stylish Mexican woman with dyed blonde hair put it while nervously wringing her hands, "*Qué vergüenza* [how embarrassing], you are probably wondering how I let this happen." But, as the interviews progressed and they became more comfortable, this initial apologetic demeanor shifted to one of determination. These Latina mothers made it clear that they were unwilling to write off their daughters as lost causes just because they were no longer virgins. Carmen exemplified this when she expressed indignation at her sister's suggestion that Minerva "was no longer worth it." Instead, mothers asserted that it was precisely because of their daughters' sexual experiences that they needed to persist in providing guidance to their daughters.

I found that mothers adopted four specific strategies to continue to offer their daughters sexual guidance after discovering their sexual behaviors. These were strategies by which they also negotiated the inequality they and their daughters faced when daughters transgressed the sexual restrictions placed on them by their families and the larger society. Mothers' strategies were (1) their continued promotion of safe sex, communicated in their redefinitions of the meanings of respect; (2) open discussion and sharing with their daughters of their own sexual experiences as a way to underscore how women's sexual biographies could exacerbate their existing disadvantages; (3) disclosure of their daughters' sexual behaviors to other women in the family and/or their husbands; and (4) making evaluative references to the sexuality of white young women. Broader cultural discourses and notions about teen sexuality, good mothers, same-sex sexuality, and race/ethnicity, as well as mothers' interactions with family members and with each other as Mexican and Puerto Rican women, significantly informed their approaches to the sex education of their daughters. As I show, their strategies were also a boundary maintenance process produced in a larger context of racialization and gender inequality, as well as heteronormativity, which refers to "both those localized practices and those centralized institutions that legitimize and privilege heterosexuality and hetero relationships as fundamental and 'natural' w/in society."[1]

Research on mother-adolescent daughter communication about sex suggests that in comparison to both black and white mothers, Latina mothers are more reluctant to discuss sexuality-related matters with their daughters.[2] Restrictions in Latina mother-adolescent sex communication are most often attributed to cultural values and norms, such as the often-cited stereotypical portrayal of Latinas as "culturally silent" on sexuality. Despite the limited sex communication among Latinas indicated by studies that have focused on this aspect of mother-daughter relationships, there are still instances in which the topic of sex becomes notably salient in their conversations. Two key moments that have been highlighted in the literature are Latina mothers' sexual socialization of adolescent daughters who are expected or assumed to be virgins and mothers' reactions to their unmarried daughters' unplanned pregnancy. I pick up on what occurs at the moment of mothers' discovery of the sexual behavior of their adolescent daughters (who are not pregnant) and what unfolds after this moment. I approach these occurrences as "magnified moments," which the sociologist Arlie Hochschild defines as "episodes of heightened importance, either epiphanies, moment of intense glee or unusual insight, or moments in which things go intensely but meaningful wrong. In either case, the moment stands out."[3] Mothers' discovery of their daughters' sexual behaviors are moments that stand out because they bring to the foreground not only daughters' emerging sexuality but also mothers' approaches to the sex education of their daughters. According to Hochschild, "magnified moments reflect a feeling ideal both when a person joyously lives up to it or, in some spectacular way, does not."[4] Little is known about the interactions between nonpregnant or nonparenting Latina girls and their mothers around sexuality *after* mothers realize that their daughters are sexually active. The narratives of the Latina mothers and daughters I spoke with call into question the often-cited explanation that Latina girls have negative sexual outcomes because their mothers are "culturally silent" about sexuality. These magnified moments and ensuing interactions between Latina mothers and their adolescent daughters provide an opportunity to explore when and how Latinas rework their gender and sexual meanings and processes.[5]

Finding Out

About an hour into our first interview, thirty-eight-year-old Aracelia asked me to wait a minute and walked out of her kitchen. A Mexican woman who immigrated to Chicago in her teens, Aracelia took great pride in having recently obtained her G.E.D. while working as a store cashier and raising her family. For most of our first hour together, she had excitedly shared with me her desire to work at a child-care center, laying out her plans to register at a community college and obtain an associate degree. With her husband at work and her two daughters out watching a movie that Saturday afternoon, the two-bedroom apartment was fairly quiet. Aracelia reemerged a few minutes later and placed a folded-up sheet of lined notebook paper on the kitchen table as she sat back down across from me. She pushed it toward me: "Look, this is how I found out." Aracelia was ready to share with me how she came to learn about her daughter's sexual behavior. I unfolded the creased and worn paper; small, neat handwriting almost filled up one side of the paper, and a few hearts embellished the outer margins. Realizing it was a personal letter written by her sixteen-year-old daughter, Soledad, I placed it back on the table. Aracelia reassured me that it was okay to read the note, but, upon seeing my hesitancy to do so, she held up the note in front of me and leaned forward, telling me, "She wrote that she was glad that she did it [sex] for the first with him [her boyfriend] and that she would never regret it, even if they were no longer together!" Aracelia explained that she found the letter in her daughter's notebook after much investigative effort.

Like Aracelia, almost all mothers became aware of daughters' sexual activities through covert searches of daughters' bedrooms, backpacks, school notebooks, or diaries or by listening in on phone calls or combing through text messages left on cell phones.[6] According to the mothers, such actions stemmed from their suspicions about their daughters' sexual propriety after they defied rules, particularly those related to curfew and/or dating, behavior that the mothers interpreted as out of character for their daughters, rather than as "normal" adolescent behavior. And, for a handful of mothers, their sleuthing activities were provoked by their discovery of a "hickey"[7] on their daughters' necks or their daughters' interest in or purchase of underwear that mothers deemed to be "too sexy," like lacy thongs or bras, as was the case for Aracelia, who was surprised when she found two animal print thongs that belonged to her daughter.

When I asked the mothers whether they had any qualms about infringing upon their daughters' privacy, they almost all emphatically responded that their actions were justified because they were tied to their efforts to protect their daughters. As Aracelia asserted, "¿Qué tiene de malo [what is wrong with that]? I do it for her own good! My obligation as a mother is to be on the watch for everything my daughters do, even if they don't like it." Most mothers were taken aback by my inquiries about their daughters' privacy, often responding that the idea of privacy for children and teenagers was an "americano" or "güero" notion ("American" was always conflated with "white"). "White parents always treat young people as if they should have the same rights as adults," stated Teresa, a Puerto Rican woman in her late thirties who has a great sense of humor. She continued, "I'm not saying that it is acceptable to abuse your children. . . . But privacy, no, to me it's an abuse not to know what your children are doing." When I suggested that perhaps it might be more effective to just ask daughters about their sexual activities rather than go through their personal items, Teresa made a face and quickly replied, "What young woman is going to say, 'Oh yeah, I'm having sex already'? I want to know about what my daughters are not telling me about so I can do something about it if I have to." Most mothers did indeed do something upon learning about their daughters' sexual behavior and did so in similar fashion.

Once armed with what they saw as evidence of their daughters' sexual activities, most of the mothers acted swiftly to address the matter. With initial feelings of anger and/or disillusionment, they immediately confronted daughters about their sexual behavior. The manner in which they moved forward with this information was a process that began with their construction of their daughters as victims. In seeking to make sense of their daughters' sexual behavior, mothers typically reported that they initially accused their daughters of being gullible, calling them *pendeja* (idiot) or *mensa* (stupid). Most mothers first understood their daughters' sexual behavior as a victimization of their daughters. That is, mothers accused their daughters of being naïve or having been taken advantage of by their sexual partners.

When Emma discovered some condoms in her sixteen-year-old daughter Miriam's bedroom, she immediately went to school to pick up her daughter. A full-time factory employee in her late thirties, Emma always handed me a plastic sandwich bag full of individually wrapped candy, such as caramels, butterscotch disks, and taffy whenever we met for an interview. She always seemed jovial when we talked, so it was difficult to imagine her being angry when she described her interaction with her daughter that day:

Oh, of course, she wanted to know why I went to get her. *No le dije nada* [I did not say anything], I was quiet all the way home. When we got home, she saw the condoms on the kitchen table and when straight into her room. Le dije, "¡¿*Que no tienes vergüenza* [Aren't you ashamed]?!" She told that me that it was none of my business and I don't know what else, but I yelled at her, "¡*Qué mensa eres, Miriam* [You are so stupid, Miriam]! You think he loves you? *Se está aprovechando de ti, ya verás* [He's taking advantage of you, you'll see]!"

Likewise, Conchita, a Mexican woman in her early forties, interpreted her daughter's actions as not being taken of her own volition. When her fifteen-year-old daughter forgot her cell phone at home, Conchita decided to go through the received and dialed text messages with the help of Carla's older sister. Much to her dismay, she found some of the text exchanges between Carla and her boyfriend to be overtly sexual. Later that evening, Conchita asked her about the text messages:

> I told her that I read her text messages and I wanted to know if she was having sexual relations with her boyfriend. She still denied it, at first. . . . I told her I wanted her to tell me the truth. . . . She then admitted it. . . . I told her how sad I was for her because she didn't know what she was doing and that her boyfriend was taking advantage of her.

Recently separated from her husband, Conchita wondered if her daughter would have behaved in this manner if her husband were still living at home, pointing out that her children were more "scared" of their father.

Carmen, who had been angered by her sister's suggestion that her daughter was a lost cause, was one of only two mothers who did not search their daughters' belongings. She recounted how she straightforwardly asked Minerva about her sexual experiences:

> I don't know, I just had a feeling she might be having *relaciones* [sexual relations] with her boyfriend, so I just asked her. She looked surprised at the question but then admitted it. I was so mad because she is so young, I began to tell her all kinds of things, I told her, "¡*Eres una pendeja! No sabes lo que haces* [You are a fool! You don't know what you are doing]!"

Within a larger societal context of patriarchal control over women's bodies, it was difficult for mothers to see their daughter as sexual subjects. Because girls are viewed as property that can be damaged, their sexual behaviors and activities are often not regarded as a choice they make for themselves.[8]

Instead, mothers initially drew on a specific cultural frame about gendered sexuality to make sense of their daughters' sexual behavior. Their anger and concern about what they interpreted as their daughters' victimization are reflective of the prevailing dominant perspective on teenage girls' sexuality in our society, namely the assumption that, when girls participate in sexual activities, that action is not guided by their own sexual desires and curiosity. While teenage boys are readily accepted as sexual beings overrun by their hormones and/or efforts to assert their masculinity, teenage girls are generally constructed as their sexual prey, susceptible to trickery by boys and men (often in the form of promises of love and romance).[9] Rather than explain teenage girls' sexual behaviors as possibly originating in girls themselves, we tend to understand their sexual activities through the sexual agency of boys and men. Latina mothers selected this prevailing cultural frame to interpret the sexual behavior of their teenage daughters. I must underscore that when I refer to Latina mothers' use of this cultural framing, I see this frame not as unique to Latinas but rather a cultural frame that is also found and made available to them within the larger U.S. society.

The cultural frame of sexual victimization was not only applied to heterosexual-identified young women. Three of the four mothers of lesbian-identified girls also drew upon this explanation as they grappled with their daughters' sexual behavior. Martina, a Mexican woman in her late forties who worked part-time at a dry cleaner shop, was one such mother. She related how, on a fall afternoon, she came to the realization that her seventeen-year-old daughter Margarita and her daughter's best friend were more than just friends:

> I saw them walking down the street, they didn't see me, though. They were saying good-bye to each other, and you know how people sometimes give each other a kiss on the cheek when they say hello or goodbye? Well, they gave each other a kiss on the lips! ¡*Me muero de vergüenza* [I almost died of embarrassment]! When she got home, I told her that I saw her. I told her that I didn't want her hanging out with the girl, *esa güera loca sin vergüenza* [that crazy shameless white girl]! I know she put those ideas in Margarita's head.

Martina, like the mothers of heterosexual-identified girls, assumed that her daughter's partner had taken advantage of her. She attributed Margarita's violation of heteronormative expectations and unabashed public behavior to the negative influence of her daughter's partner. But Martina also specifically connected this conduct to the race/ethnicity of her daughter's partner, demonstrated in her description of her as *"esa güera loca sin vergüenza."* Similarly, Gina, a Puerto Rican mother of three who worked as a hairdresser, referenced race when she first learned about her sixteen-year-old daughter's relationship with another young woman:

> I overheard them in the hallway one day, talking about being in love with each other and other things. I called Imelda's friend later that night and told her I didn't want her to come to my house anymore. I did it in front of my daughter and she started crying, that it wasn't my business, this and that. I told her that *que eso estaba muy mal y que esa blanca era una muchacha perversa* [that it was very wrong and that that white girl was a perverse young girl].

Almost all mothers discussed what they perceived to be the sexual immorality of white women, a theme I explore in more detail later in this chapter. However, the mothers of lesbian-identified girls specifically made reference to the negative influence of white young women on their daughters in their initial postdiscovery conversations with their daughters.[10] Thus, this group of mothers utilized the cultural frame of victimization to initially make sense of their daughters' same-sex attraction, but they also interpreted their daughters' actions through the lens of race/ethnicity. They found themselves having to come to terms not only with their daughters' sexual disobedience but also with their deviation from heteronormative expectations, reflecting what they took to be an undesirable assimilation to the sexual impropriety of whites. As Gina put it when I asked her why she thought that her daughter's partner was influencing her behavior, *"¿Dónde va a aprender esas cochinadas? ¡¿Con quién más, pero con esa muchacha blanca* [Where else is she going to learn such filth? With who else, but with that white girl]?!" The attitudes expressed by this group of mothers are consistent with those reported in previous studies, which found that some communities of color in the United States interpret same-sex identities, practices, and behaviors as specific to and reflective of "white culture."[11]

Talkin' Safe Sex with Daughters

All of the mothers saw themselves as the parent directly responsible for providing their daughters with sex education.[12] Prior studies of parent-child sexuality communication have found that, generally, mothers assume primary responsibility for talking to their children about sex-related topics.[13] This is not necessarily because mothers are naturally better at talking to their children about sex. One reason that mothers take on this challenging task is that they are typically the parent expected to guide their child's sexual development and the parent most blamed when a child is seen as failing to conform to normative gender and sexual expectations.

At first glance, the initial reactions of the mothers I spoke with seem to suggest that they expected their daughters to refrain from premarital sex. But most mothers insisted that virginity itself was not the overriding expectation they had for their daughters, even before learning of their daughters' sexual behaviors. In other words, the sex education they provided to their daughters prior to these magnified moments of discovery and confrontation was not limited to lessons about virginity. Despite the "victimization" reactions that affected their postdiscovery conversations with their daughters about sexuality, mothers reported that, in their prediscovery sexuality communication with their daughters, they had highlighted the importance of postponing sexual relationships until they were older and/or practicing safe sex rather than urging abstinence only. As other recent studies on Latina mothers' sexual socialization of daughters have found, in our conversations these mothers did not think it realistic to expect that their daughters would refrain from sexual activities until they were married.[14] Instead, central in mothers' accounts of their prediscovery sexuality messages to their daughters were interrelated lessons about the need to "*respetar a sí misma*" (have self-respect) and "*cuidarse*" (take care of oneself). When I asked Emma, who had found her daughter's condoms, what she meant when she told me that she instructed her daughter to have self-respect, she replied, "With so many diseases, like AIDS, I want her to be careful." She further elaborated, "I told her, 'I can't be there to watch you all the time. Sex is something normal, but very serious, nobody is going to take care of your body and your health but you. . . . That means you have respect yourself if you want people to respect you.'"

Respeto (respect) has been consistently understood as a cultural value and a familial factor that influences gender socialization practices within Latino families. Often coupled with the cultural value of *familismo* (familism), *respeto* refers to deference to the authority of elders, including parents and other adults in the family and the community. According to most cultural explanations of Latina/o sexual practices, respect is generally demonstrated in the avoidance of behavior that could bring shame to one's family; thus, there is an expectation that young women will act in a "decent and good" manner, which is tightly linked to sexual propriety. However, among the Latina mothers I interviewed, *respeto* was redefined to include the expectation of "*respetar a sí misma*"(respecting one's self), emphasizing the importance of the honor that young women bestow upon themselves, particularly by taking care of their sexual and reproductive health. The sociologist Gloria González-López also found that some of the Mexican immigrant mothers she interviewed had altered the sex education lessons they provided to their daughters. As she asserts, this suggests "a new ethic of *protección y cuidado personal* that promotes sexual-moderation" for daughters.[15] According to the mothers I spoke with, having knowledge about how to prevent pregnancy and protect oneself from sexually transmitted diseases are important components of a women's respectability.

The mothers' integration of sexual safety into the meaning of respect that they imparted to daughters was informed by the prevailing discourse of teen sexuality as risky. As I discussed in chapter 1, this discourse incorporates and reinforces problematic notions about gender, race, class, and sexuality. Though teen pregnancy was not the only negative sexual outcome that concerned the mothers, they regularly mentioned it when discussing their sexual socialization of their daughters. For instance, Emma had this to say: "Latina girls now start having sex too young! I saw in the news the other night that a lot of kids of all races are having sex, but they said that it is the Latina girls that get pregnant and have babies, more than other kids." Mothers knew some young women in their communities and/or families who had experienced early motherhood, but, as evident in Emma's comments, their perception that Latina girls were more likely to become pregnant was also informed by the broader cultural treatment of teen sexuality as perilous, a dominant approach to teen sexuality that too often homes in on the experiences of Latina and African American girls as the main example of why teen sexuality is a problem. Aware of the visibility of Latina girls in representations of teen sexuality, mothers sought to protect their daughters from negative sexual outcomes. They told me that they emphasized the importance of safe sex to daughters even before finding out about their sexual behavior, when they thought their daughters were virgins, because they were concerned for their daughters' sexual well-being in what they understood to be a context of uncontrolled teenage sexual activity fraught with harmful consequences.

Even if they were uncomfortable in doing so, the mothers thought it necessary to provide their daughters with some knowledge to help them navigate what they saw to be a precarious adolescent sexuality terrain. They cited two principal resources that facilitated their ability to communicate with their daughters about safe sex: a mother-daughter program at Casa de la Mujer and the media. Emma, for example, highlighted an HIV/AIDS workshop that she and her daughter took part in as participants of *Entre Nosotras*, the mother-daughter program at Casa de la Mujer:

I learned that it was not going to be enough for me to tell her to not have sex or not to get pregnant. There are other consequences that come with sex, like for one's health. I still tell her that I don't think she should be having sexual relations right now, but if she is, not to expect the guy she is with to protect her health—she has to do it.

The other two mothers who participated in this mother-daughter program also referred to the program as they discussed what they told their daughters about sex and how they talked to them.

The mothers who did not participate in this program mainly pointed to the media when they explained how they communicated with their daughters about sexual and reproductive health. There has been much concern about whether the media are a reliable source of information on sexuality-related issues, such as safe sex and representations of LGBTQ individuals and groups. Despite critiques of media representations of these topics, some observers have argued that certain media forms, such as TV and radio talk shows, open up opportunities for individuals and groups to have conversations about sexuality in ways that might not be possible otherwise.[16] The media forms that most of these mothers mentioned were Spanish-language TV talk shows and radio shows. They also made reference to Spanish-language newspapers and magazines, but not to the extent to which they talked about TV and radio shows. Describing an episode of *El Show de Cristina* that featured HIV-positive women, Dolores, a forty-year-old Mexican woman, said:

> The majority of them [the guests on *El Show de Cristina*] got HIV from their husbands or boyfriends, who had cheated on them with other women. They trusted them and said they felt they didn't need to use a condom or that even if they had their doubts, they felt that their husbands or boyfriends would be offended if they asked them to put on a condom. They were devastated. I told Asucena about the show and that it is the kind of thing that can happen to anyone and that is why she needs to be very careful.

Like almost all of the mothers in this study, Dolores did not go into details about how to use a condom or STD transmission routes because she did not feel comfortable and/or knowledgeable enough to go into such specifics. But, as reflected in Emma's and Dolores's narratives, mothers still managed to use the language of safe sex, such as condom use and HIV prevention, that they drew from resources such as a mother-daughter program and/or media presentations. The cultural visibility of safe-sex promotion through such outlets in our society allowed the mothers to develop some skills to communicate sex education lessons to their daughters, particularly their integration of sexual safety into their redefinition of a woman's self-respect.

Despite the significance of media and mother-daughter workshops for what mothers said and how they talked to their daughters about sexual safety, it is important to bear in mind that their notions of gender and sexuality were not fixed before their access to these resources. Prior to arriving in the United States, these women had experienced structural changes in their homelands, such as modernity and globalization, forces that have impacted how Mexicans and Puerto Ricans understand and construct their gender and sexual identities and practices.[17] In other words, we should not assume that these women's meanings of gender and sexuality had not evolved before they arrived in the United States. For instance, in her examination of generational perspectives and practices pertaining to marriage and sexuality among members of transnational families living in rural Mexico and urban Atlanta, the anthropologist Jennifer S. Hirsch found that, even before migrating to the United States, younger Mexican women had redefined the purposes of marriage and sexuality.[18] Rather than conceive of marriage as a way for women to secure respect for themselves that required them to defer to husbands (as older women did), younger women saw this relationship as needing to be characterized by companionship. And sex within marriage, for this group of women, moved beyond serving only a reproductive purpose to being a source of pleasure and intimacy. According to Hirsch, social transformations, such as young women's increased access to media in rural Mexico and their increasing age at marriage, informed younger women's stances on marriage and sexuality.

Additionally, mothers' immigration experiences have also had implications for their daughters' approaches to gender and sexuality. Scholars who have explored the relationships among gender, sexuality, and migration processes have shown that immigrant men and women negotiate and reconfigure gender and sexual relations and arrangements as they adjust to a new context.[19] Rather than interpret gender and sexual shifts as either emancipatory or subjugating,[20] this literature illustrates that various factors, such as age, class status, marital status, place of origin (i.e., urban versus rural), and employment matter for how immigrants produce and experience gender and sexuality. For example, González-López found that Mexican immigrant women's ability to provide economically for their families in the United States boosted their confidence and their sense of authority in the home, contributing to their perception of themselves as being capable of discussing sex with their children.[21]

Lessons about Inequality

The mothers continued offering messages about sexual safety after learning about their daughters' sexual activities. But this approach was now coupled with their explicit emphasis on the gender inequality associated with women's expressions of sexuality; they made connections among inequality, women's sexuality, and suffering. One way they accomplished this was by recounting the negative experiences of other women they personally knew. These experiences were relayed to their daughters to serve as lessons about heartbreak, unplanned pregnancy, sexually transmitted diseases, violence, and even poverty.[22] Gina, who found out about her daughter's same-sex relationship when she inadvertently overheard Imelda's conversation with her partner, highlighted violence as a consequence of expressions of queer sexuality and gender nonconformity by describing to her daughter the experience of a woman who lived in Gina's community in Puerto Rico: "We knew this woman *que era una deesas* [was one of those (implying lesbians)]. *Muy bonita* [very pretty], but didn't like men, acted and walked around like a man. She was raped and brutally beaten. . . . I told Imelda about this so that she knows what can happen to her for doing things like that." Gina's admonition to her daughter both emphasized her disapproval of Imelda's same-sex relationship and provided a warning about the physical consequences Imelda could encounter as a lesbian.

The majority of the mothers also now drew upon their own lived experiences, revealing previously guarded information about themselves in postdiscovery conversations with their daughters. Such was the case for Francisca, who was the only mother who took her daughter to obtain birth control after learning about her sexual behavior. The Puerto Rican medical assistant and mother of two looked much younger than her forty years. Francisca detailed how she disclosed a painful and secret aspect of her past to her seventeen-year-old daughter, Samantha:

I had always told her that I didn't leave my parents' house in Puerto Rico until I was married, but I decided to tell her the truth. I wanted her to know that I knew what I was talking about because *yo lo viví en carne propia* [I lived it myself in my own flesh]. I ran away from home with my first boyfriend. My mother warned me that I would suffer with him, but I didn't listen. Shortly after moving in with him, he started beating me. . . . I finally left him, but I suffered tremendously with him.

Likewise, Sara, a blue-eyed Puerto Rican woman with long black hair, recounted the information she shared with her seventeen-year-old daughter, Jocelyn:

> He [Jocelyn's father] kept wanting me to live with him, and I would tell him no because I was young. So one time when he was drunk he saw my father and told him that I had already been sexually involved with him. My dad kicked me out, and I had nowhere to go, so I went to live with him. He was such a jealous man . . . he wouldn't even let me work because he did not want me to talk to any men. So I didn't work, and, when he left me, he left me pregnant with Jocelyn and no money, no job. I told Jocelyn all this so she could know that all our bad choices have consequences for many years.

Through their disclosures, the mothers worked to assert themselves as knowledgeable women because, as stated by Francisca, they had lived the consequences of sexual activity "*en carne propia.*" I see the mothers' disclosures about their sexual experiences as *testimonios* (stories of lived experiences). As the Latina Feminist Group highlights, *testimonios* is a genre that has been used in a variety of ways; for example, Latin American women have employed it in their efforts to document political violence. However, the Latina Feminist Group has reconceptualized *testimonios* "as a tool for Latinas to theorize oppression, resistance, and subjectivity."[23] I utilize this conceptualization to understand the mothers' use of *testimonios* with their daughters. Mothers relied upon their *testimonios* to provide their daughters with messages about gender and sexual inequality. Thus, they also drew on the resource of their own experiences as women. They may not have had the knowledge in the "technical know-how" sense to explain the particulars of condom use or HIV transmission, but they built on the wisdom gained from their life experiences.[24] Mothers' use of *testimonios* in the postdiscovery sex education of daughters highlighted the relationship between a woman's sexual history and her life circumstances.

However, daughters made different sense of the connections between sexuality and gender inequality than that conveyed by their mothers in *testimonios*. Carefully taking sips of a hot latte, seventeen-year-old Samantha, a bright high school junior with plans to go to medical school, described how she responded to her mother upon learning of her experiences with the boyfriend with whom she ran away from home:

> But, like I told her, I really wouldn't put myself in that situation because things are different now, for one, we ain't in Puerto Rico. I wouldn't be lettin' no man kick my ass! She had it rough. . . . I think she stood with that

guy for as long as she did because she probably thought she had to, you know, since she lost her virginity to him and her mom had told her no other man would want her like that. But I tell her that with all my friends I know, guys and girls, it ain't like that no more, where you gotta stay with the first person you have sex with if you're a girl. It doesn't have to mean your life is over. She's old-school Puerto Rican like that.

Many young women, like Samantha, asserted that they would not encounter the types of negative experiences their mothers described because they would not tolerate them. The majority of girls reported that they identified the source of women's suffering described in their mothers' *testimonios* as women's uncritical conformity to gendered sexual scripts, rather than their failure to behave in a sexually acceptable manner. Seventeen-year-old Minerva, whose mother asked her if she was having sexual relations with her partner, explained this perspective:

She started going off on me, you know, that I was stupid for believing everything my boyfriend told me, but it wasn't even like that! I was like, "look, I was never going to wait [to have sex] until I was married. I'm not going to be one of those *mexicanitas* [little Mexican women implying that some Mexican woman are very traditional] that is supposed to be all pure on my wedding day, what for?!" My cousin got married the so-called right way and her husband still treats her like shit and there she is, trying to be the good wife and mother, cooking, cleaning, while he goes out and messes around with other girls. I don't think so!

Similarly, Olivia, a slender seventeen-year-old with eyes the color of honey, conveyed a similar point as she described the violence her father often inflicted on her mother:

My mom always tries to make excuses for my dad, "your dad acts that way because that is how men are, jealous." So she does stuff like let him know where she is going and what time she will be back . . . but she won't leave him because she thinks my grandma will not like it. My grandma doesn't believe in divorce, she's always saying that marriage, no matter what, is forever. So my mom puts up with my dad's bullshit because she thinks that's it, there is nothing she can do about it now that she's married.

Within the *testimonios* that their mothers imparted to them and within the experiences of other women they knew, young Latinas detected the uneven terrain in which men and women negotiate and express their sex-uality. As the narratives of Samantha and Minerva demonstrate, daughters understood such experiences to be testaments to the dangers embedded in gender and sexual hierarchies that privilege men and penalize women. Fur-thermore, Samantha's statement to her mother that "we're not in Puerto Rico anymore" and Minerva's assertion to her mother that "I'm not gonna be one of those *mexicanitas*" as they attempted to justify their behaviors to their mothers highlight the intergenerational negotiations of sexuality and gen-der within U.S. Latina mother-daughter relationships. Girls' narratives indi-cate that their second-generation status was significant in informing their adoption of gendered identities. In other words, when they considered their mothers' expectations of them, they highlighted how their social world was different from that in which their mothers grew up. Girls' responses to their mothers' *testimonios* about gender inequality suggest that they saw other possible ways to construct gendered Mexican or Puerto Rican identities for themselves. According to these Latina girls, as young women growing up in the United States, they did not want to be and could not be "old-school Puerto Rican like that" or "one of those *mexicanitas*." However, as I discuss shortly, this did not mean that they saw themselves as more "Americanized" in their sexual attitudes and behaviors, either.

This process of intergenerational negotiations of gender and sexuality was also evident when girls challenged their mothers' accusations that they had behaved idiotically and/or been deceived by their partners. Five girls did not argue against their mothers' constructions of them as victims. Instead, they relied upon a victimization explanation to help lessen their mothers' anger or disappointment. As one young woman explained: "She was already pissed off about the whole thing, I thought she was going to kick my ass. I was just like, 'I fell for his lies.' She was still mad, but not as much. More mad at him, I think." But more than half of the girls who reported that their mothers had some knowledge of their sexual activities said that, in their initial confronta-tions with their mothers, they had asserted their desire and agency in their sexual decision making. Exemplifying this, sixteen-year-old Miriam (whose mother picked her up from school after discovering condoms in her bed-room) remarked, "She kept going on about how he used me and that I wasn't '*una señorita*' [a sexually innocent young women] anymore. I told her that wasn't true . . . that no one made me do anything and that I knew what I was doing. No one played me." A petite young woman with waist-length black hair, sixteen-year-old Inés made a similar point as she discussed her effort to convince her mother that she had not been duped into sexual relations: "She was, like, exaggerating, you know, crying, and saying that he [partner] wasn't gonna want me now that he got what he wanted from me. I told her, 'How do you know I wasn't the one that got what I wanted?' She slapped me . . . guess she didn't like that answer." Inés's mother's response underscores the fact that deviance from gendered sexual conformity is not only punished through verbal sanctions but is also often met with violence to secure its stability, in this case, between mothers and daughters. In these magnified moments of discovery and confrontation, the girls attempted to make visible their sexual subjectivity and also raised questions about the gendered sexual scripts they were expected to take on.

"Pero, ¡¿cómo explico esto [But How Do I Explain This]?!":
Shame, Disclosures and Concealment within the Family

Teresa proudly showed me pictures of her two daughters as we sat in her living room. It was a humid August afternoon, and all the windows in her small, second-floor Humboldt Park apartment were open as a box fan sitting in a corner noisily blew some air. At one point, Teresa, who said she regularly searched her daughters' belongings, excused herself to lean out the window. A waitress with a head of tight auburn curls and skin the color of cinnamon, Teresa was checking up on her daughters, sixteen-year-old Irene and thir-teen-year-old Jeanne, who were sitting on the front stairs of the three-flat red brick building talking to some girlfriends when I arrived for the interview. Spotting her youngest daughter standing on the curb and talking to two Latino boys in a black Cadillac, she yelled out the window, "¡*Jeanne*! ¡¿*Qué tú haces* [What are you doing]?!" With that, her daughter walked away from the curb and the car sped off, setting off car alarms along the street with the bass from the hip-hop music emanating from it. Satisfied that her youngest daughter was behaving, Teresa moved away from the living room window, disapprovingly commenting to me that her daughters wanted to act older than their actual age. As she sat down, she added, "I've been talking to them, you know, about sex *y de eso* [and that]. I'm keeping an eye on them, no *quiero ninguna sorpresa* [I don't want any surprises]," emphasizing this point by making the shape of a pregnant belly with her hands over her abdomen.

Teresa consulted with her sister when she initially learned of her sixteen-year-old daughter's sexual conduct: "I wanted to give her [daughter] *una buena paliza* [good beating] that she'd never forget! I was so mad! I told my sister, and she made me calm down, you know? She's the one that helped me figure out how to deal with it." Like Teresa, most mothers turned to other women in the family to help them cope with their feelings of anger, disappointment, and confusion upon learning of their daughters' sexual behavior. This was typically done shortly after the mothers first confronted their daughters. But they also reached out to other women in their family to involve them in the sex education of their daughters, assistance that mothers had not actively sought out prior to their discovery. The mothers' disclosure of their daughters' behavior was not an easy task for them. Most of them described feeling shame as they revealed this information to selected women in the family, reflected in phrases such as, "¡qué vergüenza [how embarrassing]!" and "¡qué pena [what a shame]!" For instance, Emma decided to confide in her daughter's godmother, explaining, "She has daughters that are slightly older than Miriam, I thought she could advise me or give Miriam some advice. At first, sí me dio vergüenza [I felt shame] telling my comadre [daughter's godmother]." Despite their embarrassment, the mothers opened up to particular women in their families to obtain assistance for their daughters in what was interpreted as a moment of danger or crisis for them.

Several studies on gendered family dynamics reveal that, among some groups in which extended families are the norm, including Latinas/os, young women oftentimes develop important relationships with women in their families in addition to their mothers.[25] Mothers who disclosed information to other women in the family always specifically identified a woman or women that they trusted and perceived to have a close relationship with their daughters. Specifically, they involved other women so that they could provide their daughters with consejos (advice). For example, Lilia asked her sister to speak with her daughter Eva after her sixteen-year-old daughter admitted that she had already had sexual relations with her boyfriend. A soft-spoken Mexican woman who had the habit of pushing her oversized brown framed glasses up on the bridge of her nose, Lilia felt that her teenage daughter would be more receptive to the advice her aunt offered her: "I know Eva spends a lot of time with my sister, especially when I'm not there. Eva even told my sister first, when she got her period. My sister was the one to tell me that my daughter got her first period. So, I thought she could help aconsejarla [advise her]." Similarly, Luz, who volunteered as a Sunday school teacher for her Catholic parish, confided in her twenty-year-old niece after secretly reading her fifteen-year-old daughter's diary and learning about her sexual experiences. Not wanting to reveal to her daughter that she had read her diary, Luz approached her niece instead: "My niece, she's a good girl, smart, you know, going to college. . . . I told her about Iris [her daughter] and asked her if she could take her to visit her college, you know, talk to her, get her mind off the boys and back on school." Mothers' relationships with other women in the family and their daughters' relationships with these women, therefore, were a critical resource that they purposefully drew upon to offer their daughters guidance now that they were aware of some of the sexual experiences of the girls.

The mothers' strategy of revealing their daughters' sexual behaviors to specific women in their family, however, was a two-pronged tactic. Besides attempting to acquire support for themselves and their daughters, mothers also sought to perform some damage control. When talking to other women in their family, they were also certain to emphasize their proper socialization of their daughters, drawing on a larger cultural script of good mothering to deflect the blame they anticipated receiving for their daughters' sexual impropriety. Mothers generally encounter assorted scripts from various sources about the "right way to be a mother"; for instance, in terms of employment and mothering, one script can be that of a selfless mother who forgoes employment to raise her children and another script can be that of a "superwoman" who excels both as a mother and in the workplace.[26] These cultural scripts, though seemingly different, rest on the notion of an ideal mother role that women must fulfill, regardless of whether social structures actually support this expectation. By disclosing their daughters' sexual behaviors to other women in the family, the mothers I spoke with sought to demonstrate that they had not failed to be good mothers. Emma, for instance, stressed to her daughter's godmother that she had always talked to Miriam about the importance of respecting herself, explaining to her that Miriam "still did what she wanted, *siempre ha sido muy rebelde* [she's always been rebellious]." Similarly, Teresa told her sister that she had taught her daughters to behave "*como unas señoritas* [like proper young women]," pointing out that "*pero hacen lo que les da la gana* [but they do whatever they want]." Through the process of disclosure and the explanation that, despite the mothers' best efforts, the daughters did whatever they pleased, the mothers attempted to assert their respectability as good mothers.

Their effort to maintain this identity underscores the pressures felt by mothers in general within a larger cultural context of mother blaming. Since mothers are assumed and expected to be the primary caretakers of children, they are often the parents held most responsible for their children's misbehavior and failure. And, given that parents are expected to model normative gender behavior for their same-sex children, the sexual "misbehavior" of a daughter can also be read as a shortcoming of her mother's own femininity. The distance that mothers declared between themselves and their daughters' misbehavior in interactions with other women in their family indicates that they were performing a particular gendered identity, that of the good mother. This performance also reflected their internalized gendered selves. The sociologist Karin A. Martin contends that it is through such culturally constructed gendered identities that women and men are disciplined and shaped from the inside.[27] In other words, the mothers' gendered subjectivity, how they understood themselves as women, integrated a perception of themselves as mothers who had indeed fulfilled what was expected of them, unintentionally reinforcing the mother blaming that they were trying to evade.

The mothers anticipated that their husbands would also assign blame to them for their daughters' sexual behavior. To prevent the fathers from learning about their daughters' sexual transgressions, some of them decided not to consult with other women in the family about their daughters' emerging sexuality. Dolores, who discussed with her daughter the experiences of the HIV-positive women on *El Show de Cristina*, stated the following: "I don't want anyone to know about what she has done, especially her father. *Esto lo mata* [this will kill him]!" Dolores explained that her husband would react to such knowledge by blaming her for their daughter's behavior: "He's going to say that I did not take care of her." Maria, who migrated from Puerto Rico shortly after marrying her husband at the age of eighteen, expressed a similar concern about her husband's potential reaction: "I know him, he will say that it is my fault that she did this." When I asked her why she thought he would react this way, she quickly responded, "Because he always thinks that I give her too much freedom . . . *me va a echar la culpa* [he will blame me]. He is going to say that I let this happen." To avoid these interactions with their husbands, they kept the knowledge about their daughters' sexual activities between themselves and their daughters.

These mothers explained to their daughters that they would not inform their fathers about their actions because the knowledge would be especially devastating to them. Luz, who had asked her niece to reach out to her daughter, communicated this to her daughter: "I told her, you better hope your dad does not find out, you'll kill him." These three mothers described their husbands as hardworking and emotionally strong but asserted that they would not be able to handle knowledge of daughters' sexual behaviors and that they therefore felt it necessary to protect them from such news. They insisted that it was primarily their responsibility to handle such parenting challenges, especially because they were not employed outside the home.[28] They explained that, despite the financial constraints they were facing, they had decided not to work outside the home so that they could dedicate more time to their children. Like the Mexican immigrant women in the sociologist Denise A. Segura's exploration of Chicanas' and Mexicanas' meanings of the relationship between motherhood and employment,[29] almost all of the mothers that I spoke with did not feel conflicted about their employment outside the home and their ability to mother well.[30] But there were four mothers who did not work outside the home, stating that it was a voluntary nonemployment and that, like the Chicanas that Segura interviewed, they understood employment as taking away from their ability to fulfill their mothering responsibilities (rather than viewing it as part of motherhood). Holding themselves to an "idealized form of motherhood," they most likely saw themselves as failing at what they deemed to be their most important social role. These mothers, therefore, were particularly concerned that their husbands and other family members would criticize them harshly, since, as "stay-at-home" mothers, they were "supposed to be" able to be particularly vigilant about their children's activities.

However, some mothers' concerns about being perceived as bad mothers informed their decision to tell their daughters' fathers about the sexual behavior of daughters.[31] Most of these women did find that their daughters' fathers initially reacted by blaming them, a culpability that mothers rejected in heated discussions with their partners. But the mothers utilized this moment of disclosure as a way to attempt to shift some responsibility onto the fathers should their daughters encounter an unplanned pregnancy and/or develop an STD. For instance, Teresa, who was one of four mothers of heterosexual-identified girls who told her husband about their daughters' sexual activities, explained why she decided to tell her husband: "If I didn't tell him and they end up pregnant, he will ask me how come I didn't know about what they were doing. And if he finds out that I did know, he will be even more angry with me! This way, he knows what I know and we both have to be vigilant about what they are doing." Similarly, Aracelia reasoned, "I felt that, like it or not, I was going to have to tell him. He needed to know. We both needed to face this reality and think about what to do now." Most mothers did not think that the fathers would talk to their daughters about sex and did not expect them to do so, noting that the fathers would be too uncomfortable and that it was more appropriate for mothers to do so because they were the same gender as their daughters.[32] But they did expect the fathers to respond by reinforcing any rules and restrictions that both parents now placed on their daughters, such as new curfews and limits on phone use.

Additionally, mothers told their husbands because they wanted their daughters to experience shame at their fathers' expressed disappointment in them. Carmen made the following point: "Minerva *es su consentida* [is his princess/spoiled girl], and I knew that she would be very embarrassed that he knew about what she did. He told her, 'You have disappointed me. . . . I thought you were smarter than this. How could you behave like this?!' She was not talking back to him the way she did with me, she was just crying."

Like other mothers I spoke with, Carmen may have communicated with her daughter about sexual safety and even opened up about her own sexual history, but this did not necessarily mean that she was completely comfortable with or condoning of her daughter's sexual behavior. These mothers invoked the relationship that daughters had with their fathers, particularly perceptions and expectations that they thought fathers had of daughters, such as fathers' views of their daughters as asexual, sexually innocent, and obedient, to reprimand the daughters and to discourage further sexual activity. Girls whose fathers did know about their sexual behavior told me that they felt "bad" or "embarrassed" about their fathers' knowledge of their behavior. Some even said they wished their mothers had not shared this information with their fathers. Sixteen-year-old Lucy, a young Mexican woman I interviewed for an exploratory study of sexual responsibility among Latina youth, expressed how she felt when her father found out that she was no longer a virgin: "I felt bad. Just it's a different relationship I have with my mom than the relationship I have with my dad. . . . He always seen me as his little girl and I knew that at that point, he knew I wasn't his little girl anymore. I was his sweet little innocent girl."[33]

Three of the four mothers of lesbian-identified girls also told their daughters' fathers about what they had discovered. Martina, who saw her daughter kissing another girl, recounted how she demanded that Margarita tell her father about her sexual relationship with her girlfriend, "She had to tell him, because I did not want to say those words to him. I could tell that he was not expecting to hear that . . . he wanted to cry but didn't, he just kept asking her what was wrong with her. She would not even look him in the eyes because she was so ashamed." Like the mothers of heterosexual-identified girls, these mothers also relied upon the fathers' expressions of disillusionment to discourage their daughters from continuing with their sexual activities. But, unlike the mothers of heterosexual-identified girls, these mothers were also "outing" their daughters to their fathers. Fathers reacted to this information primarily as an indication of their daughter's sexual deviance or abnormality, as suggested by Margarita's father questioning what was wrong with her, rather than to their daughters' loss of virginity or sexual innocence. One of these mothers even told me that she initially hesitated to tell her husband because she was concerned that her husband might throw the daughter out of the home. This concern was based on her husband's support of a friend who had kicked his teenage son out of the home when the son came out to his parents. As scholars have noted, the repercussions for LGBTQ youth can be detrimental when they come out to their families or when they are "outed" within their families because they are vulnerable along a number of dimensions, particularly given their economic and emotional dependence on their families.[34]

Though all but one of the mothers of lesbian-identified girls told their daughters' fathers about their discovery of their daughter's same-sex attraction and sexual behaviors, all four of these mothers endeavored to conceal this knowledge from extended family members and therefore did not divulge any information to other women. Roberta, who was born and raised in a Mexican border city, was so worried that her family would find out about her daughter that she canceled our first interview three times, each time calling me back to reschedule and asking me to thoroughly explain how I would maintain the confidentiality of her and her daughter. She explained how she dealt with questions about her daughter's lack of interest in boys:

Sometimes when we get together, like for parties, my *comadres* or sister-in-law will ask me if Barbara has a boyfriend yet. I don't know what to say, so I just tell them that she's too busy focusing on school and they tell me that I'm lucky that she's so focused on school instead of boys. I don't want them to know, *ya me imagino el escándolo si supieran* [I could just imagine the scandal, if they knew]. This is different, it's not like when a girl gets pregnant or something like that because people can understand that sort of thing, *pero ¿¿cómo explico esto* [but how do I explain this]?!

Elsa, who had migrated from Puerto Rico with her family as a child and was a manager at a fast-food restaurant, also recounted how she addressed inquiries from relatives about her daughter Arely's participation in a gay-straight alliance club in school. One of Arely's cousins, who also attended the same high school, had told Elsa's sister about Arely's active role within the club.

After my niece's communion, we all went to my brother's house, and my sister asked me in front of everyone if it was true that Arely was in "*uno de esos clubs en la escuela, para esos gays* [one of those school clubs, for those gay people]." I was so mad at her for asking me that like that, everyone was quiet waiting for my answer. I told them that she was in a club for young people that were gay but also for people that weren't, to support young people that are gay in dealing with discrimination and things like that. I told them that Arely was not a lesbian but that she wanted to help out with things like that. I was like, "You know how Arely is about injustice." They seemed to believe me. But I told Arely not to say anything to them, at least not yet, you know, I don't know how they are going to react or what I'm going to say when it is known. Because I know that *tarde o temprano, se van a dar cuenta* [sooner or later, they will find out].

These mothers especially struggled with figuring out how they would explain their daughters' sexual behaviors to extended family members. While mothers of heterosexual-identified girls were able to rely upon claims of victimization, mothers of lesbian-identified girls did not feel that they could frame their daughters' behavior in this way to others (although, as discussed earlier in this chapter, they did reference victimization in their initial postdiscovery interactions with daughters). Elsa emphasized this point when she exclaimed, "*Pero¡¿ cómo explico esto*?!" This group of mothers conveyed a critical awareness of the "margin of error" that is afforded to heterosexual young women but that would not be extended to their daughters because their sexual behavior defied heteronormative expectations.[35] For example, Martina pointed out that, while people would initially perceive a young girl who was pregnant or no longer a virgin in a negative manner, this reaction would not be permanent. She animatedly explained, "People will get over it because we all know that she is not the first one and she sure is not going to be the last one." Thus, their daughters' sexual behavior could be perceived as much more deliberate than that of heterosexual young women in the family whose behavior might be attributed to their victimization.

These mothers also did not feel they could readily claim that their daughters' behavior was related to their rebelliousness, reflected in the phrase "*hacen lo que les da la gana* (they do whatever they want)." They expressed concern that extended family members would view their daughters' "doing what they wanted to do" as an indication that something was inherently wrong with their daughters. When I asked Gina how she thought her family would react if they found out about Imelda's sexual activities, she quickly answered, "*Que está loca* [that she's crazy]!" Martina, when asked the same question, similarly replied, "*Van a decir que está mal de la cabeza porque no es normal lo que hace ella* [they are going to say that she is sick in the head because what she is doing is not normal]." Mothers of lesbian-identified girls were worried that, while others might accept the explanation that their daughters were acting as they pleased, their behavior would still be understood as evidence of their moral and/or psychological deficiency. Mothers based these concerns on larger public discussions about the "causes of gay behavior" in the media and on their own experiences with informal conversations about gay or lesbian individuals.[36] Familiar with the homophobic discourses circulating in U.S. culture and within their own communities and families, they expressed legitimate concerns that their daughters would be stigmatized for their identification as lesbians and about how this would reflect on them as mothers. At time of interview, these mothers were unable to articulate how they would respond to family members when information about their daughters' sexual behavior was disclosed.

This group of mothers therefore requested that their daughters assist them in their concealment efforts by performing heterosexual femininity within family contexts. For instance, both Roberta and Gina asked their daughters to conform to normative expectations of feminity at family gatherings, figuring that family members would presume that their daughters were heterosexual because their gender presentation would be read as appropriately feminine. According to both mothers and daughters, these requests were a source of conflict between them, as reflected in seventeen-year-old Imelda's comments:

> Every time we are going somewhere where my aunts, uncles, and cousins are going to be, my mom asks me to try to look more "girly," you know what I'm saying? I say no, she starts crying, big ol' drama, and then I just do it, just to get it over with. I wear something like a nice top or something she likes. . . . I hate when she does that shit!

As she told me this, she pinched the bridge of her nose and tightly shut her brown almond-shaped eyes, trying not to cry. Eighteen-year-old Margarita, a self-described poet, also expressed frustration at her mother's attempts to impose a heterosexual feminine presentation and script on her in front of family members:

> Sometimes she tries to make me dance with guys, you know, like at *quinceañeras* or weddings . . . they come up to ask if I want to dance and I say no, but my mom is all loud, saying, "Go dance with him!" It pisses me off because I'm already trying to be cool with her about a lot of things about who I am. . . . I know it ain't easy for her . . . but I can't pretend forever for her.

These interactions between this group of mothers and daughters indicate that the mothers' strategies were especially shaped by heteronormativity and homophobia, limiting their ability to draw on other women in the family as resources in the same manner that mothers of heterosexual girls could. Their sex education efforts were constrained, if not altogether interrupted, by their efforts to present their daughters as heterosexual to family members, a pressure that they also placed on their daughters and that their daughters deeply resented.

Gendered Racial/Ethnic Boundaries and Identities

Alongside mothers' lessons to their daughters about sexual safety were notions about race/ethnicity. One key way in which these were transmitted was through mothers' judgmental references to the sexuality of young white women. Such an "assignment of sexual meanings, evaluations, and categories to others" are what the sociologist Joane Nagel calls "sexual ascription."[37] Mothers' sexual ascription of young white women marked the racial/ethnic boundary within which their daughters needed to confine their sexual behaviors. The boundary that mothers consistently referenced was not about interracial dating or marriage but about sexual behaviors and attitudes that the mothers specifically associated with white women and girls.[38] They were adamant that they did not want their daughters "to act like white girls," indicating that any flexibility that they had regarding their daughters' emerging sexuality stopped at this border.

Almost all mothers described having warned their daughters not to behave like white young women and/or accused them of doing so, even before they became aware of their daughters' sexual behavior. For example, Sara recounted an incident in which her daughter, who was thirteen at the time, asked for permission to sleep over at a friend's house: "I told her, '¿Qué te crees?! ¿Te quieres portar como las blancas?' [What do you think?! You want to act like white girls?] Their parents let them do whatever they want and then when these girls get in trouble, the parents act like they don't know why they acting so rebellious. . . . I told her no." When I probed her about what she thought young white women acted like, she immediately responded, "Esas sí tienen mucha libertad [Now, those girls have too much freedom]! Sometimes they act like they are crazy, acting like sucias [perverted women]!" Like Sara, mothers tended to characterize white young women as having "mucha libertad [too much freedom]" and/or as being "sin vergüenzas [without shame]." Aracelia, for instance, explained, "I understand that my daughter might have questions about sex . . . but that doesn't mean she can be sin vergüenza, like white girls." Mothers had limited to no interaction with white women and girls. Those who did have limited contact with white women did so through their employment in the service sector, but, for the majority of them, the media were the basis for most of their sexual ascriptions of white women and girls.

Mothers thus also utilized a discursive strategy that specifically integrated perceptions about the sexuality of white women to talk to daughters about their gendered sexual expectations for them. This particular discursive repertoire was also indicative of "how they thought through race," which, as the sociologist Ruth Frankenberg asserts, is "learned, drawn upon, and enacted, repetitively but not automatically or by rote, chosen but by no means freely so."[39] They thought of their daughters as distinct from themselves in the sense that their daughters were coming of age in a context different from that in which they themselves had done so, but they still thought of their daughters as similar to them in terms of their gendered racial/ethnic identity. They drew upon perceptions of racial differences between white women and themselves in terms of sexual behavior and attitudes as a way to assert to their daughters the importance of maintaining a gendered identity that was grounded in their identities as Mexican and Puerto Rican women. Mothers utilized this particular discursive strategy to mark the sexual boundary for their U.S.-born daughters and to assert control over their daughters' sexual behavior through their ability to question their daughters' racial/ethnic authenticity, indicating that these mothers understood their daughters' emerging sexuality through the lens of gender and race.

Furthermore, the mothers challenged negative stereotypes about themselves as Latinas through their characterization of white women as sexually excessive and out control. Dolores explained her perception of white women's sexual propriety in this fashion: "They are always criticizing us Latinas, saying that we are too traditional or this or that . . . but they should look at themselves first. They are the ones on TV almost naked and doing *pendejadas* [stupid/foolish things]." Like the other mothers, Dolores pointed out that, despite white women's visible presence in media, their sexual behavior was often treated as unremarkable within mainstream society. And, as they talked about how they understood themselves to be judged by the dominant society, the mothers regularly expressed a collective sense of themselves as Latina mothers through the phrase "*nosotras las latinas* [we Latinas]." Conchita conveyed this when she discussed the challenges she encountered in trying to communicate with her daughter about sexuality: "*Nosotras las latinas tenemos que seguir adelante con nuestras hijas* [We Latinas have to press forward with our daughters]." Thus, as a marginalized group in U.S. society, Latina mothers also utilized negative notions of white women's sexual propriety to distinguish themselves from them and to gain some power for themselves through their claim to sexual respectability.[40]

Latina girls, however, rejected their mothers' accusations that they were adopting the sexual behavior and attitudes of white young women, declaring that they were not like them.[41] Sixteen-year-old Juanita strongly asserted this as she discussed why she disagreed with her mother's and aunt's ideas of virginity and other gendered sexual expectations: "I guess it's different to me 'cause I grew up here, but, at the same time, it's not like I want to be like them crazy-ass white girls . . . virginity doesn't mean anything to them, it's like, 'Whatever!'" Similarly, fifteen-year-old Carla recalled that she denied wanting to be *"como las güeras* [like white girls]" in a heated argument with her mom: "She thinks I act the way I do 'cause I just want to be *'como las güeras.'* I told her, 'Not even! I ain't trying to act like that, having sex whenever with whoever, showing my boobs on TV and kissing girls so guys can just look at me. . . . I ain't a 'ho' like that!"[42] Latina girls made it clear that, although they did not fully embrace their mothers' ideas about women's sexuality, they did not identify or want to be identified with what they also perceived to be the sexual excessiveness of white young women (as I discuss in chapter 4, this also was communicated within their peer groups, which were predominately homogeneous along racial/ethnic lines). Daughters utilized the very same sexual ascriptions of young white women that their mothers communicated to them to simultaneously construct their own gendered sexual identities and challenge accusations that they were losing their racial/ethnic identities in the process.

It is worth noting that there was a general silence about the sexuality of African American women and girls in the narratives of both mothers and daughters. While most of the women and girls I spoke with lived in predominantly working-class Latina/o neighborhoods, a significant number of the girls attended public schools in which Latina/o and African American students made up the majority of the student body. Thus, they had more opportunities to interact with African American girls than they did with white girls. Although I cannot offer a conclusive analysis of the invisibility of African American women and girls in these Latinas' narratives about sexuality, one possible explanation could be the pervasiveness and effectiveness of larger racial discourses that already construct African American as the "other."

"Ya sabes como son...": On Mexican and Puerto Rican Women

Both Mexican and Puerto Rican mothers drew contrasts between themselves and Latina mothers who belonged to other ethnic groups. Though both groups occasionally mentioned other Latina groups, such as Guatemalan or Ecuadorian women, they most often contrasted Mexicans and Puerto Ricans when talking about the challenges they faced in raising their daughters. Their perspectives on the other group were often based on their interactions with women from that group, usually as neighbors, friends, or co-workers. This was exemplified by Francisca when she discussed her efforts to talk about sex with her seventeen-year-old daughter, Samantha: "My neighbor, she's *mexicana, buena gente y todo* [nice and all], but she never talked to her daughter about *de eso* [that (meaning sex)], and now she is pregnant. *Pobre nena* [poor girl] . . . I don't know, you *mexicanas*, you can't talk about that at home *para nada, ¿verdad?* [at all, right]?"

Early in our interview process, mothers would inquire about my specific racial/ethnic identity, usually taking a guess as to which Latina group I identified with before even allowing me to answer.[43] Mexican women usually prefaced their comments about Puerto Rican women with "*tú sabes como son* [you know how they are)]," while Puerto Rican women would generally initiate their commentary on the gendered behavior of Mexican women by asking me to tell them if it was true or not ("*dime si es verdad o no*") or to explain something to them ("*explícame algo*"). But, regardless of how they broached the subject, both groups of mothers expressed their ideas about the other group's socialization of its daughters. For example, discussing why she thought her daughter's friend was a bad influence, Betina criticized what she saw as Puerto Rican mothers' lack of supervision of their daughters:

> She [her daughter's friend] always wants to be out on the street. Sometimes, she tries to *sonsacarse a* [coax] Rita [her daughter] to go hang out with her on the street, but I won't let her. *La mamá la deja que haga lo que le da la gana* [Her mom allows her to do whatever she feels like doing], but I see that a lot of Puerto Rican women do that with their daughters. That's why you see the girls hanging all over the boys on the street. . . . *No les ponen las riendas a las hijas* [they don't place any restraints on their daughters].

Emma shared a similar perspective on Puerto Rican mothers when she described an argument she had had with her daughter over her unwillingness to allow her to attend a coed weekend trip organized by a local community center. The mothers of two of her daughter's friends, both Puerto Rican, had attempted to persuade her to allow Miriam to participate in the trip. As Emma explained her unwillingness to permit her daughter to participate in the weekend activity, she commented, "*Yo pienso que las puertorriqueñas les dan más libertad a sus hijas que nosotras, pero a veces es demasiado* [I think that Puerto Rican women allow their daughters more freedom than we (Mexicans) do, but sometimes it's excessive]. . . . *ya ves, a veces les vale* [but as you see, sometimes they could care less]!"

While Mexican women generally perceived Puerto Rican women as not placing enough restrictions on their daughters, Puerto Rican women tended to regard Mexican women as being too conservative in their expectations of their daughters. Maria conveyed this perception to me one day while we were watching a *telenovela* (Spanish-language soap opera) in her living room. In the *telenovela*, the protagonist, a young Mexican woman, seduced by a man discovered shortly thereafter that she was pregnant. As the protagonist dramatically cried about being taken advantage of in typical soap-opera fashion, Maria and her *comadre* loudly scoffed at her predicament, calling her a *pendeja* (an idiot). Maria then turned to me and remarked:

> Let's see, tell me if I'm right or wrong, but *las mexicanas son más cerradas sobre el tema del sexo* [Mexican women are more close-minded on the topic of sex]. I think that is why you see so many young Mexican girls having babies or getting married. Their mothers don't tell them anything. I mean, I think we [Puerto Rican women] talk to our daughters more about it.

Likewise, Francisca described Mexican women as being less willing than Puerto Rican women to talk to daughters about sex: "Sometimes, they [Mexican mothers] can be too strict with them. . . . But I think we [Puerto Rican mothers] might be more honest with our daughters about the topic, even if it embarrasses us . . . it is not fair to think that they are going to know everything they need to know about *de eso* [that (referring to sex)]."

As illustrated by Francisca's comment, marriage was a topic that emerged quite often when Mexican and Puerto Rican mothers assessed each other's approaches to the sex education of daughters. Betina, who had described Puerto Rican mothers as failing to supervise their daughters adequately, discussed what she understood to be differences in Mexican and Puerto Rican women's attitudes toward marriage as we sat at her kitchen table drinking coffee and talking about her family. On that October afternoon, her fifteen-year-old daughter, Rita, was still at school. As Betina recounted how she and her sister had immigrated to Chicago in their late teens, the telephone rang, and she excused herself to answer it. After asking who it was, she visibly stiffened, and her tone changed as she replied rather curtly, "*No, Rita no está aquí ahorita. No sé cuándo va a llegar, okay? Aha, Michelle, yo le digo que llamaste. Hasta luego*"[No, Rita is not here right now. I don't know when she'll get home, okay? Aha, I'll tell her you called, Michelle. So long]. Hanging up the telephone, she shook her head and stated:

> *Esa muchacha no me gusta para nada* [I don't like that girl at all]. I already told Rita that I don't want her hanging out with her [Michelle]. *Es muy callejera* [She is always hanging out in the streets]. . . . *Y la mamá es igual de loca, ya sabes como son las puertorriqueñas* [And her mom is just as crazy, you know how Puerto Rican women are].

When I asked Betina to explain what she meant by the comment about Michelle's mother, she hesitated before she replied, thinking about how to answer my question. She explained that her mother raised her, along with her sister, to be *señoritas*. As a testament to this socialization, Betina pointed to her status as a virgin when she married Rita's father. She insisted that, while she lamented that Rita, her daughter, was no longer a virgin, she was still endeavoring to raise Rita appropriately: "I don't want her to just live with different men. . . . *todavía se puede casar bien, aunque ya no es virgen* [even though she is no longer a virgin, she can still get married properly]." She hesitated and continued, "But I don't think marriage is that important to Puerto Rican women, it's like, *se conforman con* [they are content with] just living with a man." She was quick to explain that, although she had left her husband when Rita was four years because he physically abused her, she had never lived with any man after that because that would have set a "*mal ejemplo*" (bad example) for her daughter, emphasizing that she would not live with another man unless they were married.

Betina's statement about Puerto Rican women's attitudes toward marriage was in line with comments made by other Mexican women about Puerto Rican women and marriage. For example, Aracelia was critical of what she perceived to be Puerto Rican women's inability to allow for mistakes within the context of marital relationships.

> *¿No sé, como que son muy exageradas para todo, ¿verdad* [I don't know, it's like they make a big deal about everything, right]? The slightest thing goes wrong in their marriage and just like that [snapping her fingers], they leave their husbands or divorce them. *Como que son más rencorosas que nosotras las mexicanas* [Like they are more spiteful than us Mexicans]. I understand if there is abuse or something like that, but just because you fought *por una tontería* [because of a foolish act], you don't leave. Marriage is hard work! *No aguantan* [they don't tolerate].

Lilia made a similar comment about the inability of Puerto Rican women to tolerate the hardships that sometimes accompany marital relationships, adding that this attitude among Puerto Rican mothers negatively influences their daughters: "I think young Puerto Rican girls get pregnant and do not get married because of the example they get from their mothers. Like my neighbor, she left her husband because he would come home drunk sometimes." Rolling her eyes, she continued, "And now, her eighteen-year-old-daughter has two babies from two different men. . . . *Ellas se conforman con vivir de esa manera* [They are satisfied to accept living that way]." That Lilia herself was never married did not prevent her from asserting her evaluation of Puerto Rican women's stance on marriage.

Puerto Rican women, on the other hand, utilized the idea of "*conformando* [accepting]" differently when speaking about Mexican women and their marital situations. For example, Gina described how, unlike her Mexican friend, she left her husband rather than put up with domestic violence:

> I left him like that [snapping her fingers]! . . . I don't know how some women put up with it, like my friend, *ella sí se aguanta, es mexicana* [She does put up with it, she's Mexican]. I see that Mexican women might stay married more than us, but they put up with a lot more than us *puertorriqueñas . . . se conforma con la situación* [she resigns herself to the situation].

Whereas Mexican women took on a judgmental tone in their critiques of Puerto Rican women's attitudes toward marriage, Puerto Rican women expressed a pity for Mexican women when considering their attitudes toward marriage.[44]

Teresa connected her perception of Mexican women's ethos of suffering to shame, pointing out that Mexican families relied too heavily on marriage as a solution to daughters' mishaps: "I think marriage is important, but not the answer for everything. . . . I wouldn't make them [her two teenage daughters] get married if they weren't ready just because *metieron las patas* (got pregnant)." She paused here as she thought about how to explain why she would not demand marriage of her daughters:

> *Yo veo* [I see] that when Mexican girls get pregnant, they want to make them get married right away. . . . *Como que la familia se conforma con que esté casada la muchacha* [Like the family can deal with it if the girl is married]. . . . I think that making them get married when they aren't ready makes it worse for them. We aren't in México or Puerto Rico. Things are different here, you know what I mean?

Teresa's acknowledgment of the need to take into account how living in a U.S. context may pose different challenges in raising daughters was certainly echoed by all mothers.

Gendered racial/ethnic notions were part of mothers' strategies of action to meet the challenges of raising U.S.-born daughters, specifically in their efforts to mark for their sexually active daughters the limits of what was acceptable, as well as to set themselves apart from white women and from each other. But they also made distinctions among themselves as Mexican and Puerto Rican women, evaluating their performance as mothers vis-à-vis the performance of members of the other ethnic group. While both groups of mothers perceived white women as too sexually permissive, Mexican mothers perceived themselves to be more sexually conservative than Puerto Rican mothers, and Puerto Rican mothers thought of themselves as being less conservative with regard to their socialization of daughters. Both groups of mothers expressed an awareness of and a concern about pregnancy and about birth rates among Latinas in general, but, as evidenced in their interviews, they offered the differences in mothering between Mexican and Puerto Rican women as one explanation for these outcomes, particularly the degree to which mothers in each group were willing to discuss sexuality with their daughters and each groups' approach to marriage. Thus, while they were able to point to how some social forces, such as immigration and racialization processes, had shaped their common experiences as Latina mothers, they also maintained the boundaries between themselves as Mexican and Puerto Rican women by drawing on a repertoire of explanations for Latina girls' sexual outcomes, specifically the larger societal cultural narrative of mother blaming and the cultural distinctions they made between themselves. This form of boundary making may be a way for these two groups of Latinas to distance themselves and their daughters not only from the sexuality of white women but also from the "problem" of Latina teen pregnancy.

Conclusion

I do not present these mothers' strategies to evaluate how effective they are in "truly" empowering mothers and daughters or the extent to which they are "truly" reflective of a feminist consciousness. Approaching the relationship between mothering practices and empowerment in such dichotomous ways, as has often been done with women of color, distracts us from appreciating the complex and sometimes contradictory forms that resistance takes place.[45] Instead, I invite readers to consider how mothers' strategies for addressing the emerging sexuality of their daughters, along with their daughters' interpretations of these strategies, provide insight into how Latinas engage and begin to rework their meanings and processes of gender and sexuality.

A larger cultural framing of adolescent sexuality as dangerous has informed Latina mothers' perceptions of their daughters as "at risk" for negative sexual outcomes. But, rather than adopt the prevailing sex education approach at the time—sexual abstinence until marriage—these mothers chose to focus on sexual safety in their conversations with their daughters. While their emphasis on sexual safety could be interpreted as a relaxing of Latinas' sexual "values" due to assimilation, it is more complex than just an indication of their assimilation. The notion that changes in sexual behavior and values among Latinas/os are a direct reflection of their "Americanization" is problematic because it suggests not only that sexuality in relation to assimilation follows a linear path in which "American" sexual values are placed at the end of the continuum but that "American" sexual values, attitudes, and behavior are somehow more liberal than those of other groups. That Latina mothers' incorporation of sexual safety lessons was not a marker of their assimilation was made especially evident in their assertions that they did not want to identify and be identified with the sexual behaviors and attitudes they ascribed to white women. Instead of focusing on the prescribed sex education of sexual abstinence, mothers decided on sexual safety as a lesson to transmit to their daughters because they wanted to be responsive to the sex education needs of their U.S.-born daughters, who are overrepresented in broader discussions of the "problem" of teen sexuality. On one level, then, the Latina mothers I spoke with wanted to protect their daughters from negative sexual outcomes and from gender inequality, continuing to emphasize the safe-sex lessons they had already been providing to their daughters while now also sharing with them some of their own experiences and recruiting other women in their family to help them. Their experiences indicate that we need to better understand how different groups of parents engage larger discourses about teen sexuality and what they consider to be responsible parenting in relation to the sex education they provide to their children.

Furthermore, the discussions that unfolded between these Latina mothers and their daughters provide some insight into how gender and sexuality among Latinas are given meaning through intergenerational interactions. Too often, it is assumed that only mothers produce and transmit cultural knowledge to their daughters.[46] It is also necessary to consider the ways in which daughters contribute to the production and transmission of meanings of gender and sexuality in these mother-daughter relationships. While many of these initial conversations between Latina mothers and daughters were fraught with tension, the interactions created opportunities for daughters to articulate their perspectives on gender and sexuality and to reconfigure gender and sexual meanings and processes with their mothers.

Mothers' sex education of their daughters after discovering daughters' sexual activities, however, were also elaborated upon in a context of gender inequality. Though they provided their daughters with lessons about safe sex, it was still quite painful for them to learn of their daughters' sexual behaviors. Mothers' construction of their daughters as victims is indicative of the broader societal negation of the sexual agency and desire of young women. And this particular reaction on the mothers' part seemed to contradict the messages of sexual safety that they were communicating to their daughters. This reminds us that we cannot lose sight of the patriarchal constraints under which women and girls negotiate and make sense of sexual subjectivity. As for most parents, it is not easy for Latina mothers to talk with their daughters about sexuality. It is undeniably a challenging task and one that mothers are primarily responsible for because gender organizes family life and parenting. And it is mothers who are typically blamed when their children deviate from gendered sexual expectations, particularly their daughters. Their daughters' behaviors also have implications for them.

Thus, on another level, mothers' strategies for responding to their daughters' emerging sexuality were also about identity and boundary maintenance for both themselves and their daughters. They were now mothers of daughters who were sexually experienced, a relationship that jeopardized their identities as good mothers, and so they were also trying to hold onto this respectable gendered identity. The significance they assigned to their identities as mothers especially emerged when they were defining themselves in opposition to each other as Mexican and Puerto Rican mothers, citing differences in their attitudes about marriage and in how they communicated with their daughters about sex. But it was also reflected in their attempts to manage knowledge about their daughters' sexual behaviors and perceptions about their parenting through their disclosures to some family members.

The mothers may have challenged patriarchal practices when they reached out to other women in their families to create more opportunities for their daughters to learn about sexuality and when they asked their daughters' fathers to ask them to share responsibility for parenting daughters. But these actions were coupled with both an emphasis on their own proper parenting and a distancing from their daughters' behaviors. Thus, these strategies also accommodated the belief that mothers are primarily to blame when their children misbehave. In other words, mothers' adoption of their specific strategies occurred in a context of patriarchal bargains that defined and shaped their options.[47]

The approaches of mothers of lesbian-identified daughters were particularly constricted not only by patriarchy but also by heteronormativity. In other words, their claims to identities as good mothers were especially jeopardized by these intersecting systems of inequality. Unlike mothers of heterosexual-identified daughters, these mothers were not able to "normal-ize" their daughters' sexual behavior to family members by drawing on claims of victimization or youth rebelliousness. Instead, they rejected the possibility of same-sex identities for their daughters, constructing these identities and related behaviors and desires as "foreign" to Latinas/os; their fear of stigma-tization of both their daughters and themselves informed their decision to conceal this information from extended family members and to demand that their daughters cooperate with this strategy. In this way, they were able to hold on, even if briefly, to their identities as good mothers and to protect their daughters, but, in doing so, they also bolstered sexual hierarchies.

Mothers also deployed strategies to maintain an identity and a bound-ary grounded in gendered racial/ethnic distinctions. Mothers were teaching their daughters about sexuality, but they did so by constructing themselves and their daughters in opposition to white women and girls and to Mexican or Puerto Rican women—reflecting how race/ethnicity, sexuality, and gen-der are brought together in the maintenance of boundaries.[48] They may have based their assumptions about Mexican or Puerto Rican women on their everyday interactions with members of that opposite group, whereas they relied on their very limited interactions (if any) with white women to form opinions about their practices, but, nonetheless, they relied upon gendered racial/ethnic stereotypes about both groups of women to set themselves apart and to garner some power for themselves. Their strategies, then, in part, were also a response to their racialization as U.S. Latina women, demonstrating that their identities as women and mothers are constructed in relation to how others define them. Their deployment of sexualized racial/ethnic stereo-types about each other and about white women in their elaboration of strate-gies provides further evidence that racial, gender, and sexual identity prac-tices are interdependent processes.[49] However, when they defined themselves on the basis of racial, class, gender, and sexual stereotypes of others—like the "*mexicana sufrida*" and the "*puertorriqueña rencorosa*"—these controlling images also limited their ability to fully see and comprehend the social forces that shaped all of their mothering experiences.

Latina mothers' responses to their knowledge of their daughters' sexual behaviors indicate that we must take into consideration the sociocultural context in which they provide sex education to their daughters. They were not "culturally silent" about sexuality in their interactions with their daugh-ters; their approaches to sex education were related to broader discourses about adolescent sexuality, racial formations, gender and sexual ideologies, and sex education policies. In other words, we cannot thoroughly under-stand the content of the lessons that mothers provide to their children if we do not appreciate the social location from which they take on this challenging parenting task. By focusing on the magnified moments of mothers' discovery of daughters' sexual behaviors and the conversations between mothers and daughters that unfold after this discovery, we are able to grasp some of the ways in which they are cultural actors, rather than just understanding them as women who have culture bearing down on them.

3

The Sexual (Mis)Education of Latina Girls

For our first scheduled interview, I met Samantha, who had character-ized her mother as "old-school Puerto Rican," at Centro Adelante, where she was organizing poster-size diagrams for a presentation she was prepar-ing on safe sex.[1] The professionally printed diagrams illustrated female and male reproductive organs and different birth control and safe-sex methods. Samantha, along with Carolyn, a young African American woman, had been training to be a peer health educator at the Chicago Committee on Youth Health (CCYH). Under the supervision of a CCYH youth coordinator, the two young women of color led an engaging one-hour workshop on safe sex for a group of fifteen to twenty young women and men that afternoon. Their audience, composed mostly of Latina/o youth, listened attentively and asked pointed questions about access to sexual health resources in the community and about safe-sex methods. A young man asked where one could obtain an HIV test and whether parental consent was required for such a test, while a young woman inquired about parental consent for access to birth control. With minimal assistance from the youth coordinator, Samantha and Carolyn confidently addressed questions directed at them. Later, I asked Samantha whether she had been nervous during the workshop. She confidently replied, "I'm just trying to spread some knowledge other teens might want to know about. Please, especially when a lot of these schools don't really do a good job of telling it like it is, they don't care about what we wanna know or need to know, just what they think we should know and shouldn't be knowing and doing."

Samantha, like the majority of girls I spoke with, expressed her dissatisfaction with school-based sex education.[2] Describing some of her own experiences with sex education in the classroom, the honor roll student stated, "Everyone is always telling us, like, 'Knowledge is power,' this and that. But when it comes down to it with some things, like sex ed., some teachers are like, 'Uh-uh, that's too much information for you. You only need to know this.'" School-based sex education, whether abstinence-only or comprehensive, left much to be desired in terms of the knowledge that was imparted to the Latina girls who shared their experiences with me.

Research on sex education has revealed that sex education policies are informed by national and local struggles over the meanings and consequences of gender, race, class, and sexual categories.[3] The implementation of sex education has generally been guided by the perceived need to protect the sexual innocence of youth or to protect youth from the dangers of their own sexual curiosity. Decisions about which objective to pursue are often guided by assumptions about race/ethnicity.[4] While middle- and upper-class white youth are often perceived to be in need of intervention to guide them through their "normally abnormal" hormone-besieged adolescence, youth of color are typically constructed as always "at risk" and a source of danger.[5] And feminist scholars have pointed to the ways that gender and sexual inequalities are produced and maintained through sex education lessons.[6] Thus, it should not be assumed, as the sociologist Jessica Fields contends, that all young people encounter sex education curricula in the same manner.[7]

In this chapter, I explore Latina girls' accounts of their school-based sex education experiences in middle school. Their interactions with teachers and sex educators were tied to various assumptions about Latinas and were central to their stories of school-based sex education in middle school. Their experiences reveal not only how sexism, racism, and the presumption that all girls are heterosexual structure the content and delivery of school-based sex education for Latinas girls but also how these young women relate their need to be informed sexual subjects to their educational plans. Their narratives indicate that their ability to be academically successful is also an important component of their crafting of femininity, a process that entails negotiation of their sexual subjectivity and respectability. The intersection of Latina girls' multiple identities—as U.S. Latinas, as daughters of immigrants and/or migrants, as students, and as sexual subjects—shapes their understandings of the role of education in their lives and the importance they assign to their future success.

Sex Education and Public Schools

Presently, sex education curricula are grouped into two broad categories: abstinence-plus (also called comprehensive sexuality education) and abstinence-only-until-marriage (also called abstinence-only). Comprehensive sex education does cover abstinence but also teaches about contraception, sexually transmitted diseases, HIV, and abortion. Slightly more than half of the girls I spoke with described access to this type of sex education. The rest of the young women were provided abstinence-only education. Abstinence-only education does not teach about contraception or abortion. When sexually transmitted diseases and HIV are referenced, it is typically to highlight the negative consequences of premarital sex.

With the exception of two girls, all of the young women who participated in this study were or had been at one point Chicago Public Schools (CPS) students.[8] Since the average age of young women at the time of interview was sixteen, their middle school sex education generally occurred between 1998 and 2002, a period marked by increased federal funding for abstinence-only programs. Although the Reagan administration had made federal funding available for abstinence-only sex education beginning in the early 1980s, the support and promotion of abstinence-only programs intensified in the mid-1990s. More than $1 billion were channeled to abstinence-only sex education programs between 1996 and 2006, while federal funds were not made available for comprehensive sexuality education.[9]

Although girls discussed their sexuality education experiences at all grade levels, it was their experiences in the sixth through the eighth grades that they elaborated upon in great detail.[10] During the years, while these young women were middle school students, the Board of Education of the Chicago Public Schools did not take an official stance or provide guidelines on sex education. Thus, it was possible to have variations in the quality and content of sex education in CPS. However, there were similarities in the girls' descriptions of their sex education in terms of how they participated in it and who was designated to teach it. For example, the majority of the girls said that female and male students generally received sex education together in the classroom, whether it was comprehensive or abstinence-only sex education.

Guest speakers, most of whom were women, typically taught sex education in middle school, according to most of the young women.[11] But teachers also figured prominently in the girls' discussions of their sex education.[12] In what follows, I discuss themes and patterns that cut across both types of sex education curricula, allowing us to further understand how inequalities emerge and are reinforced through sex education in general.

Maintaining Inequality through School-Based Sex Education

The girls' narratives reveal that heteronormativity was central to the content and delivery of both types of sex education curricula. In girls' descriptions of their sex education experiences, lessons were crafted around heterosexuality and heterosexual norms. And heterosexuality was most often discussed in relation to masculinity and femininity. In other words, masculinity and femininity were tightly linked to heterosexuality, and femininity was connected to the good-girl/bad-girl dichotomy within sex education lessons. However, the institutionalization of heterosexuality via sex education also entailed the incorporation of racialized gender stereotypes to produce specific lessons for Latina youth about how they should engage sex education in the classroom and what kind of sex education information was most relevant to them.

Lessons about Engaging Sex Education in the Classroom

Whether they were speaking of abstinence-only or comprehensive sex education experiences, many girls told of interactions with teachers and sex educators in which students were invited or expected to ask questions but were then disciplined for their level of engagement with sex education. Much as my friends and I did when we were middle school students, they characterized their male peers as "acting foolish," "not taking it seriously," or "saying ignorant things." Quite often, girls told of incidents in which boys were scolded or disciplined by teachers for misbehaving during sex education. Girls, on the other hand, were described as being reprimanded for their active engagement with sex education in the classroom. In other words, it was possible for female students to be too interested in learning about sex. Such was the experience of seventeen-year-old Minerva, whose mother, Carmen, rejected the idea that Minerva was a lost cause because she was no longer a virgin. Not one to shy away from speaking her mind, the talkative young woman often made comments that elicited either laughs or gasps from her peers at Hogar del Pueblo. Raising her arm as she described doing to ask a sex educator whether it was "true" that the morning-after pill could prevent pregnancy, Minerva said, "Anyways, she [sex educator] was starting to answer me when Ms. Phyllis [her eighth-grade teacher] was like, 'Now why do you want to know about that, Minerva? You don't got anything to worry about if you're behaving and, anyway, we are out of time.'" Other girls told of similar exchanges with teachers and sex educators in which their inquiries were met with suspicion, suggesting that they were perceived as "knowing girls" and therefore assumed to be sexually active because they displayed some knowledge and/or curiosity about sexuality.[13] By publicly questioning Minerva about the motives behind her inquiry, her teacher communicated to the students not only that certain questions were invalid but that they could shift girls unto the wrong side of the good-girl/bad-girl dichotomy.

The young women vividly recalled that their teachers and sex educators prefaced or followed lessons with a statement about the need for girls to be mindful of their respectability, emphasizing that they should behave like "good girls" or "young ladies." A young Puerto Rican with pink-streaked hair and a small silver hook ring on her eyebrow, seventeen-year-old Imelda, told me of how her eighth-grade teacher interjected this message during a guest speaker's comprehensive sex education presentation:

Like the woman [the sex educator] was talking about sex as being a personal choice and not letting anyone pressure us, and that when we were ready we should remember to be safe, and all that, you know? And Mrs. Damenzo [the teacher] is like, "Yeah, but they shouldn't be doing it, right? They should act like young ladies so that the boys will respect them."

According to girls, these contradictory lessons left them uncertain about what to do with the information presented to them. Inés, whose mother slapped her when she found out about her sexual behavior, frustratingly explained, "I don't get it, they tell you all about being safe, then turn around and tell you, 'But you really don't need to know this, unless you a hoochie.'" Teachers and sex educators were never described as warning boys that their respect was tied to their sexual behavior. These gender-specific messages implicitly communicated to girls and boys not only that girls were the intended recipients of sex education but that there are limits to their sex education, given that the knowledge sought should reflect sexual modesty.

Yet, the girls' narratives also suggest that these gender-specific messages were fused with perceptions about them as Latina girls. Teachers and sex educators inscribed the good-girl/bad-girl dichotomy with racialized sexual stereotypes of Latinas that functioned to specify the kind of "bad girls" they should avoid becoming (i.e., the pregnant Latina teen or the sexually promiscuous Latina). The majority of young women described interactions with teachers and sex educators in which references were made to these particular "bad girls." Olivia, who desired to be a social worker, encountered such a lesson from her seventh-grade abstinence-only sex educator:

> The lady [the sex educator] talking to us was all about how true love waits. Every time I asked a question she didn't like or whatever, she would say, "That is not something someone your age should even be thinking about." . . . I think I was annoying her 'cause she just said, "Maybe a lot of girls you know are having sex, but you need to be better than that. When you ask things like that, it makes people think you are like those girls."

Like Olivia, other young women reported that teachers and sex educators assumed that they already knew or were acquainted with "those girls," who were perceived to be prevalent in students' neighborhoods. This was seventeen-year-old Elvia's experience. A cadet in her high school JROTC (Junior Reserve Officers Training Corps) program, Elvia shared how her eighth-grade sex educator responded to her when she questioned her suppositions about Latinas: "She got all embarrassed . . . and just said, 'Well, I'm just telling you how it is. Numbers don't lie, there are a lot of teenagers in your community who are making real poor choices when it comes to sex.'" The mention of "those girls" and "a lot of teenagers" by these young women's teachers referred not to girls or youth in the general sense but specifically to Latina youth.

Latina girls' sex education experiences reveal that their interactions with teachers and sex educators constituted a heterosexualizing process that supported gender inequalities between boys and girls and among the girls themselves. Teachers and sex educators not only presumed that all students were heterosexual but also invoked a good-girl/bad-girl dichotomy that kept boys' sexual behaviors invisible and unchecked. Furthermore, this dichotomy was racialized, in that it both borrowed on and supported the notion that Latinas are culturally predisposed to fall on the "bad" side of it.[14]

Lessons about "Latino Culture" and Pregnancy Prevention

Another point that was widely discussed in the girls' accounts of their school-based sex education experiences was the emphasis placed on pregnancy prevention lessons. Although these young women were warned not to be like "those girls," their narratives suggest that they were still viewed as a particular type of girl—a Latina teen always at heightened risk for pregnancy. Minerva articulated her awareness of how this perception of Latinas figured into her sex education:

Sometimes they come at us like we are these ghetto-ass kids who just make babies and drop out of school . . . like we all have single moms on welfare that don't show us how to be responsible so they talk down to us, like, "OK, we know that in the Hispanic culture it's okay for girls to get pregnant young and become mothers, but not in American culture, okay?"

Minerva, like many other young women, criticized teachers and sex educators for often connecting Latina girls' risk for pregnancy to a "Latino culture" in which not only were Latinas presumed to be sexually oriented toward Latino men but also gender relations among them were assumed to be shaped by a unique machismo system oppressive to women ("machismo" is commonly conceptualized as a strong and exaggerated sense of masculinity specific to Latinos). Loudly popping her gum every so often as she thought about my questions, sixteen-year-old Miriam, a self-described "tomboy," recounted with much annoyance such a lesson provided by her seventh-grade sex educator: "[She] started talking about Latino culture and saying that because of machismo, guys were always gonna try to control us and tell us how many babies to have, and that they were too macho to wear condoms." Experiences such as Miriam's illustrate how the heterosexual parameters of femininity are maintained through gender and race/ethnic-specific sex education lessons; such lessons depict young Latinos as sexually manipulative and ignorant about condom use and also communicate to young Latinas that their main task as unmarried young women is to develop the skills necessary to effectively fulfill their sexual gatekeeper role.

The significance of racialized gender stereotypes of Latinas was particularly evidenced in the ways in which information about the Depo-Provera shot was provided to girls. Some young women related that sex educators spent a considerable amount of time emphasizing the shot as an effective form of birth control. Their narratives suggest that sex educators generously supplied both information and advice about the effectiveness of this particular birth control option. Sitting cross-legged on a sofa across from me, sixteen-year-old Maritza remembered how a sex educator introduced "the shot" to the young women in Maritza's eighth-grade class:

So this woman [the sex educator] has the nerve to get up there and say, "I ain't gonna spend too much time on condoms 'cause you probably won't use them anyway. Guys usually don't wanna wear them 'cause of all the machismo and stuff. So if you are gonna have sex, and you really shouldn't, then you should wear a condom and at least know about the pill or shot so you won't get pregnant."

Similarly, fifteen-year-old Marta, who always seemed to be taking pictures of her friends at Hogar del Pueblo and was a cadet in her high school JROTC program, told of how the sex educator presented information about Depo-Provera to her eighth-grade class: "She [the sex educator] said something like, 'Too many Hispanic girls feel that having a baby is no big deal, but don't believe it . . . the shot is a good way to help you be safe.' . . . I felt that she thought we were all *pendejas* [idiots or stupid], like the shot would be easier for us since all we worried was about getting pregnant."

The pregnancy prevention lessons that Latina youth encountered in their sex education are informed by the heteronormative designation of sexual relations and bodies as reproductive. The experiences of Maritza, Marta, and many other Latina girls reveal that they are assigned hetero-sexuality but that they are seen as failing to conform to idealized hetero-normative standards. Their bodies, read through a racial-gender lens, are interpreted as excessively reproductive. Historically, there have been racial-ized gender stereotypes about the reproductive decision making of Latinas in the United States, such as in depictions of them as wanting large fami-lies and refusing or unable to use birth control. However, scholars have asserted that Latinas' sexuality and reproduction have recently received intense scrutiny entrenched in a larger concern about the immigrant "invasion."[15] Anti-immigrant discourses and policies have fueled public ste-reotypes about the "hyperfertility" of Latinas, which inform the develop-ment of social policies directed at them, particularly at their bodies.[16] For example, there has been controversy surrounding the 1992 FDA approval of the Depo-Provera injection; among the key issues are the unethical test-ing of this form of birth control on women of color in developing coun-tries and the heavy marketing of this form of birth control to women of color in the United States.[17] These scholarly insights on societal perceptions of and responses to Latinas' reproduction provide a way to make sense of the experiences Latina girls encountered regarding the presentation of birth control information in sex education. And, as the girls' narratives indicate, they perceived their sex education to be limited; they attributed this to racial-gender biases, exemplified by Marta's statement that the Depo-Provera shot was emphasized because the sex educators assumed that all Latina girls "worried was about getting pregnant." The racialized heteronormative assumption of Latina bodies as potentially overreproduc-tive that girls encountered often constrained their access to information, particularly the knowledge sought by young women who in middle school were exploring the possibility of identities not defined by heterosexuality, as I discuss in the next section.

Learning to Conceal Same-Sex Desire

Young Latinas who identified as lesbian said that, while in middle school, they had not yet identified themselves as such but that they had an awareness of their emerging sexual identity during this time. Several shared with me that they had had "crushes" on girls at this age. As Margarita put it, "I thought this girl in class was nice, but it was such a crush!" Recollecting her attraction to her middle school friend, the high school senior, whose mother saw her kissing another young woman, occasionally smiled and laughed out loud. Similarly, Imelda reflected, "I knew that I liked girls, but I don't think I saw myself as a lesbian at that point." This group of girls often described being confused during middle school about the feelings they had for other girls.

These young women indicated that they did not experience school-based sex education as a supportive context in which to explore their feelings and questions. As eighteen-year-old Cristina explained, "I knew I didn't look at guys the way I looked at girls, but, hell, no, there is no way the teachers were gonna wanna hear that!" Cristina, a young Puerto Rican with short, curly brown hair imagined out loud how teachers would have responded had she dared asked a question about "getting it on with girls." Shaking her head at the possible scenario, she said, "They would've been like, 'You must be crazy!' and probably just ignore me or call my mom to tell her I wasn't behaving in school or something." With the exception of only one young woman, this group of girls did not report asking questions during their sex education lessons in middle school.

Seventeen-year-old Linda was the only lesbian-identified girl who reported venturing to ask a question, albeit anonymously, while in middle school. Taking a moment to pull back her straight black hair into a pony tail, she recalled that her eighth-grade teacher instructed the students to write down their questions so that she could "pick some" to provide to the sex educator the next day. As the teacher reviewed the questions out loud, she came upon Linda's question:

> She started yelling, "Who asked this?! Who asked the question about books about lesbian teenagers?!" Shit, I did, but I wasn't gonna say anything! . . . She got more pissed off and was like, "I don't know who did it, but I hope it wasn't one of you girls, because you should know better than to act so immature."

The response to Linda's anonymous question is yet another example of how teachers directed gender-specific comments exclusively to girls about acceptable sexual behavior. Such a response is also reflective of the expectation that girls will assume "femininized responsibility" for helping maintain order within the classroom.[18] However, the dismissal of Linda's question as "immature" once again reflects an assumption that all the students were heterosexual and reinforces the message that that anything outside of heterosexuality is abnormal.

The middle school classroom for this group of girls was generally not a site in which they felt safe exploring their sexual identity. Like Linda, the other girls stated that they were "not gonna say anything" that would draw unwanted attention to their same-sex attractions. To further ensure this, they also spoke of making efforts to be recognized as "straight" by peers and school authorities. Eighteen-year-old Barbara, whose mother told family members that Barbara was too dedicated to her studies to be interested in boys, recounted how and why she performed a heterosexual femininity in the eighth grade:

> There was this guy in our class who everyone thought he was gay. . . . Anyway, the guys would always pick on him a lot, calling him "*maricón*" [fag]. During a workshop, some of the guys were being smart-asses and said, "So, Manolo wants to know about having sex with other guys, 'cause he's a fag." Most of the class laughed and the messed-up thing was that the sex educator ended up laughing, too, even though she told them to be respectful. I didn't want to be treated that way, so I just acted like I was just a regular girl, you know, saying that I thought this boy and this boy were cute, even though I had a crush on a girl in my classroom.

Like Barbara, other lesbian-identified girls explained feeling intense pressure to conform to heterosexuality to avoid mistreatment by peers, which they saw as especially being inflicted upon gender-nonconforming boys. While a couple of these young women described themselves as also being gender nonconforming (i.e., "tomboyish"), they still felt compelled to express desire for boys to deflect their peers' potential suspicion and thereby avoid verbal or physical attacks. Barbara's description of the sex educator's laughter at the comments made about Manolo resonates with other studies that have found that teachers, intentionally or inadvertently, support heteronormativity in both their response and their lack of response to expressions of homophobia.[19]

However, two girls told of instances in which they did attempt to challenge the heteronormativity they encountered in their middle school–based sex education classes, specifically the virginity pledges presented to them in abstinence-only sex education. As part of abstinence-only programs, young women and men are often asked to pledge to refrain from premarital sex, typically in the form of signed contracts. A friendly olive-skinned young Puerto Rican woman, seventeen-year-old Arely related that her seventh-grade teacher made her stand outside in the hallway during the remainder of a sex education presentation as punishment for "ripping the virginity pledge" form that she had been asked to sign by a sex educator. When I asked her whether she thought this was fair, she responded, "I didn't care. It's not like I really wanted to listen to that bullshit about the only right way to have sex is when you are married and with a person of the opposite sex. She [her teacher] never really asked me why I ripped the form. . . . I don't think she wanted to know, know what I mean?"

The teacher's reaction to Arely can be interpreted as indifference to her students' thoughts on the subject matter presented to them (i.e., as being focused more on having "docile" bodies in the classroom than on taking the time to find out what provoked the behavior), but it can also be reflective of teachers' lack of training and their discomfort in addressing the needs of LBGTQ and gender-nonconforming students, especially within an absti-nence-only sex education context.[20] Arely's challenge to heteronormative mandates by refusing to sign a virginity pledge may have briefly created an opportunity to destabilize heteronormativity, but it was quickly shut down by her teacher's refusal to engage the "teachable moment" presented by Are-ly's contestation. Arely's interaction with her teacher, along with the narra-tives of girls who identified as lesbian, reveal that same-sex identities, prac-tices, and desires remained unacknowledged within sex education, which reinforced heterosexuality as the norm and assumed that the only significant identity for Latina/o students was a racial/ethnic identity already rooted in heterosexuality.[21]

Latina girls' own understandings of how their identities mattered for their access to school-based sex education and for their larger educational ambitions, which I turn to in the next section, make evident the ways in which they negotiated their development of themselves as informed sex-ual subjects in relation to their futures. They expressed a determination to secure for themselves successful futures, which, for them, was a neces-sary component of their femininity. Their narratives indicate that they also sought to claim sexual respectability for themselves through an emphasis on their educational plans. The importance that Latina girls assigned to their education and futures was shaped by the complex ways in which their racial/ethnic, generational, and class identities intersected with their gender and sexual identities.

Risking Educational Failure

The setting sun cast a warm glow in the large second-floor hall at Hogar del Pueblo. The hall was usually utilized for the preschool program and the weekly high school tutoring program, but on this June evening it had been transformed into a ceremony and reception space for the graduating seniors of the tutoring program.[22] Tucked away on the low shelves lining the walls were children's toys and puzzles, and the only remaining evidence of the preschool program was the children's summer-themed artwork that decorated the large windows on the perimeter of most of the hall. The usual long folding tables and chairs used for the high school tutoring program had been replaced by rows of festively adorned chairs that raced the small stage area. Several people were congregated toward the back of the room near a buffet table of appetizers and beverages that included items such as empanadas, flautas, guacamole and chips, and *agua de horchata* (rice water). Instead of wearing their usual wardrobes of jeans, t-shirts, sweatshirts or the school uniform of polo shirt and khakis, almost all of the youth participants of the tutoring program, whether graduates or not, were dressed up for the occasion. The pride that the young men and women took in their outfits was evident in their smiling compliments to each other on their dress shirts, shoes, ties, blouses, and summer dresses. A few of them blushed at the flattery but still seemed pleased with it. Many of the graduates' parents and siblings were also in attendance. As we waited for the ceremony to commence, a projector screen displayed a slideshow of various activities the youth had participated in over the course of the year. Many of the images showed them studying, working on computers, or discussing homework with their mentors. Some pictures illustrated their volunteer activities and various outings, such as sports games, festivals, and college visits. Occasionally, there were outbursts of laughter as the youth recognized themselves and their friends in pictures that they had not realized were being taken at the time.

During the ceremony, graduating students were asked to approach the front of stage to be individually acknowledged. I, along with others who participated in the tutoring program as staff, mentors, or students, was pleasantly surprised to see Nancy because she had stopped participating in the tutoring program toward the end of her pregnancy. That she was there with her family, including her baby boy, indicated that she had managed to graduate from high school. Her mother and father, both in tears, enthusiastically applauded for their daughter, clearly very proud of her accomplishment. As the ceremony came to a close, the director of the organization reminded all of the young people to not let anything "stand in the way" of their education and told them that, as alumni of the high school tutoring program, they had a "responsibility" to continue with their educations.

I decided to head home after assisting with some of the reception cleanup. Outside I found seventeen-old Jocelyn and Stephanie, who were waiting for Jocelyn's older brother to arrive and give them a ride home. "Next year, it'll be your turn to graduate," I told them. "Can you believe you only have one more year left of high school?!" They both nodded, "For real! It's gonna go real fast, I bet!" exclaimed Jocelyn. Stephanie then said, "Did you all see Nancy's baby? He's a lil' *papi-chulo* [handsome/cute young man]!" "Man, I'm glad that Nancy didn't drop out of school!" Jocelyn added. After a pause, she continued, "She kinda messed up though. She should've waited." At that moment her brother arrived, so we were unable to continue our conversation.

I walked away from that conversation puzzled by Jocelyn's comment that Nancy should have "waited." I wondered whether she meant that she thought that Nancy should have waited to have a baby, waited to have sex, or waited for both? I was trying to make sense of her remark in light of our first interview, during which the tall young woman said that it "annoyed" her when adults told young people to "wait" until marriage to begin having sex. A few weeks later, during her second interview, I asked her about it.

LORENA: When you said that Nancy should've waited—were you talking about her waiting to have sex?

JOCELYN: No, I didn't mean it like that! I meant like waiting to have a baby. I mean, she finished high school and that's all good, but she should've waited and finished college so she can get a good job and then have a baby.

Like many of the other young Latinas, Jocelyn thought there was specific order in which certain milestones should be achieved in the transition into womanhood. For instance, Lourdes, a young Mexican with plans to become an accountant, told me, "I'm gonna graduate, go to college, work and enjoy my social life first. Then maybe marriage. But I'm gonna be able to take care of myself and a baby when I have one." And Annabelle, who wanted to be a police officer, had this to say about her future plans: "I just gotta do what I gotta do for me now, know what I'm saying? I'm going to college, gonna get a job, maybe a car and a house. Then maybe get married. And have kids. But I need to have my shit together first, I just want to make sure I'm stable." Every single girl I spoke with mentioned her intention and her desire to go to college, suggesting that these young women did not see a high school diploma as sufficient to guarantee their future opportunities. Without prompting, almost all of them formulated in similar order how they wanted these milestones to play out in their lives, with education and career at the top of the list.[23]

According to Latina girls, the sequence of these achievements was important for their ability to have better life chances, as Rosalba expressed to me when she shared with me her desire to have a "business-type" career: "I just want to do things the *right way* [my emphasis] so that way it ain't so hard in life." In other words, they expressed a belief that, if they pursued these milestones in the order in which they were "supposed" to, successful futures would be possible for them. As I became more attentive to how they described their aspirations, I came to realize that Latina girls' perspectives on their pathways to adulthood reflected their attempt to assert some control over their futures and to shed the stigma of being identified as young women who were "at risk." Linda, for example, prefaced her plans to become a school counselor with this comment: "Most people look at me and other girls like me and probably just think we ain't shit and ain't gonna do nothing with our lives." Young women constructed their sexual respectability not only through that which they would not do or become, as I discuss in chapter 4, but also through that which they gained, namely their educational and career credentials.

The weight that they placed on their need to do well academically was significantly informed by their identities as second-generation Latinas. They saw their educational aspirations as having implications not only for them as individuals but for their families, as well. For instance, though uncertain as to the career that she wanted for herself, Margarita insisted that she had to graduate from high school and go to college "Because my parents never could do that. They got here and just been working hard. I got a chance to go to school because of all they've been through." Likewise, Celia stated that she wanted to attend college to become a nurse:

Partly 'cause I feel like it would be disrespectful to my mom not to, 'cause she's been bustin' her ass working at that school cafeteria all these years. And then, too, when I went to PR [Puerto Rico], I seen how she used to live, and some of my cousins still live, and I think, it would just be messed up if I didn't go to school when I could.

Latina girls thus incorporated their knowledge of their parents' sacrifices and their sense of transnational ties into their articulation of the place of education in their lives. When they shared with me their educational aspirations, every single girl I spoke with referenced her parents' im/migration experiences, and some, like Celia, also pointed to the living conditions and the lack of opportunities for improvement that faced their relatives in Mexico or Puerto Rico.

The Latina girls I came to know were not immigrants or migrants themselves, but they were daughters of immigrants and/or migrants, and thus their parents' immigration and migration experiences had significance for them, too. According to almost all of them, on various occasions, their parents had shared with them details about the harsh living conditions that informed their decision to im/migrate to the United States. In the case of many of the Mexican girls, their parents described the difficulties they had encountered when they made their way across the U.S./Mexican border as undocumented immigrants. It is important to note that, with the exception of two girls, these young Mexican and Puerto Rican women reported that they could speak and understand Spanish. This bilingual fluency allowed them to communicate with their parents and other adult family members and also enhanced their ability as second-generation Mexican and Puerto Rican girls in the United States to identify with their parents' homelands.[24] Moreover, some girls reported that their families had made trips to their parents' hometowns for events such as weddings and quinceañeras and for the holidays. Some of them described spending one or more summer vacations in Mexico or Puerto Rico visiting relatives without their parents. These experiences therefore were all important to their development of transnational orientations.

Latina girls' approaches to education reflect their dual frame of reference.[25] Scholars such as the anthropologist Marcelo Suárez-Orozco have found that immigrant students compare their current circumstances in the United States to conditions in their country of origin, seeing their current situation as improving their life opportunities despite the various challenges they encounter in their new context.[26] Furthermore, through interactions with their parents and also by witnessing their parents' efforts in working at one or more physically demanding jobs, these students often develop an awareness of their parents' sacrifices as they strive to provide their children with opportunities. The value that some immigrant students assign to education is shaped by this dual frame of reference, through which they come to see educational advancement as a way to meet their obligation to their families and to make their parents' struggles worthwhile. Like their peers who are immigrants, the second-generation Mexican and Puerto Rican girls I spoke with also assigned importance to their academic success as a means to build upon their parents' efforts to improve their family's socioeconomic circumstances.[27]

But the girls also specifically highlighted their mothers' experiences and efforts when speaking about their educational ambitions. Celia did this when she asserted that it would be disrespectful to her mother if she did not go to college, given her mother's struggle to provide financially for her family on a school cafeteria worker's wages. Other young women also expressed a sense of accountability to their mothers when it came to their educational pursuits. For instance, Minerva said that her mother often expressed how she would have liked to have a chance to go to school as a young woman, especially when she saw Minerva doing her homework. In my interview with Carmen, Minerva's mother, she revealed a great desire to go on to college. Because of her family's poor economic circumstances in rural Mexico, Carmen was unable to attend school beyond the sixth grade. According to Carmen, her family could afford to send only her older brother to school; as the eldest daughter, she was expected to help out at home with household chores and to care for younger siblings. She was nearly in tears when she told me, "I was so sad about that, especially when I would see him [her brother] with his books." All of the mothers reported frequently communicating with their daughters about the value of education, emphasizing, "*que se preparan para una carrera* (that they should prepare themselves for a profession)." My interviews with their daughters confirmed the importance that their mothers assigned to education.

Like mothers interviewed in other studies on gender and sexuality socialization among poor and working-class Latina and black women, these mothers stressed educational success as a way for their daughters to gain more independence and avoid economic reliance on men.[28] While mothers attempted to restrict their daughters' movement outside the home to sexually "protect" their daughters, they did describe being flexible about their attendance at educational activities. One key manner in which many mothers promoted the importance of an education was by encouraging their daughters to seek additional educational opportunities at community centers, such as tutoring or summer enrichment programs. In some cases, the girls' participation in these types of enrichment activities was met with opposition from other family members. For example, some of the mothers reported that their daughters' fathers were worried that the daughters would not be properly supervised at these places. And some relatives, such as grandparents, aunts, and uncles, criticized the mothers for permitting their daughters "*demasiado libertad* (too much freedom)" outside the home. Yvette told me that her mother responded to her aunt's criticism of the time Yvette spent at Hogar del Pueblo: "She told her [Yvette's aunt] that this was helping me with school, so that I wasn't doing anything bad. I am keeping my grades up so that when I go to college, my mom could be like, 'See, I told you so.'" A young Puerto Rican who always seemed to have neatly manicured nails with interesting designs, such as hearts or imitation jewels, Yvette went on to detail her plans to become a teacher. As their narratives indicate, some Latina girls felt that their mothers risked having their parenting skills questioned in allowing them to participate in educational activities outside of school; they did not want to let them down.

However, the girls' educational aspirations also revealed another frame of reference, one grounded in their identities as U.S. Latina youth. Specifically, as they talked about their desires and plans for their futures, they defensively rejected stereotypes about them. Lisa, for instance, shared with me that she was initially wary about the motivations underlying my project. The young Mexican with dyed-blonde hair and blue contact lenses raised this during our second interview as she was telling me about her goal to become an elementary school teacher: "Man, at first, when I saw you around here, I was like, 'Oh oh, she's probably some kind of reporter or something and wants to talk to us about [shifting to an imitation of a TV reporter] why Latina girls want to be baby mommas and not finish school.' I was like, 'I ain't talking to her!'" After we both laughed at her impersonation of a TV reporter and her first impression of me, Lisa told me, "I wanna be a teacher, like maybe a sixth-grade teacher. I think that that's when kids start maybe feeling like just confused about a lot of stuff. I wanna be the kind of teacher that helps them believe that they can be whatever they want, no matter all the negative stuff that people say about them." I asked Lisa, "Like what kind of negative stuff?" She replied, "You know! At least for me, I be getting tired hearing all the time that we're all gangbangers, or going to jail, having babies, stuff like that. I'm like, 'I do good in school,' and watch, I'm gonna become a teacher and show people that we all ain't like that!" Other girls also stressed educational success as a way to counter notions about who they were as young urban Latina women, particularly the expectation that they would fail. In line with the findings of some studies on the educational perspectives and outcomes of students of color, this group of Latina girls did not associate educational success with a desire to "act white."[29] In other words, these young women did not interpret academic achievement as assimilation into the dominant society, or what the late educational anthropologist John Ogbu called an "oppositional stance."[30] Like the second-generation young Caribbean girls that the sociologist Nancy Lopez interviewed, these young Latinas' "race-gender" experiences and identities shaped their perspective on education as an important vehicle for contesting gendered-racial stereotypes about them.[31]

While Latina girls' articulations of their educational and career aspirations can be understood as characteristic of the experiences of all young people as they undergo the process of adolescent development, their narratives demonstrate that we must attend to how young people's experiences of adolescence also intersect with other aspects of their identities, such as gender, race/ethnicity, class, and sexuality.[32] Drawing attention to young women's current constructions and experiences of femininity, some girls' studies scholars have asserted that, in the current neoliberal context, a new category of girl or young womanhood has emerged that is defined by individualization, choice, and capacity.[33] Citing what they describe as the emergence, in the 1990s, of a "successful girls' discourse" that highlights girls' academic achievements and advancements as evidence of the weakening of gender inequality and of girls' ability to move beyond it, these scholars argue that this discourse has interfaced with neoliberalism to reproduce a new young womanhood grounded in disciplinary notions of meritocracy. The sociologist Jessica Ringrose writes, "Girls' new found 'equality' and power becomes a meritocratic formula, a signifier, a 'metaphor' for the hard work needed to attain educational and career success."[34] This reconstituted normative femininity is promoted to girls through their encounters with media and popular literature and through their educational experiences and is seen as re/producing the regulation and control of young women—but now it is young women who are self-monitoring themselves. Thus, these Latina girls' plans, particularly the order in which they wanted to pursue key achievements, and their policing of their sexual behavior and that of other young women from whom they distance themselves (as I discuss in more detail in chapter 4) may reflect how they engage with this discourse of success as young women of color who already cannot afford to fail.

Desires for Informed Sexual Subjectivity

In view of the importance that Latina girls assigned to their ability to achieve academic success, I wondered what place they thought sex education should have in their larger educational curriculum. In other words, did young women perceive sex education to be a central component of their overall education? When asked about this, all of the young women replied without hesitation that sex education should be offered in schools. Marta, for instance, had this to say: "How are we going to know about that [sex education] if not in school? It ain't like everyone's mom or dad talks to them about it, I mean maybe to tell you not to do it [sex] or whatever, like my mom does sometimes!" Other young women shared Marta's perspective on school-based sex education. Yvette insisted:

Some stuff you gotta know right now and some stuff you gotta know it for later. But you should still learn about it, even if you don't need to know it like right this minute. . . . We might not get tested on sex ed like with those tests we take, like the Iowa Test [Iowa Test of Basic Skills (ITBS)] or whatever, but someday we gotta know some stuff about sex ed, too.

Marta's and Yvette's viewpoints indicate that these young women understood sex education to be relevant knowledge to which they should have access in the classroom.

Yvette's comment also draws attention to the emphasis on standardized tests in schools—a theme that repeatedly surfaced in my interviews with young Latinas. I was surprised by how often standardized testing was referenced in narratives about their school-based sex education experiences. An aspiring artist with a pixie haircut and large hazel eyes, sixteen-year-old Irene recounted how her seventh-grade teacher pressured her classmates to forgo their scheduled sex education lesson to allow more time for test preparation:

He got up there and was like, "You all really don't want to learn about this stuff right now, right? What's more important to know, stuff about sex or getting ready for the Iowa Test?" I could tell everyone wanted to say they wanted to learn more about sex, shit, at least I wanted to! But everyone was too scared to say something, so nobody said anything and he was like, "Okay, then, here are a couple of brochures and handouts for you to check out at home, if you got any questions, just let me know." He then played some phony-ass video about this girl who gets HIV and *ya, nada más* [that's it, nothing more].

And seventeen-year old Minerva described how her eighth-grade teacher framed sex education as subject matter disruptive to test preparation:

She [her teacher] went to some meeting and came back all pissed off, slamming the door and telling us that she needed to let a speaker come talk to us about sex. . . . She started saying all this stuff about how we weren't supposed to be learning about sex in the classroom, that we shouldn't even be thinking about perverted stuff like that, and that we were just gonna be wasting time we needed to get ready for the Iowa Test. I don't know, she made us feel like we were doing something wrong for even being curious about any of it, you know what I mean? And since she stood [remained] in the classroom when the speaker [sex educator] came, nobody really wanted to ask anything.

Thus, another challenge that young women encountered in their access to school-based sex education was the priority placed on standardized testing preparation, such as for the Iowa Test of Basic Skills (ITBS)[35] and the Illinois Standards Achievement Test (ISAT).[36] Both Irene's and Minerva's teachers communicated to their students that sex education consumed time that should be dedicated to test preparation, with Irene's teacher going so far as to frame sex education as a choice to his students, a choice that was ultimately incompatible with their need to perform well on their standardized tests. Teachers, it is recognized, also find themselves under pressure to ensure that their students perform well on standardized tests.[37] The narratives of Irene and Minerva demonstrate that sometimes their teachers had to make decisions about how much time to allocate for sex education in a high-stakes testing climate. And Minerva's experience with her teacher who openly expressed her opinion that sex education was a "perverted" matter indicates that sometimes this decision making was informed by teachers' own attitudes about the usefulness of sex education in the classroom. In such a context, sex education may be cast as superfluous and not necessary to students' overall educational development.[38]

However, girls believed that sex education should indeed be a part of their larger education curriculum. As their narratives indicate, they often emphasized the "need" for students to have this particular knowledge. When I asked them to elaborate upon why they felt that school-based sex education was necessary, the majority of them first made sure to preface their responses as Olivia had when she asserted, "Cause, it ain't like I'm a pervert or something, I'm just saying whether people like it or not, it don't matter, 'cause some kids do have sex." Other young women made sure to point out that their own interest in sex education was not based upon their sexual desire. Irene, for instance, had this to say: "I don't want to learn about sex in school because I'm a freak and shit. I just wanna know what I need to know to take care of myself and avoid drama. Some people say that to do that, just don't have sex. Okay, but what about for those of us who do have sex? What are we supposed to know?" The "drama" that Irene and other girls referenced related to the potential negative outcomes associated with sexual behavior and the impact of such results on their plans for the future. As they explained why they needed sex education, they always related it their educational and career ambitions, incorporating a discourse "of not getting in trouble" or "avoiding drama." For this group of girls, preventing an unplanned pregnancy or an STD and avoiding parental detection of their sexual behavior were seen as particularly critical for their ability to pursue their educational aspirations.

The majority of young women expressed worry that their parents would not support their plans to leave home for college if they uncovered their sexual behavior; they feared that their parents might, for example, withhold financial assistance. Alicia, who switched from using the birth control pill to the Depo-Provera shot to minimize the chance that her parents would find about her sexual activities, conveyed this when she outlined her "game plan" to obtain a four-year college scholarship, telling me, "I just gotta make sure not to mess it all up now and end up like pregnant or something stupid like that. I seen too many girls get themselves into drama like that. I ain't trying to end up like that." Alicia, like most of the young women, understood that her sexuality potentially posed a risk to her plans. In other words, Latina girls cited their educational and career goals as another reason why they needed to be vigilant about their sexual respectability—suggesting that their school identities were also significant for their fashioning of their identities as sexually respectable young women. These young women did not report "saying no" to sexual activities as a way to secure these educational achievements; rather, they emphasized their need to know about safe sex as a way to protect their ability to continue with their education.

Sex education, according to girls, should provide them with an opportunity to develop themselves as informed sexual subjects. When young women considered their sex education experiences, they often specified what they wanted to learn from sex education lessons. For instance, when I asked seventeen-year old Carla why she asked her close girlfriends about using condoms, the petite young Mexican, who wore a shiny gold name tag necklace, explained: "Like they [sexuality education instructors] actually didn't want to say any real words. It was interesting because they assumed that we knew everything there was to know leading up to what they were saying, know what I mean? Like, to say, 'use a condom,' they assumed we knew what it meant about how to use it." Similarly, Celia turned to some friends for information: "When I first started messing around with him and we were gonna actually do it [sexual intercourse], it was weird because I really didn't know how to bring it up [condom use]. I did, but I remember thinking, 'Why don't they teach you about this in sex ed, you know, the stuff that really happens and how to handle it?'" As Carla's and Celia's comments indicate, girls sought to learn practical knowledge and skills that would enable them to practice and negotiate safe sex with partners.

Unlike the academically successful young black women observed and interviewed by the sociologist Lea Hubbard (1999) who said "no to boys" as a strategy for school achievement, the heterosexual-identified girls I spoke with did not see it as impossible or irreconcilable to be in a relationship with a boy and remain focused on school, so as long they "handled their business."[39] Though some of them characterized their relationship as a romantic/love relationship, in general, most heterosexual-identified girls expressed some doubts about being able to rely on their male partners for support, whether financial or emotional, should they experience an unplanned pregnancy.[40] Of her boyfriend, Jocelyn said, "It ain't like I'm gonna be believin' that he'll be there no matter what. In the end, if I get pregnant I gotta deal with it, I got no choice. He can walk away like nothing happened 'cause he ain't the one pregnant. I ain't letting no guy keep me from going to college." Thus, these girls' interest in such pragmatic details was also connected to their understanding of their disadvantaged gendered position in the face of such a sexual outcome.

Noticeably absent in their expectations of school-based sex education was mention of an interest in learning more about their sexual desire and/or pleasure. Girls' silence on lessons or queries about their own sexual desire and/or pleasure is a reflection of their awareness of both the potential for pleasure and the threat of danger that their desire holds for them, which is communicated to them within a larger culture "that denigrates, suppresses, and heightens the dangers of girls' sexuality."[41] In such a cultural context, girls often come to understand their ability to be academically successful as dependent upon their behavior and sexual morality, which for them means that desire, when imagined, is often interpreted as representing complete loss of control.[42] The girls I interviewed asserted control through their claims to sexual respectability, which included their knowledge and practice of sexually responsible behavior. One significant reason why this was important to them was that it would facilitate their control over their educational and career aspirations. Knowledge about their own sexual desire and/or pleasure perhaps was not seen as essential to what they needed to know to protect the achievements they sought for themselves. With little validation of themselves as desirous sexual subjects in and outside school-based sex education, girls who do engage in sexual activities may also find themselves having to prioritize what information is essential to their claims to sexual respectability. Latina girls' emphasis on the links between their sexual respectability and their educational and career achievements are reflective of what the educational researchers April Burns and María Elena Torre term "anxious achievement," which "results in a reordering of the erotic, away from an erotics of the body as a site of pleasure and the self as sexually desiring, to an erotics of achievement and material success."[43] While the Latina girls I came to know did not adhere to a school-sanctioned femininity that deemphasizes the sexuality of young women,[44] they nonetheless saw themselves as performing a school-oriented femininity that was a pathway to better academic and life chances. This school-oriented femininity allowed space for their sexual behavior as long as they safeguarded their educational and career aspirations through their sexual respectability, namely their knowledge and practice of safe sex, leaving little room for their claims to sexual desire and/or pleasure.

Conclusion

When considering school-based sex education, we typically focus on the debate about whether abstinence-only or comprehensive sex education is the most appropriate and effective approach to teaching students about this subject. All too often in these discussions, we lose sight of the fact that students do not encounter similar educational contexts and that their location in our current racial/ethnic, gender, class, and sexual hierarchies matters for the quality of their schools and education. We need to remember this when we consider the purpose and merit of school-based sex education. What are the lessons we can learn when we ask different groups of young people about how they experience school-based sex education, what they think of it as part of their larger educational development, and what they would like to gain from it?

The experiences of Latina girls show how the interplay of heteronormativity, sexism, and racism in their sex education simultaneously reproduces, normalizes, and conceals inequalities, further constructing these girls as "at risk." Thus, in this context, Latina youth can be understood to be more broadly "at risk" of these oppressions, a view that arguably poses greater danger to them than sex or pregnancy. For instance, one especially troubling lesson that they are taught is to regard the masculinity of young men in their communities as a threat; however, they are not invited to critically examine the larger societal culture (and not just "Latino culture") that privileges male sexuality. Latina youth are thus taught that, while they have control of certain things, such as whether they will or will not get pregnant, they are also taught that they have no control over disrupting gender inequalities. Another risky lesson that they are taught is that survival in and outside their schools necessitates an adherence to heteronormative imperatives and that queer subjectivity is not possible within a Latina/o subjectivity. Together, such lessons contribute to their already vulnerable status as young women of color in this society.

The emphasis that Latina girls in this study placed on their educational and career aspirations as they discussed their experiences and expectations of school-based sex education reveal that they were well aware of their vulnerability. We generally assume that girls who engage in sexual activities must not be thinking about their futures, especially African American and Latina young women, who are already designated as being "at risk." We particularly home in on the negative educational and occupational experiences of those young women who encounter an unplanned pregnancy and/or become mothers to lay out for girls the ways in which expressions of their sexuality at this point in their lives threaten their futures. But the young Latinas I came to know did not interpret their sexuality as incompatible with their future plans so as long as they practiced and maintained their sexual respectability. They did not want to jeopardize their futures and, as sexually active young women, sought to develop themselves as informed sexual subjects through sex education.

Building on their desire to give meaning to the sacrifices made by their parents and families, their desire to push back against their racialization, and their desire to secure their futures, they placed importance on their acquisition of success. And they saw this as possible if they followed a well-organized plan for their life and achievements. I am proud of them for envisioning such possibilities for themselves and am excited for their futures, but I also cannot help wondering if such ambitions will be met with the necessary resources and opportunities, given the challenges already present in their lives. Sex education, however, if thought about differently, does have the potential to enhance their ability to navigate them. I draw upon Jessica Fields and Deborah L. Tolman's assertion that we work toward teaching young people to critically engage sexual risk in a way that confronts social inequalities, rather than operate on the idea that sexual risk can be completely eliminated via sex education.[45] As Fields rightly points out, the development of a liberatory sex education necessitates that we move beyond a dichotomous approach to sex education (abstinence-only or comprehensive sex education).[46] Similarly, Michelle Fine and Sara I. McClelland assert that sex education must be situated within structural contexts and linked to other human rights struggles, such as that for LGBTQ rights, reproductive rights, and education reform. In this way, sex education can be part of the process of teaching students to claim an entitlement to learning the skills necessary to confront and disrupt the intersecting inequalities that shape their lives.[47]

The sex education experiences of Latina girls reveal that, to truly appreciate the processes by which young women come to negotiate and develop their identities as students and informed sexual subjects, it is also necessary to understand that their desire for success is also shaped within a neoliberal educational context that emphasizes high-stakes testing, the need for achievement, and individualization. Latina girls' articulations of their educational and career aspirations can also be understood as a way in which they distanced themselves from those young women whom they saw as not assuming responsibility for their sexual behavior and for their futures. As the sociologist Angela McRobbie asserts, "The acquisition of qualifications comes to function then as a gendered axis of social division. Young women are in effect graded and marked according to their ability to gain qualifications which in turn provides them with an identity as female subjects of capacity."[48] Though there were many instances in which the girls I interviewed expressed an awareness and a critique of the structural inequalities they encountered as young women of color, they still pointed to the role of individual effort in determining one's success. I contend that Latina youth are at risk but that the real risk here lies in the fact that they are being taught a particular lesson about who is to be held accountable for the inequities in their sexuality education, their general education, and in their social worlds—that they are the ones who will be held primarily accountable.

4

"Handlin' Your Business"

Sexual Respectability and Peers

The cool air inside Las Palmitas, a small Latino-owned grocery store in the West Town community, offered us a welcome relief from the muggy weather outside. Hearing the bell attached to the door jingle, a middle-aged Latino man near the register looked up from the newspaper he was reading to greet us. Centro Adelante youth often strolled to Las Palmitas, only a couple blocks away, to buy their snacks of choice, a small bag of potato chips and a can of pop. I had joined sixteen-year-old Irene and Asucena and fifteen-year-old Felix that afternoon to buy a snack. As we paid, Magdalena walked into the store; Irene and Asucena immediately greeted her with a hug and kiss. Magdalena, a petite and shy Puerto Rican young woman, had regularly participated in the youth program when I first began my fieldwork but had not been back to Centro Adelante for quite some time. Irene gently touched Magdalena's round belly: "Damn, girl, what you been up to!?" she said jokingly. Her cheeks flushing, Magdalena sheepishly giggled as she looked down at her belly. After talking briefly about Magdalena's due date and the sex of the baby, the girls hugged goodbye, and our group exited the store. We were silent as we opened our ice-cold cans of pop and slowly walked back to the center. Asucena, looking behind us to make sure that Magdalena was not around, broke the silence: "That's crazy, huh?" Tall and lanky, Felix also looked cautiously behind us and replied, "I know . . . she should've used some protection. Too late now." Irene, slighting nodding in agreement, added, "Guess some females just don't know how to handle their business."

I frequently heard the phrase "handle your business" in interviews with Latina girls and in my fieldwork observations. Generally, it was within the context of being challenged to take charge of a specific task or an affair in need of attention, such as confronting someone who had publicly offended you, addressing disagreements with others, or even setting your academic affairs in order. And, although, like many people, I had heard the phrase before, it seemed to take on an especially powerful meaning for the girls I spoke with. When they talked about "handling their business," as Irene did when she considered Magdalena's pregnancy, it was with an understanding that the stakes were especially high in the context of girls' sexual experiences. Sexually handling one's business, according to Irene and other young women, was certainly about safe sex in that it referred to the ability to effectively avoid pregnancy and STDs. They equated safe sex with the prevention of STDs and pregnancy through the use of condoms and/or "protection," a meaning drawn from the widely circulated safe-sex rhetoric available to them. But, as I delved deeper into the safe-sex discourse that they articulated, it became clear that the girls' vigilance against negative sexual outcomes was not just about their reproductive and sexual health. Sexually handling one's business was also about sexual respectability and the formation of one's sexual subjectivities as young urban Latinas. They expressed much anxiety about the implications for their social status if they failed to practice safe sex, pointing to another meaning that they assigned to safe sex. They associated safe sex with the kind of Latina girls they understood themselves to be and wanted others to see them as—sexually responsible girls. The girls I got to know were invested in being the type of young women who knew how to handle their sexual business, resisting being classified as "bad girls" because of their sexual behavior.

All young women are subjected to being placed within the good-girl/bad-girl dichotomy that is designed to both socially control women's sexuality and to privilege men's sexuality. One significant strategy by which these girls negotiated their sexual subjectivity and their positioning in the good-girl/bad-girl dichotomy was to establish a symbolic boundary of sexuality between themselves and other "sexually active" girls, with the lines drawn around sexual respectability. As the sociologists Michèle Lamont and Virág Molnár explain, symbolic boundaries "conceptualize distinctions made by social actors to categorize objects, people, practices . . . they are an essential medium through which people acquire status and monopolize resources."[1] Sexual respectability among Latina youth operated as a gendered sexual and racial/ethnic boundary formation that distinguished them from other Latina girls and from white young women and affirmed their identities as sexually responsible girls among their peers. It allowed them to participate in sexual activities and still be "good" girls on the basis of their constructions of themselves as sexually "handling their business" and other girls as sexually irresponsible. This symbolic boundary of sexuality was a tool by which they attempted to delineate their identities and status as sexual "good" girls. But this boundary formation process also restricted their ability to fully explore their sexuality, evidenced in their interactions with close friends, to whom they turned in their efforts to enact safe-sex practices and to claim sexual respectability for themselves. Their accounts of these exchanges with friends point to how their constructions of sexual respectability and safe sex limited their engagement with their sexual desires and pleasures.

Avoiding Unplanned Pregnancy and STDs

The majority of girls primarily understood sex as referring to sexual intercourse. Heterosexual-identified girls thought of sex as primarily meaning penile-vaginal intercourse, while lesbian-identified girls understood sex to include both vaginal intercourse and oral sex.[2] And it was upon these comprehensions of sex that they developed their ideas about safe sex. Rolling her neck and pointing to herself with her right index finger, Celia explained, "To me, safe sex is about using protection like condoms 'cause, you know, you gotta take care of yourself." As if they were giving well-memorized answers to a sex education quiz, girls consistently cited the phrases "using protection" and "using condoms" in their interviews when asked what safe sex meant to them. The manner in which they initially responded to my questions about what safe sex meant to them reminded me of how children respond to adults when they are asked to explain what they will do if someone offers them drugs ("say no") or if a stranger approaches them ("don't talk to strangers"). Sixteen-year-old Norma, a thin and light-skinned Puerto Rican with an inviting smile, illustrated this when she asserted that information about safe sex was readily available: "Come on! Everyone knows that safe sex means you gotta use protection!" Asucena, who joined Irene at the store in asking Magdalena about her pregnancy, told me that anyone who did not know what safe sex meant was "ignorant." The devoted soccer fan insisted, "I mean, you gotta be really stupid or not ever seen anything, and I mean *anything*, about sex to at least know that to have safe sex, you should be using condoms or some other kind of protection." Like Celia, Norma, and Asucena, almost all the girls tended to equate safe sex with the use of condoms and/or "protection."[3]

Latina girls were well versed in the ubiquitous rhetoric of safe sex that has unfolded since the 1980s. The safe-sex concept, initially developed in the early 1980s by gay communities as a response to the devastating impact of HIV on this group, began to be applied to HIV-prevention education campaigns directed at heterosexuals by the late 1980s, when it became evident that HIV and AIDS were not just a "gay man's disease."[4] The adoption of the safe-sex concept as a strategy to curb the sexual transmission of HIV among heterosexuals was informed by encouraging evidence of gay men's behavioral changes, particularly the adoption of condom use. The safe-sex concept has been a valuable tool for disseminating information about the transmission and prevention of HIV and has been extended to educate young people on other STDs and on teen pregnancy through school-based sex education and public health campaigns[5] and has even been incorporated into films, TV shows, and music that are produced for a teen audience. In a highly sexualized culture such as ours, the cultural visibility of the concept of safe sex is undeniable. In a sense, safe sex, as an idea and as a practice, is now part of the everyday ways we talk and think about sex. Like the adults around them, young people may not all consistently adopt safe-sex practices, but it certainly is now part of the vocabulary they use to talk about sex and make sense of their sexual experiences.

I often witnessed Latina girls draw on the rhetoric of safe sex in their interactions with peers. Late one afternoon, for example, Stephanie, an athletic Mexican young woman with deep dimples in her cheeks, was in the Hogar del Pueblo computer lab diligently trying to finish writing a paper on teen pregnancy for her English composition class. She wanted to do well on this paper, and I was helping her organize her main points. Her friend surfed the Internet as she waited for Stephanie because they were going to walk home together. As Stephanie tried to wrap up her conclusion, her friend impatiently whined, "Girl, come on! Just write something like, respect yourself, protect yourself, and use a condom, *y punto* [and that's that]!" Stephanie exasperatedly exclaimed, "I can't just end the paper like that!" "Why not?" asked her friend, who then turned to me for affirmation and commented, "It's true, ain't it?" I did not have a chance to reply because Stephanie instantly answered, "Yeah, but it's really more about respecting yourself, though. Just give me five more minutes, I'm almost done." With that, the opinionated high school junior turned her attention back to the computer screen and continued to type. Before printing out her paper, Stephanie asked me to look over her concluding paragraph, in which she stated that the "problem of teen pregnancy" had many causes and that among these was the "issue" of girls not being taught enough about "respecting themselves." Elaborating on this point within her conclusion, she explained that a girl's self-respect also had to do with the respect she wanted others to show her.

The theme of self-respect surfaced frequently in the girls' talk of safe sex with me. As if reading from a public health poster, they matter-of-factly stated that everyone should have sexual self-respect and use protection. But, like Stephanie, they felt that it was especially critical for young women to be mindful of their self-respect. One key reason that they offered for this was the possible physical consequences of sexual activity, namely an unplanned pregnancy or an STD. Sixteen-year-old Soledad, whose mother, Araceli, had found a letter she wrote to her boyfriend after searching her personal belongings, explained, "If I didn't respect my body and I didn't care then I would be one of those girls that just had sex with anyone and didn't really care if I got pregnant." Like the other young women, Soledad particularly raised concerns about the implications of an unplanned pregnancy. Adjusting her high pony tail, the soft spoken young woman with an interest in teaching kindergarten added, "And I don't want to have a kid right now. I gotta do what I gotta for me right now, like finish school and get a good job. No taking care of babies for me right now." An unplanned pregnancy, according to the girls, would interfere with their educational and career ambitions, which, as discussed in chapter 3, were seen as within reach so as long as they were sexually responsible and pursued these goals in a pre-scribed order. However, Latina girls also were concerned that an unplanned pregnancy would more immediately constrain their already limited freedom outside the home, a restriction they witnessed occurring to young moms around them.

Arriving early at Hogar del Pueblo for the weekly tutoring program, Marta and Yvette, both sophomores, were excitedly talking to me about their MySpace pages and trying their best to convince me to join the popu-lar online social networking site. Marta, who regularly wore her long, black, and curly hair in a tight bun to meet JROTC uniform and self-presentation requirements, commented to Yvette, "Oh, I saw a picture of Ruthie's son! He's so cute!" Ruthie was Yvette's cousin, who was only a year older than she. Yvette, whose shoulder-length loose brown hair and hot pink acrylic nails stood in contrast to Marta's hair style and short nails, smilingly replied, "He looks just like her, right?" Sighing, she continued, "I feel kinda sorry for her, though." "Why?" I asked Yvette. She explained that Ruthie was pretty much "stuck at home" because her parents babysat her eight-month-old son only when Ruthie went to work at her part-time job at a local shoe store. "I think they're even more strict with her now that she had a baby!" she exclaimed, disapprovingly shaking her head. She added, "My parents would probably put me on lockdown, too, if I had a baby. So not trying to do that . . . they barely let me do anything now! I'm lucky they even let me come here!" Frequently, like Yvette, the young women expressed frustration with the close monitoring they received from their parents. As their developing bodies began to signal their emerging sexualities, the girls found that their parents responded by restricting how much time they could spend outside the home, which many of them already felt was limited because of their responsibility for some household tasks.[6] The gendered division of labor in their households that they described set them up to take responsibility for cooking, cleaning, and/or taking of younger siblings while their mothers worked outside the home. Many girls noted that male siblings were often exempt from household responsibilities. One significant way in which they carved out freedom for themselves was through their participation in youth activities at community organizations. For more than half of the girls I interviewed, this was the only afterschool activity they were permitted to join; it represented one of the few sanctioned spaces outside the home where they could move about without parental scrutiny and/or criticism that they were *callejeras* (street-roaming girls) or *en la calle* (on the street) too much. Thus, for the young Latinas I spoke with, handling their business, particularly the prevention of an unplanned pregnancy, was also a means by which they protected this small degree of autonomy.

The girls' avoidance of an unplanned pregnancy was also related to their perspective on abortion. Abortion, most of them believed, was not an acceptable way to sexually handle one's business. Dramatically rolling her dark-brown, almond-shaped eyes, eighteen-year-old Fabiola explained, "Girls can't be just like, 'Oh, if I do get pregnant, then I'll just go and have an abortion.' That shouldn't be how you think about safe sex . . . that you always have that resort there." Slightly more than one-third of girls firmly asserted that they were opposed to abortion, citing their Catholic upbringing. Jocelyn, who had commented that her friend should have "waited" before having a baby, declared, "I couldn't ever have an abortion if I did get pregnant, though," adding, "I don't believe in abortion. That's the worst thing you could do." Other young women, however, talked about abortion without explicitly stating their position on it. Instead, they imagined out loud how those close to them would react if they were to ever consider or have an abortion.[7] Soledad, who stated that she was not ready to have a baby because she wanted to focus on school and a career, speculated, "My parents would be real mad if I got pregnant, but they would be more pissed off at me if they found out that I had an abortion." And Inés, whose mother slapped her during their initial confrontation about Inés's sexual behavior, told me, "I don't know what I'd do if I was pregnant, but my boyfriend would never go for that [abortion] anyway." As evidence of her boyfriend's stance on abortion, she went on to explain that her boyfriend had not spoken to his sister for six months after she had an abortion.

When these young women shared with me their fears of an unplanned pregnancy and having to grapple with abortion as option, none of them utilized the language of "choice" that has framed mainstream discussions and debates about abortions.[8] But they knew that it would not just be their own perspective on abortion that they would have to contend with if they encountered an unplanned pregnancy. Juanita saw what happened to her older sister, who had a baby girl when she was a senior in high school. Juanita, whose heavily made up face made her look older than her sixteen years, said to me, "I don't know how they [parents] found out she was pregnant and that she was thinking about an abortion . . . they told her not to even bother coming home if she did that. I think she was scared of what they would do, so she just didn't do it." After detailing her sister's experience, Juanita avowed, "I'm just going to keep takin' care of myself 'cause I don't ever want to have to go there and even deal with that kind of drama!" Like Juanita, other girls expressed great concern about the possibility of having to negotiate the outcome of an unplanned pregnancy with those close to them; thus, handling their business meant that they had to work to avoid being placed in such a predicament.

Latinas/os have long been described as being anti-abortion, a stance that has been attributed primarily to their Catholic faith and to familism. However, recent surveys, such as a 2007 joint survey conducted by the Pew Forum on Religion and Public Life and the Pew Hispanic Center, suggest that a shift in attitudes on abortion may be occurring among Latinas/os depending on their generational status.[9] This survey showed that, while 65 percent of first-generation U.S. Latinas/os believed abortion should be illegal, only 48 percent of second-generation U.S. Latinas/os felt the same way.[10] One possible explanation offered for this difference has been the second-generation's movement toward assimilation, given its longer period of residence in the United States. However, these shifts in abortion stance among Latinas/os cannot be interpreted only as a product of assimilation, nor can it be understood solely as a reflection of mainstream pro-life and pro-choice discourses. As reproductive justice activists and scholars have long argued, the reproductive lives of women of color unfold at the intersection of various systems of oppression, such as patriarchy, heteronormativity, and racism.[11] Latina girls' narratives reveal that their viewpoints on abortion are also shaped by their perceived vulnerability and by their ability to enact their agency—not feeling equipped with the skills and resources to negotiate abortion in the face of an unplanned pregnancy, they instead try to claim some control over their sexual and reproductive lives by developing strategies for practicing safe sex, particularly the prevention of an unplanned pregnancy.

Young women's concerns about an unplanned pregnancy, however, did not mean that they were dismissive of their potential risk for contracting an STD and the sexual and reproductive health consequences associated with STDs. Girls cited several different STDs they wanted to avoid in their safe-sex efforts, but they were especially apprehensive about HIV. As an example, Linda, who was the only lesbian-identified young woman who asked a question about same-sex attraction during sex education, said to me, "Supposedly I should be okay and not worry about HIV because I only have sex with girls. But I still worry about that shit and just try to be safe." Celia, who had told me that one needed to use protection because "you gotta take care of yourself," adamantly stated that she would never have sex without a condom, insisting, "I'm scared to get pregnant, but I'm scared to get AIDS, too. It's just not worth it to me . . . it's not worth my life."[12]

The life that Celia pointed to was her physical well-being, but she also placed value on the social dimensions of her life. In other words, Celia, like the other girls, was equally worried about the social consequences associated with STDs, as well as those related to an unplanned pregnancy. This was made evident in the anxiety they expressed over the constant threat that their peers would designate them as "dirty" or "sucia." The term "sucia" literally means "filthy" or "grimy," such as when one gets dirt or mud on him or her. But the term can mean that one's actions, words, or thoughts are sexually perverse. Young Latinas fiercely sought to avoid this label because it made distinctions between "good" and "bad" girls, specifically marking some girls as infected with a sexually transmitted disease and therefore also as infectious. Lisa, who initially assumed that I was a reporter investigating Latina teen pregnancy, confided in me that she had recently taken an HIV test upon the unrelenting urging of one of her girlfriends. She had discovered that her boyfriend had been "playing her" (seeing another young woman), explaining, "My friend, she told me, 'If he's been with her, imagine who else he's been with?' She got me all paranoid, 'cause, you know, it was true and I know the girl I found he was messin' with!" Pausing for a minute and crinkling her nose in disgust, she continued, "She is nasty 'cause she's been with half the guys on my block. Everyone knows! I didn't want people thinking I was the *sucia* [dirty one] if he ended up giving me something . . . 'cause you know people always think it's the girl who was all out there." Inés, who had stated that her boyfriend was strongly against abortion, also conveyed frustration about what they saw as a double standard: "See, guys, they can get away with a lot of shit when it comes to sex. Not girls, though. We don't only gotta worry about getting pregnant but like other stuff, like people talking shit about us 'cause we have sex." Similarly, Margarita, who self-identified as lesbian, sat forward in her chair and angrily pointed out: "Everyone's always like it ain't no big deal for guys, it's what guys are supposed to do or whatever! But when it comes to girls, people are always trippin' and I hate that!" All of these young women felt especially vulnerable to the possibility of getting a bad reputation because of their sexual behavior.

Girls felt little control over whether others would badmouth them because of their sexual behavior and instead tried to manage how their peers interpreted any such attacks. For instance, Stephanie, who wrote the paper on the connections between teen pregnancy and girls' self-respect, asserted, "I don't like that someone can say I'm a ho or something because I'm having sex, but ain't nobody can say I'm dirty or that I have some disease." She believed that she did not deserve this designation because she used condoms. And Miriam insisted, "My boyfriend might tell someone I had sex with him, but he ain't gonna be able to say I let him hit it [have sex with her] without a condom. No one is gonna be thinking I'm a skank who doesn't respect her body." As reflected in Stephanie's and Miriam's comments, the young women anticipated that negative things would be said about them and tried to control what types of things could be said by pointing to their practice of safe sex. They reasoned that they may have engaged in sexual activity, but this did not mean they were "dirty" or "skanks," like some other girls, because, like wearing "badges of dignity,"[13] they made it clear that they embodied sexual respectability because they sexually handled their business. This, according to them, set them apart from girls for whom they did not want to be mistaken, namely girls that they saw as sexually irresponsible.

Not Like One of Those Girls

As a volunteer with the youth program at Hogar del Pueblo, I occasionally joined in on various field trips throughout the city. Field trips typically generated much excitement among the young people, who enjoyed taking excursions together outside the center. On one oppressively humid summer day, I sat in the back of the yellow school bus with Marta and two of her friends. The three girls were attentively looking out the window trying to see if they would spot anyone from the neighborhood as the bus pulled away from the center. Marta suddenly exclaimed in surprise, "Aww, hell no! It's true! She did get pregnant!" The group turned their attention to a young pregnant Latina who was slowly crossing the street. Looking straight ahead, she had not noticed her peers on the bus, or at least she pretended that she did not see them. As Marta continued to observe the young woman, she loudly commented, "And people always thought I would be the first one to get pregnant . . . whatever!" One of her friends quickly chimed in, "People can talk all the shit they want about me, but that ain't gonna be me." When I asked them what they meant, they glanced at one other as they considered how to explain their comments. Marta, who wanted to join the Marines after high school, responded with frustration: "It's like everyone just thinks we're going end up pregnant or something. It feels like they are watching and just waiting for us to fuck up . . . not me, I ain't trying to end up like that."

As they had done when they talked to me about their educational aspirations, the young women expressed a keen awareness of the negative perceptions others had of them as they explained how and why they wanted to practice safe sex. They referenced stereotypical notions of urban African American and Latina women and mentioned derogatory slang names such as "baby mommas," "bitches and hos," "skanks," and "hoodrats" when they described how other perceived them and expected of them. And they were resentful that they could so easily be classified in such negative ways, a sentiment that many of them had conveyed in our initial interactions with one another.

Seventeen-year-old Graciela expressed this when I ran into her at a local laundromat on a frigid Saturday morning. As the slim young woman quickly sorted clothes into three large washing machines, she glanced in my direction, rolled her big brown eyes, and explained that she was doing the laundry for her family, asserting, "But it's all right 'cause at least it gets me out the house for a bit, 'cause sometimes they all be getting on my nerves." Prior to this chance meeting, Graciela had never directly spoken to me, although she saw me regularly at Centro Adelante. After she inserted quarters into the washing machines, she walked in my direction to grab a *Sun-Times* newspaper that was on a seat nearby. Plopping down a couple seats away from me, she abruptly asked, "So . . . why do you want to interview Hispanic teenagers about safe sex?" Her question caught me off guard. I began to explain, but Graciela immediately interrupted: "But why? Who wants to know about that? I mean, people think that we should not even be having sex. And if they know we have sex, they think we all don't know what we're doing or that we're just hos." Somewhat satisfied with my explanation that I did not agree with such assumptions, Graciela shifted the rest of our conversation to her curiosity about what exactly sociologists did on a day-to-day basis. While Graciela and I did regularly interact at Centro Adelante after our laundromat exchange, she did not approach me about participating in the study until two months after our initial encounter. When we sat down for her first interview, she began by jokingly warning me, "All right, I'm going to answer some of your questions, but remember, you better not make me look like some of these girls who don't know what they're talking about and being baby mommas and all that." The strong desire that Graciela had to be differentiated from particular girls was echoed by almost all of the young women. Their meanings of sexual respectability and their assertion of their identities as sexually responsible girls were reflected in the way they talked about and categorized other girls.

As feminist scholars and writers have pointed out, girls encounter an omnipresent and powerful good-girl-versus-bad-girl dichotomy that sets limits on their sexual agency.[14] On the basis of gendered expectations surrounding women's expressions of their sexuality, "chaste" women have traditionally been classified as good women, while "sexual" women have been designated as bad women. While the categories of "chaste" and "sexual" remain central elements of this dichotomy, as a socially created way to classify women, this dichotomy sometimes shifts to incorporate certain expressions of women's sexuality that may be more culturally acceptable at a given time. For instance, young women regularly come across both implicit and explicit messages that stress the importance of producing an "emphasized femininity" that is desirable to men, particularly the performance of sexy.[15] Set within a heterosexual erotic system and a larger context of gender inequality, women may produce such a femininity to garner some privilege for themselves.[16] In other words, girls and young women may deploy their femininity, particularly their heterosexuality, as a "gender strategy" to gain power and status among their peers.[17] However, in doing so, they also run the risk of crossing the fine line between being a "sexy good girl" and a "sexy bad girl." Therefore, while there seems to be some room for girls to express aspects of their sexual selves, what marks good and bad girls can seem to change capriciously at any given moment because girls' sexual behavior is scrutinized in ways that boys' sexual behavior is not. One wrong move and a girl can suddenly find herself on the "bad" side of the dichotomy. Furthermore, the categories of race/ethnicity and class serve to differentially position girls within the good-girl/bad-girl dichotomy, in which poor and working-class girls and young women of color are assumed to embody an inappropriate femininity, marked by sexuality that is out of bounds.[18] This becomes especially evident when one considers how we typically discuss girls' expressions of their sexualities and the "interventions" we think that they need; concerns about white, middle-class young women tend to center on the implications of their behavior for their social and emotional health, whereas concerns about young women of color and poor and working-class girls concentrate on their sexual precociousness and their "culture" of teenage motherhood.[19]

Latina girls were attuned to the good-girl/bad-girl dichotomy and, finding it inescapable, incorporated it into their identity-making repertoires. However, they elaborated on this dichotomy to make room for themselves on the "good" side on the basis of their sexual respectability, which, according to them, was reflected in their self-protective sexual practices. And this meant that there needed to be "bad" sexual girls if they were to be able to define themselves as "good" sexual girls and to be acknowledged as such by their peers. Like Graciela, girls who saw themselves as sexually handling their business set themselves apart from girls who they felt had not been sexually responsible. As they shared their sexual experiences and choices with me, they consistently and resolutely pointed to girls they were not going to be like, establishing boundaries between themselves and two specific types of "bad" girls in their communities: those they described as "hos" and "skanks" (sexually promiscuous girls) and "baby mommas" (teen mothers). They insisted that they did not want to be "one of those girls."

Perspectives on Girls with "No Self-Respect"

The girls I spoke with were adamant about differentiating themselves from young women they depicted as "hos and skanks." One criterion that they used to determine which girls fell into this category was the number of sexual partners the girl had had or was perceived to have been with in the past. Jocelyn communicated this to me one afternoon as she explained what made certain girls "hos and skanks": "There's a girl on my block who's always having sex with a different guy! I would never do some shit like that. She's just a ho! I mean, she's got no kinda respect for herself." When I asked her how many sexual partners were too many, Jocelyn crossed her long legs and tilted her head as she thought about it; she finally responded, "I don't know, like more than two or like more than four, I think." Like Jocelyn, many other girls could not definitively state how many sexual partners they thought were too many. They provided me with a range of numbers, mostly between one and five, when I inquired about what constituted too many sexual partners. As discussed earlier, they felt that the sexual restrictions typically placed on girls, such as limits on their display of sexual desire and number of partners, were unfair. Yet, they relied on such gendered sexual restrictions to set themselves apart from certain girls. And, to further mark their difference from such young women, they emphasized their established relationship with their sexual partners, which for slightly more than half of the girls was one that should ideally be defined by "love."[20] This is not surprising, given that romantic heterosexual relationships are key for young women seeking to negotiate their sexual behavior in an acceptable way, allowing them to remain "good" girls in the adolescent sexual terrain.[21]

Furthermore, according to the girls I talked to, young women who had too many partners also had no self-respect because they did not care for their sexual health. They were assumed to have some type of sexually transmitted disease acquired through their indiscriminate sexual partnering with various individuals. I witnessed both young men and women participate in constructing young women as diseased and therefore, as "hos" and "skanks." For instance, one gray and damp spring day, some of the young people from Centro Adelante pitched in to help with a block clean-up. A couple of Latinas in their late teens casually strolled by and waved to Nestor, a charismatic and popular young man who also participated in the Centro Adelante youth program. The athletic soccer player with a head full of wavy black hair nonchalantly waved back and went back to halfheartedly raking the litter off a patch of grass near the sidewalk. A few of the other Centro Adelante youth noticed this brief interaction and smirked and gave each other knowing looks. Waiting until the girls were around the corner, Graciela, whom I had met at the laundromat, teasingly asked Nestor, "Is that your lady?" Nestor made a face and told her to shut up. "Don't deny it, bro! You were all up on her at that party," said a young man who was close friends with Nestor. "Eww . . . you probably got something from her," taunted Graciela. Nestor, turning slightly red, exclaimed, "Hell, nah! I ain't messing around with that bitch!" Fifteen-year-old Rita, who was listening in on the conversation, dramatically placed one hand on her hip as she warned, "I hope not 'cause if you are, you better go get checked out 'cause she's a dirty skank!" Both young women and young men depicted some girls, like the one that the group talked about that afternoon, as infectious, making them stigmatized individuals.[22] With the exception of one time, I never heard young men who had multiple sexual partners described as diseased or as contaminating to others, though they were often characterized as "players" or "dogs."

Perspectives on Teen Mothers

Girls also talked at length with me about young mothers, as eighteen-year-old Camila did one afternoon as we sat in a second-floor office at Centro Adelante.[23] Every so often during her interview, the serious young woman with a sprinkling of freckles across her cheeks and nose would glance out the closed window as she thought about how to answer my questions. At one point, she focused her attention on a group of three Latina teens animatedly talking to one another near the street corner. Keeping her eyes on them, Camila commented to me, "See, that's what I mean, that girl," referring to a petite girl in the group with a toddler who kept trying to yank free from her hand. "I know her, she had a baby, and now what? I know some girls who are like that, who don't do anything to take care of themselves. That's just stupid. I sure as hell ain't gonna be no baby momma." After a brief pause, she turned to me and continued, "I'm not saying that you shouldn't be having sex, 'cause I won't be a hypocrite, 'cause I do and I don't think that is wrong! But what I think is bad is when you don't make sure you know what you are doing so you don't end up like that," using her thumb to motion toward the young woman outside. Similarly, Arely, who refused to sign a virginity pledge during a sex education class, expressed the following to me: "You wanna have sex or get your freak on, fine, no problem, but be smart about it, there ain't no excuse for getting pregnant . . . there's no need for that."

In her ethnography of a Chicago Mexican community more than twenty years ago, the sociologist Ruth Horowitz found that many young unmarried women in this community did not live up to the ideal of virginity, despite the value that was placed on it. Instead, girls worked to manage how their peers interpreted their sexual behavior. Though they possessed knowledge about birth control, the girls that Horowitz became familiar with did not think it acceptable for unmarried young women to use birth control. Horowitz's interviews and fieldwork revealed that girls needed to demonstrate that they possessed a "bounded sexuality," which required not only that they be seen as sexually "surrendering" only to a boyfriend that they loved but that they not use birth control. According to Horowitz, the use of birth control placed a stigma on young women because it reflected "unbound sexuality, the open expression of passion, which is legitimate only for men."[24] In other words, a girl was no longer able to explain her sexual behavior as being "swept away by passion" if she used birth control because it served as an indicator that she was planning to have sex and could do so with whomever she pleased. Furthermore, Horowitz found that the use of birth control was also perceived as a "denial" of the importance of motherhood, an identity the community tightly linked to notions of appropriate femininity. In contrast, I now found that, while many Latina girls emphasized the importance of engaging in sexual behavior in the context of relationships, they, like Camila and Arely, firmly believed that an unplanned pregnancy could be prevented and perceived young women who failed to do so as foolish, sexually deviant, and falling short of meeting the standard for appropriate femininity.

Despite the stigma attached to being pregnant or a young mother, it was possible for the stigma to be lessened if one appropriately took on and performed motherhood, according to girls.[25] They explained that young mothers could make up for their lapse in sexual responsibility by taking on the role of "good mother," which for them meant working and/or continuing with school while caring for one's child.[26] Juanita, whose parents had threatened her sister with eviction from their home if she had an abortion, highlighted the possibility of redemption for young mothers when she talked about her sister: "At first, I thought she was a *pendeja*, you know, for getting pregnant. But then I've seen that she takes really good care of my niece. Like, she works part-time and uses most of her money for what my niece needs and she goes to school at night. She's a real good mom, no joke." And, while adamant that they themselves did not want to be young mothers, some of the girls even considered motherhood to have a positive effect on some girls who they thought might have ended up in the "promiscuous" category. For instance, describing the challenging mothering experiences of a close friend, Imelda, whose mother feared that family members would think that Imelda was mentally unstable if they learned that she was sexually attracted to women, commented about her friend: "It was too bad she got pregnant and had a shortie, 'cause we used to be able to hang out more. But she was getting kinda boy crazy, so this calmed her down, you know, being a mom." This was similar to Horowitz's finding that young unwed mothers could gain respect through motherhood. She noted that, within the Chicago Mexican community that she studied, the "the act of becoming a mother does not, of itself, alter a woman's identity, if she keeps being sexually active or seen as not being a good mother. . . . If she is not seen as responsible and devoted to her child, her identity as a mother is disallowed."[27] The Latina girls who spoke with me distanced themselves from both the category of "hos and skanks" and that of "baby mommas," but they did not see these categories as equally denigrated groupings of bad girls. Perhaps they felt this way because almost every one of them knew and/or was close to at least one young woman who was a mother. This was in contrast to their lack of relationships with girls whom they thought of as sexually promiscuous, who lived in their neighborhoods and with whom they attended school but whom they seemed to know only casually.

Latina girls' meaning of safe sex, therefore, was not just about the adoption of self-protective sexual practices to guard against pregnancy and STDs; it was also about protecting their social status as young women within their communities. Their categorization of other sexually experienced girls and the ways in which they talked about them suggest that, for this group of girls, "doing" appropriate femininity included being sexually responsible by practicing safe sex.[28] In other words, they critiqued the sexual "bad" girls because they assumed that they had not taken up safe-sex practices, but, even more important, they saw these young women as failing to meet normative gendered sexual expectations by not being sexually responsible (even though, as discussed in the next chapter, there were moments in which they themselves lapsed in their sexual self-protective practices). The girls I spoke with, then, "handled their business" in part to avoid the social stigma encountered by girls who were seen as falling short of demonstrating what the community thought of as appropriate femininity.

Perspectives on Good Girls

When girls talked about young women they saw as having failed in "handling their business," they initially attributed their sexual irresponsibility to ignorance and/or a lack of concern about negative sexual outcomes. Samantha, who co-facilitated a safe-sex workshop at Centro Adelante, first told me, "Some girls just don't think, like they don't care about what happens if they don't protect themselves. They are, like, 'Whatever' and keep taking all kinds of chances!" As revealed by their meaning of sexual respectability, girls believed it was imperative that young women have some knowledge about safe sex. As Samantha and I kept talking, the slender young woman with tight chestnut brown ringlets that framed her face noted, "Some girls do worry too much about *lo que dirán* [what will people see or think] . . . they have sex, but then so people won't think they want to, they don't have protection or whatever 'cause everyone says girls ain't supposed to be like that, which is stupid." Samantha, like many of the young women, offered another explanation that was centered on gender-sexual restrictions placed on young women.

According to them, some girls' sexual irresponsibility was related to their uncritical adherence to notions of "proper" sexual behavior, especially those they felt older generations espoused or what they often called "old-school thinking about sex." For instance, Lourdes stated the following:

It's the quiet ones that always surprise everyone. Here they are doing their work, being good girls and shit, minding their own business, and then, boom, out of nowhere you see them, you know, they got pregnant. I sometimes think that they're too busy trying to be good and don't know what to do or act when the first guy comes along trying to get some from them.

But this did not mean that girls viewed virginity as a stigma or as a sign of a young woman's prudishness.[29] As Lourdes explained:

One of my girls, she told me she don't even wanna bother with the drama of sex right now, so she's still a virgin. And I told her that I thought that was cool, 'cause it not 'cause she's just doing what *mami y papi dicen* [mom and dad say], you know? Or, because "*las señoritas no hacen esas cosas*" [proper young ladies don't do those things (she emphasized this by making quotation marks with fingers)]. She tells me that she ain't got time for that right now 'cause she's taking care of her school stuff, you know?

The girls frequently told me that they respect those young women who choose to be virgins, stressing, like Lourdes, the element of choice when referring to their esteem for this category of young women. But, as expressed by both Samantha and Lourdes, they were critical of young women they thought of as too concerned with presenting themselves as "good" girls in a very narrow way.

The girls that they tended to classify into this particular "good"-girl category were those who were born or raised for some length of time in Mexico or Puerto Rico. Some research suggests that early motherhood is more prevalent among first-generation Latina girls (also referred to as the immigrant generation) than in second-generation Latina youth. One finding, for example, indicates that 26 percent of first-generation Latina young women between the ages of eighteen and nineteen are teen mothers, whereas 16 percent of second-generation Latina girls in the same age range are teen mothers.[30] The differentiation that Latina girls made between themselves and their first-generation peers was perhaps their way of making sense of the experiences of this group of Latina girls with early motherhood.[31] For instance, Lisa described Magdalena (the pregnant young woman we ran into at the corner store) to me in the following way: "I think we were all like, 'What?! Magdalena is pregnant?!' 'Cause she was always so sweet and quiet, never hanging out with guys or whatever, like some girls are, you know, all innocent when they first get here from Puerto Rico or Mexico." When I asked her what she meant by this, Lisa tried to find the right words to articulate her observation:

"You know, like their parents won't let them have a boyfriend or be around too many guys or like hang out with friends, you know, like all proper and shit." Annabelle also made a similar point when she recounted a recent argument with her mother about curfew in which her mother asked why Annabelle could not be more like her eighteen-year-old cousin, who had immigrated from Mexico to Chicago when she was eleven years old. The athletic young woman with a salon spray-on tan told me, "My cousin is really sweet, but I think she's kinda too innocent about guys. For real! I think she thinks I act too wild or something, probably 'cause she lived in Mexico for a long time and thinks girls should always act like good *señoritas* [proper young ladies] or something." Thus, as second-generation Latina girls, they also articulated some distinctions between themselves and first-generation girls in terms of their gendered sexuality. Specifically, they characterized some first-generation Latina peers as "too good," which, according to them, could be detrimental to girls because it could get in the way of their ability to handle their business.[32]

Confronting and Creating Racial Sexualized Representations

Girls also moved beyond discussing the implications of these gendered sexual stigmatized identities for individual girls and connected them to larger characterizations of their communities. As I discussed in chapter 3 and earlier in this chapter, Latina girls were cognizant of how they were represented within the larger society. Elvia, who had questioned a sex educator's assumptions about Latina girls, shared how she thought others viewed her and other young women in her community: "I think people just think, 'Oh, she's Puerto Rican or Latina or whatever, she probably just wants to have babies really young or something.' People think that we are all like those girls on them shows, like on *Jerry Springer* or that *Maury* guy, trying to find out who their baby daddy is or talking about how they want to have a baby at fifteen." After a brief pause, the JROTC cadet with plans to join the Navy continued, "And I ain't saying that there ain't girls out there that are like that, but we aren't all like that . . . there are a lot of us who are not like that, who want to do other things with our lives and can take care of ourselves." Elvia, like the other girls, resented the assumption that she was sexually irresponsible because of her racial/ethnic identity.

Despite their recognition that such misconceptions were informed by racism, they still assigned some blame on girls they thought of as sexually irresponsible for these stereotypes. Camila, for instance, told me, "Regardless of what we do, white people are always gonna talk shit about us [Latinas], but people talk about us being ghetto and baby mommas and hos 'cause of some these girls who act like *pendejas* [idiots], too!" Thus, Latina girls also connected their sexual self-respect to the responsibility they felt for contributing to the integrity of their communities, articulating a politics of sexual respectability. That they were expected to do this was also communicated to them by some of the adults around them, as one of the Centro Adelante youth staff members did one muggy summer afternoon after the group returned from a trip to the Art Institute of Chicago. The staff member, a Latina in her mid-thirties, was angrily scolding the young people for their various misbehaviors during this trip. At one point, she turned to a couple of girls who were wearing midriff shirts and "Daisy Duke" shorts and chided them, saying, "And you all should know better than to dress like that. What do you think people think about us when they see you lookin' like that?" Then, addressing the entire group, she continued, "Remember, the young folks of Centro Adelante only look as good as you all make us look!" The girls, feeling embarrassed, just rolled their eyes and crossed their arms over their chests, obviously now self-conscious about their appearance.

The politics of respectability that Latina girls articulated was not grounded in a desire to emulate the sexual behavior of young white women, as was also evidenced in their interactions with their mothers when they were accused of wanting to "act white." In other words, they did not interpret the sexual behavior of young white women as the model of sexual propriety. Latina girls had limited opportunities to interact with white young women on a regular basis, given that they lived in predominately working-class Latina/o neighborhoods. When they spoke of the sexual behavior of young white women, they relied on the images they encountered through the media, such as the notorious *Girls Gone Wild* videos, talk shows like *Jerry Springer*, and popular films. As Latina girls made sense of how and why they were hypersexualized within the larger society, they resentfully brought up what they perceived to be the invisibility of young white women's sexual behavior. Carla, who vehemently denied wanting to be like white girls when her mother confronted her about her sexual behavior, expressed this to me: "White girls can do whatever they want, hook-up with all kinds of guys, but they ain't hos?! Yeah, right!"

White young women, it is certain, would disagree with Carla's claim that they are free to do as they sexually please without repercussions. Feminist scholars have illustrated that interpretation of white girls' sexual behavior is also shaped by a good-girl/bad-girl dichotomy.[33] But what Carla was also perceptively noting was how race/ethnicity mattered for how different groups of girls were judged within the larger society. Most of the young women I spoke with, like Carla, believed that the sexual behavior of young white women was not scrutinized, criticized, or pathologized to the degree that their own behavior was because of their white racial privilege.

Characterizing some white girls as hos, these young women asserted that they did not want to be described as sexually "acting like a white girl."[34] I witnessed this play out at a Halloween dance hosted by one of the other youth programs in the West Town neighborhood. As they sang along with the lyrics to Lil' Kim's hip-hop song featuring 50 Cent, "Magic Stick," a mixed-gender group of young people, including Isela and Graciela, was dancing in a circle to the popular tune's beat. One of the young men in the group began to slightly push Isela toward Graciela, saying, "Come on, kiss her!" The other two guys in the group began to egg them on as well, chanting, "Go, Isela, go, Isela!" Trying to ignore them, Isela finally spun around and angrily shoved the young man, exclaiming, "What the fuck?! Get off me! Do I look like a white girl to you?!" With that, she walked off the dance floor, with Graciela following her. When I asked Isela about this interaction a few days later, the tan young woman with bright hazel eyes explained to me that she "hated" when guys behaved like that, adding, "They just love to see girls kissing each other, you know, like some white girls be acting, kissing each other, showing their thongs, acting like hos! I ain't no white girl." As a lesbian-identified young woman, Isela distanced herself from white young women as a way to resist her objectification and the commodification of her sexuality for the sexual pleasure of men.[35]

It would be easy to simply interpret or dismiss the remarks of the young women I got to know as judgments or gossip about other girls' sexual behaviors. But an appreciation of the social location from which they attempt to construct their sexual respectability demonstrates that this behavior is more complex than girls just being mean to one another. Feminist scholars have broadened our understanding of girls' antagonistic interactions with one another by laying out the connections between these particular intragender relations and the gender inequality embedded throughout society.[36] On the basis of interviews she conducted with over four hundred girls, the psychologist Lyn Mikel Brown, for instance, argues:

> Simply put, girls' treatment of other girls is too often a reflection and a reaction to the way society sees and treats them. While we may not want to admit or even believe it, girls and women—by their association with conventional understandings of femininity—have less power and garner less respect in our culture. . . . Girls' meanness to other girls is a result of their

struggle to make sense of or to reject their secondary status in the world and to find ways to have power and experience feeling powerful.[37]

With very few culturally acceptable ways for girls to claim respect for themselves, sexuality, particularly interpretations of sexual behavior, often becomes a central way for them to do so. Confronting gendered-sexual prescriptions for their behavior and racial sexualized stereotypes about themselves, the Latina girls I spoke with struggled to create respect for themselves among their peers and within the dominant society. They did so by defining themselves as sexual "good" girls, in part through their construction of girls whom they saw as not embodying sexual respectability. Unfortunately, these young women also inadvertently participate in their own subordination by positioning themselves as superior to other young women on the basis of sexual behavior. The advantaged position in the good-girl/bad-girl dichotomy that they seek, predicated on appropriate gendered sexual behavior and race/ethnicity sexual difference, depends upon and sustains, as the sociologist Amy Wilkins notes, "the maintenance of a gender hierarchy that positions men over women and good women over bad women."[38]

Building the Tool Kit of Safe-Sex Skills and Resources

The day I first met Maritza, she came to the teen health center for a scheduled appointment. As we talked about the circumstances that brought her to the health center, she revealed her intention to obtain an HIV test. Since Maritza was there to obtain an HIV test, I expected her to have been motivated to do so because of an unsafe sexual experience. But, instead, the energetic young woman with brown cornrows that ended at her shoulders told me that she had decided to take the test after a conversation with a close circle of girlfriends about HIV:

> Me and my girls sometimes talk about sex. It's not like we put our business all out there, but if one of us got a question about sex, we put it out there and try to see if we can figure it out. Like I knew to come here to this clinic for an HIV test because one of my girls heard about this place in a presentation they did at her school.

Maritza explained that some of her friends had already been tested for HIV and had encouraged her to take the test even if she felt she had been practicing safe sex. She said she had decided to get tested to be "on the safe side . . . and to let my girls know that, like them, I am also 'handlin' my business.'" Maritza's intention to demonstrate to her friends that she was sexually responsible highlights once again the importance that Latina girls assigned to their ability to claim sexual respectability. But her story also underscores the importance of peers to the process by which Latina girls put into motion their plans to practice safe sex.

It is well noted that peers inform the sexual attitudes and behaviors of young people. Indeed, many popular teen movies often humorously depict the embarrassing predicaments that young people find themselves in after heeding the sexual advice of friends, especially young men. And research on the sexual development of youth has tried to ascertain the degree to which peers influence the sexual decision making of young people. But little attention has been given to how peer influence operates in the sexual lives of youth—that is, we really do not know much about how peer influence in relation to sexuality is exerted among youth and its extent.[39] It is readily assumed that young people are incapable of providing each other with reliable information about sex, especially safe sex. This is especially so with young women of color, who are persistently categorized as sexually "at risk." But, as I describe, Latina girls found their close friends to be credible sources of safe sex information.[40]

When I asked the girls to name all the organizations they were familiar with that offered sexual and reproductive health care and/or information to youth in the Chicago area, they were all able to identify at least two such organizations. These young women were likely able to do so because they were a highly self-selected sample of Latina youth who were practicing safe sex and whom I had met through community organizations. Therefore, they may have possessed more knowledge about local resources than girls who do not access community organizations on a regular basis. While a few of the girls came to know about at least one organization through their school-based sex education, most of the girls identified these sites with the assistance of close friends. Many had already visited at least one organization and had first done so in the company of at least one close friend. Such was Jocelyn's experience; she shared with me that her friend had volunteered to accompany her to a health center when she was having second thoughts about keeping an appointment to inquire about birth control options. The young woman, who had decidedly told me that she did not believe in abortion, said, "I was so glad she came with me 'cause I don't think I could've gone in there by myself, you know, I'm too shy to ask stuff sometimes."

And close to half of the girls I spoke with me told me that they had encouraged close friends to seek out safe-sex resources. Norma was one such young woman. Recounting her most recent visit to the teen health center, the charismatic young woman explained that she had accompanied her best friend to her first health center appointment:

> So she confessed to me that she had, you know, had sex with her man for the first time. 'Cause you know, she knew I had already had sex, but she was still a virgin, or at least I thought so! When I asked her, "Are you taking care of your business?," she was like, "No." I was like, "Girl! What you doing?! You trying to get yourself in trouble or something?" So the next day, I made her go with me to the teen health center. . . . So I took her there and now she's using the shot, so at least she ain't gotta worry about getting herself in trouble.

I was not surprised that Norma had persuaded her best friend to visit the teen health center. Norma had told that me that she frequently "looked up stuff about sex" at the library and on the Internet for her close friends. At various points in our interviews, she shared with me that she took pride in being someone whose friends consistently approached for advice, especially about boys and relationships. On multiple occasions, I witnessed Norma in deep conversations with her tight circle of girlfriends at Hogar del Pueblo, who always seemed to be hanging on her every word.

Lesbian-identified girls, however, described locating institutional resources through their own efforts. Arely, for instance, told me she that came across some LGBTQ organizations that provided safe-sex workshops when she was considering entering into her first sexual relationship with another young woman. Twirling the silver angel necklace pendant she always wore, she said:

> I was curious, but also nervous big time because I had only messed around with a guy before! And let me say that even the first time I kissed her, I felt right. I found myself wanting to learn more about being with women, you know, sexually, so for a while, I tried to read stuff, mostly erotic fiction and forums on the Internet.

She explained that her sexual partner had also helped her identify reading materials as she was exploring the possibility of a same-sex relationship with her, but this information was not about specifically about safe sex. According to Arely, her search for information when she was questioning her sexuality contributed to her awareness of safe-sex resources. She explained, "I mean, through all that, I kinda ending up knowing where to find more information about safe sex that is for queer folks . . . so I was like, 'Hey, I remember read-ing that this organization over here or over there has folks that can tell me more about having safe sex with my girlfriend.'" Like Arely, other lesbian-identified girls also discovered organizations when they began to question their sexual identities and searched for information to help them negotiate their feelings and perspectives on their sexuality. Though they did not find organizations through their friends, they did speak with their close friends about safe-sex practices. As an example, sixteen-year-old Gloria told me that she was aware of the importance of using dental dams for oral sex with her partner but did not begin using condoms and saran wrap on sex toys until a close friend shared information about safe-sex techniques with her. The high school junior with an interest in journalism explained, "I was thinking I was doing all right with safe sex, but then when she [her friend] was talk-ing about covering up sex toys . . . that's when I was like, 'Hmm . . . maybe I should do that, too.'"

This was also the experience of heterosexual-identified girls. Maritza, for instance, communicated how her close friends influenced her choice of method for practicing safe sex:

> Since the idea is that you ain't supposed to be it doing until you are mar-ried, no one really tells us much anyway. But it's like me and my friends, we all talk about it anyway, you know? Like, the condoms I use are the Trojan ones, I wasn't sure which would be the best, you know what I mean, like the safest. They all pretty much said that they used those condoms. So I make my boyfriend get those if we are gonna get busy.

And Annabelle, who thought her cousin was "too sexually innocent," shared that she had used condoms "all the time" when she initially began having sexual intercourse with her partner, primarily because he provided them. But, shortly thereafter, she decided that she did not always want to rely on her partner to bring condoms, especially since there were instances in which he attempted to convince her to have sex without one. She considered the birth control pill and the Depo-Provera shot but had reservations about these methods because of the possible side effect of weight gain associated with these hormonal contraceptives. She decided on the birth control pill after discussing it with her friends:

> Two of my girls were using the pill, and they recommended it. They even told me which brand to ask for when I went to the doctor. And they didn't get fat or whatever. Besides, like one of them said, "I'd rather get a little fat,

like five pounds, than, like, big fat, like pregnant." So, I've been using the pill and condoms for two years, and I'm cool with it.

As these narratives reveal, Latina girls perceived their close friends to be credible sources of information, particularly when these friends shared knowledge gained from their firsthand experiences with safe-sex methods. And, as I discuss in next chapter, these friends were also instrumental to their negotiation of safe sex with partners. In considering how young Latinas were able to locate institutional resources and accumulate some knowledge to facilitate their engagement with safe-sex practices, it is critical that we appreciate the sociocultural context in which they did so, particularly the challenges they navigated in their effort to claim sexual respectability for themselves. Their vulnerability as sexually active young women of color became painfully evident when they shared the strategies they had developed to avoid parental detection.[41] One hurdle they encountered was the limited mobility they were afforded outside the home, which made it difficult for many of them to access institutional resources. Norma, who had convinced her friend to visit a teen health center, detailed how she and her best friend had managed to keep her friend's first appointment: "We had to cut school for like a half-day so that her parents wouldn't find out, 'cause they like always wanted her home straight after school. They like time her, 'cause they are, you know, straight up, like old-school Mexican." Like Norma and her friend, the girls had to be resourceful to buy themselves time to be able to seek resources or keep appointments; to do so, they told their parents that they needed to go to the library to work on a project, bribed siblings to cover for them, skipped the youth program for an afternoon, and/or missed school or classes.

Girls also collaborated with their close friends to figure out how to conceal their possession of condoms, birth control pills, dental dams, and/or sex toys. Most of them felt that they had little to no privacy in their homes, particularly since they often had to share bedrooms with siblings. The young women told me that they learned from friends how to discreetly hide such items in their school lockers or in "secret" locations in their homes, such as under mattresses or in shoeboxes, or carried them around in their backpacks. These were risky strategies because family members or school authorities might discover them at any time and also because they might not always be accessible. One young woman, for example, described her frustration when she forgot her birth control pills at school one weekend.

Another factor that contributed to the girls' vulnerability was their economic dependence on their parents. Since they were concealing their sexual behavior from their parents, the girls were unable to request money from their parents for items such as birth control pills, Depo-Provera injections, or condoms. And those young women had health insurance through their parents' coverage did not utilize it for their sexual and reproductive health care. Even in cases in which parents already knew about their sexual activity, most of these girls did not feel it appropriate to ask for money for pay for items related to safe sex. Thus, the majority of the girls relied heavily upon confidential, accessible, and age-appropriate sexual and reproductive health care services that were free and/or inexpensive, such as those that used a sliding fee scale.

Both lesbian-identified and heterosexual-identified girls negotiated obstacles to their ability to handle their business, but the oppressive forces of patriarchy and heterosexism especially heightened the vulnerability of lesbian-identified girls should they get "caught" by their parents and/or other family members. Isela, who had walked off the dance floor when a male peer kept insisting that she kiss another girl, conveyed this concern:

> I'm always feeling like I gotta be looking around, to make sure there ain't nobody around that knows me. I hate that! If my mom or dad knew, I think they'd kick my ass or even kick me out! It's bad enough they trip when they think I'm out messing around with boys. They think Rebecca is my best friend, and her mom thinks I'm Rebecca's best friend, so we're always saying that we're at each other's house studying or just hanging out. But, lately, my mom has been saying *cositas* [little things] here and there, like maybe's she's starting to suspect. So my friend told me to have a guy friend call my house, so my mom would think that I was seeing a guy, you know, stupid shit like that!

The anxiety conveyed by Isela underscores the harsh penalties that young lesbians may face because of their sexual identity and/or behaviors. This is not to imply that heterosexual-identified Latinas did not report fearing or encountering violence as a response to their sexual behavior, but lesbian-identified girls are particularly at risk because they are overtly challenging the patriarchal definition of their sexuality as subordinate to that of men. As I discussed in chapter 2, while parents can possibly construct an explanation of their heterosexual daughter's sexual activity as a form of victimization, the sexual activity of a lesbian-identified daughter makes her own desire and agency undeniably visible, an incongruent component of women's sexuality in a culture with strong patriarchal expectations for women.[42] In response to this transgression, parents might attempt to "persuade" their daughters to conform to heteronormative expressions of female sexuality not only by physically disciplining the body through violence but also by imposing economic sanctions, including eviction from the home.[43]

Regulating Sexual Desire and Pleasure

Through the distinctions that they made between themselves and other "sexually active" young women and the safe-sex resources and skills they gathered through their friendships with other young women, the Latina girls I came to know fashioned their identities as sexually respectable young women. However, this identity-work had implications for their ability to explore their sexual desire and pleasure in their interactions with close friends (and, as I explore in the next chapter, also shaped how they negotiated safe sex with partners). This was particularly so for heterosexual-identified girls. References to sexual desire and pleasure in front of their peers, according to this group of girls, could undermine the credibility of the image for sexual respectability that they were trying to establish for themselves. Fabiola, a high school senior with a two-year university scholarship, expressed this when I asked her whether she discussed what she enjoyed about sex with her friends. She had just finished animatedly describing the condom tips her friends shared with her when I posed this question. Noticeably less enthusiastic, the honor roll student replied:

No, I can't say we really like talk about *de eso* [that (referring to pleasure)] too much . . . sometimes we say that it was good, you know, sex. But I don't think we get into details and stuff . . . if I was like, "Oh, I like the way this position feels or this and that," they'd be all weird about it and probably talk about me when I wasn't around.

Yvette, whose aunt had reservations about the amount of time she spent at Hogar del Pueblo, responded to my question in a similar manner:

We all just kinda keep it at that level where we do talk about sex, but just certain things. Like, I mean, it's okay to talk about having sex, but not what you like to do, 'cause then they might be there listening to you and thinking you some kind of ho and maybe even talking shit about you behind your back.

Though girls conversed with me at times about desire and pleasure, the subject came up rarely and was even avoided in the conversations they described having with close friends, as indicated by Fabiola's and Yvette's experiences.

Nevertheless, they did not completely avoid the topic of sexual desire or pleasure in their conversations with friends. The majority of the girls wanted to be able to discuss this topic in more detail with their close friends and suspected that their friends also wanted to do this. Graciela, whom I had bumped into at the laundromat, communicated this to me when she discussed her friends:

> I think we all kinda think about it, you know, but won't say it. It's there, in the back of our minds when we are talking about sex! Like I could tell we all really do wanna know more about orgasms and stuff like that, but we're either too embarrassed or scared to just bring it up 'cause you don't want your girls to be thinking you're a freak or something like that! We'll talk about this or that, like using condoms, no problem, but when it comes down to other things like that, we get all real quiet.

Finding it too risky to directly divulge their feelings of desire and/or pleasure to their friends, heterosexual-identified Latina girls instead cautiously wove this topic into more acceptable sexual discussions among their peers. Patricia, whose mother, Maria, felt that it was necessary for mothers to openly discuss sexuality with daughters, was one such young woman. Uncertain as to whether she had indeed experienced an orgasm during sexual intercourse with her boyfriend and not wanting to seem either too sexually inexperienced or too sexually eager to her friends, Patricia described how she had indirectly raised this issue by asking them about condoms: "We were talking about how guys sometimes act like condoms don't fit them and I was like, 'Hey, do you think sex feels better with or without a condom?' That's when some of them talked a lil' bit about how they felt when they were doing it, so that kinda helped me a lil' bit." Thus, some girls explored their sexual desire or pleasure in conversations they had with close friends about safe-sex methods, such as the impact of condom use on bodily sensation or decreased sexual drive as a side effect of the birth control pill.

Another key manner in which heterosexual-identified girls touched on their sexual pleasure and desire in these interactions was through the process of demonstrating the solidity of their relationships with their boyfriends, which for some of them was one of the grounds on which they established their sexual respectability. They made references to pleasure and desire to convey their commitment to their partner, most commonly expressed through the touting of the partner's sexual prowess and, occasionally, their own sexual skills. For example, Graciela recounted how she had responded to her friends' inquiries about the possible infidelity of her boyfriend:

> I don't let them know all our business, like what he likes to do to me or what I do to him, but they know that it's all good between us. Like, I tell them that he's all good in that department, you know? My man knows how I like it! Or they'll know that I know how to treat him good, that I ain't no little girl.

Likewise, Yvette asserted to her friends the stability of her relationship with her boyfriend: "I ain't gonna be there and be like, okay, I did this and that to him, 'cause they ain't gotta know all that. But if they ask me if I like it, I'll tell them I do, because I do! He ain't got no reason to hook up with anyone else 'cause everything is cool with us when it comes to that." As illustrated by the experiences of Graciela and Yvette, this group of girls relied upon comments about sexual pleasure and desire to lend creditability to their sexual relationships.

Furthermore, rather than highlight their own pleasure and desire in these conversations with friends, they described their focus on their partner's experiences of pleasure and desire. For instance, Stephanie described how she and her friends sometimes disclosed to one another the specific things that sexually excited their partners:

> I don't really know how we get to talking about it, but like just the other day, one of my girls was telling us how her man likes her to wear thongs, you know, stuff like that, and then everyone was like, "Oh yeah, well, my man is a freak, he likes this or that or I read in *Cosmopolitan* that guys like it when you do this or that."

In our interviews, almost all of the young women listed the varied sources from which they culled specific knowledge on their own pleasure and desire—the Internet, romance novels, magazines (typically *Cosmopolitan* and *Glamour*), movies, and videos—but this was often undertaken as an individual endeavor, rather than being done in the company of a group of girlfriends.

While many heterosexual-identified girls found it easier to discuss their partners' pleasure and desire rather than their own with their close friends, lesbian-identified girls described feeling less restricted in talking to friends about their sexual pleasure and desire. Lesbian-identified young women were more willing to elicit specific information about enhancing their own

pleasure from other young women, mostly other young women who identified as lesbian or bisexual. A self-described "hard-core" salsa fan, Cristina
recounted how she approached a close friend to inquire about the subject:

> Each time I get with her [her partner], I feel like I'm just beginning to
> learn about sex, it's cool, but it also feels so weird. I mean, she's the first girl
> I've been with, 'cause before her, I had only been with my boyfriend. But,
> with Melissa, I remember thinking, "Damn, so this is what it's supposed to
> feel like" . . . 'cause I didn't really have those feelings before. I was talking
> to my friend, she's been out since she was like fifteen, and I was asking her
> about different things she likes to do, just to kind of see what I might want
> to check out for myself.

As Cristina's experience illustrates, she actively sought information about
her own pleasure through her conversations with a friend whom she perceived to be more experienced with this issue. Two lesbian-identified girls
even recounted how they had tried to introduce the topic of pleasure and
desire when hanging out with their heterosexual-identified friends. Linda,
who had asked a question about same-sex desire during a sex education lesson, described the reaction she had received from a close circle of girlfriends
when she attempted to introduce the topic of sexual desire after they had
watched a show about the sexual lives of teenage girls on *Oprah*:

> Of course, it was mostly about white girls from nice suburbs and some
> black girls . . . but they made it seem as if girls just have sex to fit in and
> were being used by boys. We were saying that how come they don't ever
> talk to girls like us, you know, like Latinas from around here . . . then I
> was like, "And girls like to get their freak on, too, right? It's not just guys."
> Then they got kinda weird about it, like they didn't know what I was talk-
> ing about.

Although Linda and her friends were critical about the lack of diverse perspectives on the popular talk show, the conversation focused on race/ethnic-
ity and class, rather than on notions of gendered sexuality, even when Linda
attempted to initiate a conversation about girls' sexual desire and pleasure.
For many of the young women I spoke to, talking about pleasure and desire
with friends was risky because it might invite speculation about the appropri-
ateness of their sexual behavior. Open to her friends about her identity as a
lesbian, Linda was already challenging heteronormative prescriptions of gendered sexuality and was more willing to critique such limited representations

of girls' sexuality. But her heterosexual-identified friends' silence about pleasure and desire helped to ensure that they themselves would remain within
the boundaries of sexual respectability.

Conclusion

The Latina girls I came to know made no apologies for their sexual interests and activities. Though they acknowledged that virginity was important
to some of their female peers, they did not see themselves as having violated
notions of proper femininity because they were no longer virgins. Rather,
they believed that sexual respectability, a key element of proper femininity,
was something they were still entitled to claim because of their self-protective sexual practices. In other words, Latina girls coupled sexual respectability and safe sex to negotiate their sexual subjectivity in the face of the good-
girl/bad-girl dichotomy that, while seemingly increasingly open to women's
expression of their sexualities, continues to be characterized by a sexual double standard that privileges men.

The power and pervasiveness of the good-girl/bad-girl dichotomy makes
it extremely challenging, if not altogether impossible at this time, for young
women to form sexual identities and subjectivities outside that dichotomy.
As girls who engaged in sexual behaviors, the young women I spoke with
knew that they were perpetually at risk of being defined as bad girls and
therefore sought to define themselves and to control where they were situated in this patriarchal gendered sexual construct. They did so by establishing a symbolic boundary of sexuality between themselves and other "sexually
active" girls that was predicated on sexual respectability; they set themselves
apart from girls in their communities who they believed had not been sexually responsible and from young white women, whom they saw as sexually
out of control. Thus, sexual respectability functioned as a gendered sexual
and racial/ethnic boundary formation that distanced them from these other
young women and affirmed their identities as sexually responsible girls.

Gender scholars have asserted that we cannot currently exist outside the
gender order but that we can decide how we are going to participate in it,
particularly how we will challenge it.[44] While I agree that this is one promising route by which we can effect positive social change, we cannot lose sight
of the constraints under which differently situated groups in our society must
do so. For instance, the stories of the lesbian-identified Latina girls in this
study provide further evidence of the need to account for the specific conditions under which different groups of queer-identified girls negotiate their
sexual identities and, more important, the consequences that process entails

for them socially, politically, and economically. The experiences of all of the Latina girls I spoke with provide insight into how they negotiated some of the gendered, sexual, and racial constraints under which they must form their sexual subjectivities. They walked a fine line between being good girls and bad girls, one riddled with gender-sexual and racially sexualized classifications of girls. Latina girls' meanings of safe sex and sexual respectability and the ways they connected them to gender, sexuality, and race illustrate how these categories construct each other and are relied upon to stabilize and destabilize them.[45] With few or no resources and little of the support that would allow them to step back and try to determine alternative ways to proceed with their sexual agency, this group of young women instead attempted to make room for their sexual lives and experiences on the "right" side of the good-girl/bad-girl binary. In a sense, they expanded what it means to be a "good" girl. However, this also legitimated the very dichotomy that restricted their sexuality. Much of their sexual agency was spent on their effort to be able to claim sexual respectability for themselves, particularly by articulating who they were not going to be—those "other" girls. This means that there was little space for them to explore and articulate whom they wanted to be as sexual beings on their own terms and without positioning themselves vis-à-vis other young women, which, as I explore in the next chapter, also had consequences for how they negotiated safe sex with partners.

5

Playing Lil' Games

Partners and Safe-Sex Strategies

Stephanie was an hour late for our second scheduled interview. As I waited for her in the lobby of Hogar del Pueblo, I began to worry that she had changed her mind about participating in the study after our initial interview. I checked my cell phone again to make sure I had not missed her call and decided to head home. As I walked down the street on that cold and blustery November afternoon, I spotted Stephanie and her friend hurriedly walking toward me. Greeting me with a wide smile, the charismatic young woman shook her head and exclaimed, "Girl, I had me some drama!" After settling down in a private room at Hogar del Pueblo, Stephanie pulled out a small, crumpled paper bag from her backpack. Inside the paper bag was a small blue and white package labeled *Plan B.*

She shared her drama with me, recounting that the previous evening, after "doing it," she and her boyfriend realized the condom had "broke." Upset and scared, she placed the blame on her boyfriend:

I was like, "You probably didn't put it on right!" So he got all pissed off when I said that and he was like, "I know what I'm doing, you're the one that don't know how to put one on! I never see you tryin' to put one on me!" I mean, damn, what the hell does he want!? I'm the one that usually gets the condoms 'cause I know he'll say he forgot to get some.

Stephanie, who had highlighted the importance of self-respect in her paper on teen pregnancy, explained that she was late for our meeting because she had had to wait for an available appointment at a health center to obtain the morning-after pill. Her friend helped her locate this resource and accompanied Stephanie because her boyfriend had to work that afternoon. When I asked her if she and her boyfriend had ever made it a point to discuss their perspectives and practices related to safe sex, she shrugged her shoulders and replied, "We've never been like, 'Okay, time to sit down and talk about safe sex.' But, we kinda do sometimes. Like if we know someone who got pregnant or something like herpes, we start talking about how we gotta be careful." She continued:

Once or twice he's tried to do it without a condom and I like start telling him why it ain't gonna happen like that and he's like, "All right, all right! I know!" He got mad that one time 'cause I told him, "Well, you act like someone who don't know." I think he was mad 'cause he's a guy and don't want no female telling him stuff like that.

Like Stephanie, most girls described encountering resistance from their partners to discussions about safe sex. They expressed a desire for more safe-sex communication with their partner, referencing gender as a key reason why it was difficult for them to sustain a dialogue with their partners on this topic. However, heterosexual-identified girls and lesbian-identified girls pointed to gender in different ways.

Heterosexual-identified girls characterized young men as being generally uncomfortable with sharing their thoughts or feelings about many things, including safe sex. For example, Maritza, who sought an HIV test after a conversation with some close friends, explained, "He [her boyfriend] doesn't really like to talk all serious about stuff and I think that makes it hard for him to even talk about stuff like that [safe sex], at least like all serious about it." Likewise, Camila, who thought that some girls' behavior sustained stereotypes of Latinas, stated, "It's just harder for guys to 'talk talk' [she emphasized this by making quotation marks with fingers] the way girls do, they're like, 'Oh no! Is this going to be one of those feelings conversations?'" This group of girls connected their boyfriends' reluctance to engage in safe-sex discussions to their concern about not seeming "too" expressive or talkative—traits most often associated with femininity (and for which women are often criticized). Furthermore, these girls thought that their partners assumed that they would take responsibility for safe-sex practices or expected them to do so. As Juanita conveyed to me, with frustration, "He thinks I know more about that [safe sex], you know, 'cause I'm a girl, so he's just like, 'Ain't much too say, you got it covered.'" A few even speculated that their partner avoided such conversations because they did not want to reveal how little they did know about safe sex. Camila, for instance, added, after stating that young men were uncomfortable with "feelings" conversations: "Talking about sex with girls, especially about being safe, might be hard for guys. Sometimes I think that he doesn't want to talk about it 'cause maybe he doesn't know a lot about it." Thus, heterosexual-identified girls attributed their limited safe-sex conversations with boyfriends to the boys' sense of masculinity.

Lesbian-identified girls also connected their partners' resistance to safe-sex communication to gender, but not in terms of traits associated with masculinity and femininity. Rather, they believed that partners were dismissive of the need for safe-sex communication because of their shared gender and sexual identities and their partners' perceptions that they were at lower risk because of their sexual practices. For instance, after sharing with me some of the personality traits she admired in her partner, Linda added, "She gets me in a lot of ways so it's easy to talk to her, but one thing that she don't feel like we gotta talk about that much is that [safe sex] since we are both females, you know? For her, that means we should be okay when it comes to safe sex." Similarly, Imelda, whose mother called her girlfriend to inform her that she was no longer welcome in their home, stated, "She [her partner] don't want to talk about it [safe sex]! She's like, 'We're all right, that's something that girls who have sex with guys need to worry about.'" According to this group of girls, their partners attempted to evade the topic by insisting that, as women having sex with women, they were not at risk, at least not to the extent that heterosexual and/or bisexual women were.

Gender has now consistently been identified as a significant factor contributing to women's negative sexual-related health outcomes.[1] As researchers have noted, notions of appropriate femininity and masculinity inform one's ability to enact safe-sex behaviors. A heterosexual woman, for example, who is knowledgeable about the importance of condom use for minimizing sexual risks may still not purchase male condoms because she may believe this is inappropriate for women to do, or she may be intimidated by how others will react to her behavior. Or she may feel empowered enough to purchase male condoms but still need to rely on her partners' cooperation to use the condoms, a negotiation that is both complex and conflict laden because it unfolds in a gender order in which men and women do not hold equal social status.[2] Moreover, access to knowledge about safe-sex practices is uneven for differently situated groups, such as LGBTQ communities, which often encounter information that presumes sexual actors to be heterosexual. Among these groups, there have also been gender discrepancies in access to sexual health information, such as HIV awareness and prevention campaigns directed primarily at gay men. Lesbian women, along with other sexual minority women, at least until recently, have often been rendered invisible not only by dominant discourses on heterosexual women's sexual health risks but also by those related to gay men.[3] Thus, the constraints under which women and men negotiate their sexuality and risk-reduction behaviors are shaped to a significant degree by gender inequality and heteronormativity.

In this chapter, I analyze Latina girls' accounts of their safe-sex communication with their partners to explore how they negotiate sexual safety and sexual pleasure in interactions with their partners. I focus on the strategies Latina girls develop and employ to deal with the obstacles of gender inequality and heteronormativity in their safe-sex communication with partners. As discussed in chapter 4, Latina girls' cultivation of their sexual respectability entailed boundary construction that set them apart from other girls along the lines of gendered sexuality and race/ethnicity. A significant component of this distancing between themselves and girls they characterized as sexually deviant was their self-perception as young women who sexually "handled their business" by practicing safe sex. Their ability to claim this particular gendered sexual identity, however, also required that they negotiate their sexual-safety perspectives and practices with their partners. Encountering resistance to safe-sex communication, these young women did not just "talk" to their partners about safe sex. Instead, they developed and employed strategies that drew on notions of risk, expectations about femininity and masculinity, and education to engage their partners in sexual safety talk. Their stories of their safe-sex communication with their partners reveal how their understanding of sexual respectability carried over into their sexual relationships. Their narratives also demonstrate how their efforts to stay within the symbolic boundary of sexuality they constructed both permitted and constrained their negotiation of safe sex with partners.

Finding and Creating Opportunities for Safe-Sex Talk

The majority of the heterosexual-identified girls with whom I spoke did not have structured conversations with their partners about safe sex.

Instead, they indirectly engaged their partners in these conversations during moments that lent themselves well to the topic. The most common manner by which girls drew their partners into such dialogues, even if briefly,
was, as Stephanie described, through a discussion they were already having
about the sexual-related misfortune(s) of someone they personally knew,
such as family members or friends. Olivia, who was critical of her father's
controlling behavior toward her mother, recounted a conversation she had
had with her sexual partner (a young man she identified as her friend) after
they discovered that his fifteen-year-old sister was pregnant.[4] She described
angrily reacting to his perception that his sister "put herself" in the predicament: "I snapped at him! I was like, 'What the fuck?! She didn't just get pregnant by herself!' And then I was like, 'That better not happen to us,' and then
we started talking about it for a while that time." Instances such as these, in
which young women and their partners reflected on the sexual-related circumstances of those close to them, briefly opened up a space for this group
of young women and their partners to express their concerns and ideas about
sexual safety with each other.

However, six of them said they had talked with their partners about safe
sex upon having their own scares about negative sexual outcomes. Four of
these young women told me that they experienced pregnancy scares after
failing to use condoms and/or birth control. Of these four girls, one revealed
to me that she had received treatment for chlamydia in the past. Another
shared with me that she had obtained an abortion. And one young woman
told me that she sought an HIV test (and got a negative result) after discovering that her boyfriend had cheated on her. Consider how Fabiola, who had
insisted to me that girls should not utilize abortion as a birth control method,
described the exchange she had with her boyfriend when her period was two
days late:

> We were trippin' 'cause we had done it one time and not used anything
> a few weeks before. He was telling me, 'We are so stupid, why did we do
> that?' When I finally got my period, we were like, "Fuck that, we don't ever
> wanna go through that again!" We told ourselves that we had to always to
> use something, no matter what. We were even too scared to have sex again
> after that for at least a couple months!

Like Fabiola, these six young women identified such "scare" experiences
or negative-outcomes as hard lessons that meant that they and their partners "had to talk" about safe sex.[5] Despite their sexual self-protective lapses,
these girls still asserted their claim to sexual respectability, something they

denied to other young women with similar experiences. Fabiola explained away this inconsistency to me: "I could see if I was always not doing what I needed to handle my business, but it ain't like that. I fucked up and I learned the hard way and never again, for real!" Thus, they felt able to hang on to their sexual respectability because they interpreted their lapses as isolated instances from which they had learned harsh lessons about the consequences of unsafe sex.

The other manner by which heterosexual-identified girls entered into communication about safe sex with partners was through their commentary on TV shows, films, and/or magazine articles that focused on the topic, such as the notorious paternity-test episodes featured on the *Maury* show and sex-related "surveys" and quizzes featured in *Cosmopolitan* magazine. For instance, Lourdes told me of her unplanned extended safe-sex conversation with her boyfriend after watching the film *Real Women Have Curves*: "We were saying how they showed the girl [the film protagonist] and that she was the one with the condom. And we started talking about how girls ain't really cool with doing that, especially Latina girls, and we just kept talking about that while we ate." Thus, media culture sometimes presented opportunities for girls and their partners to have some safe-sex-related discussions. The media have been identified and accepted as an influential source of information for young people.[6] In relation to their sexual development and sexual understanding, the media and cultural studies scholar Meenakshi G. Durham asserts that "it is virtually incontestable that adolescents rely heavily on the mass media for learning about sex."[7] Media are often criticized for having a negative impact on young people's sexuality. But it is critical to consider how young people's consumption of media may also facilitate their ability to question and negotiate sexuality and its overlap with other aspects of their identity, such as gender, race/ethnicity, class, and age.[8]

Some girls, however, drew their male partners into safe-sex conversations by inquiring about their reaction to hypothetical scenarios. These four girls specifically posed scenarios about unplanned pregnancy. Camila, for example, told of how she waited for her boyfriend to raise the subject of safe sex as their relationship progressed. When he failed to do so, she broached the topic with him:

> He was talking about how much he wanted to do it [sex] with me and how much he loved me . . . and I was like, "Okay, what would you do if I got pregnant?" And he was like, "I don't know, that wouldn't happen to us." I was like, "How do you know that for sure?" I told him nothing was gonna

happen unless we were both sure and knew what we were doing . . . we talked about using condoms, who would get them . . . girl, I even made sure that both of us knew how to put it on before we ever even did it!

Instead of accepting her boyfriend's self-assured response that they would not encounter the problem of an unplanned pregnancy, Camila insisted that they both needed to be well informed in their sexual decision making, leading them into a conversation about condom use, a specific safe-sex communication I explore in more detail later in this chapter. These young women never described posing a scenario about STDs to their boyfriends, even though they were also concerned about STDs, as I discussed in chapter 4. One reason for this may be that an STD scenario could arouse a boyfriend's doubts about the fidelity of his girlfriend. Whereas the pregnancy scenario invites a boyfriend to imagine his response to a "crisis" that is understood to be co-created in the context of a relationship, the STD scenario asks a boyfriend to respond to a "crisis" that he or his girlfriend introduces into the relationship as a result of stepping out on the partner. While these orchestrated discussions were limited to the topic of pregnancy, girls' use of hypothetical scenarios was still a way in which they created some opportunities to talk with their partners about safe sex.

As is evident in their stories, most heterosexual identified girls consistently described themselves as the initiators of safe-sex communication with their male partners. I made it a point not to ask them if they took on this task because I wanted to explore how such communication unfolded and the contexts in which it emerged for young women. I did not assume that young women initiated safe-sex communication with their male partners, nor did I want girls to perceive my questions as suggesting that they should be the ones to do so. Nevertheless, the majority of girls indicated that they indeed took on this responsibility.

One important reason why this occurred was that girls perceived the young men to be unable to fully express themselves in conversations with young women, as pointed out earlier. Their view that there were gender differences in communication was certainly informed by their experiences with their partners, but this notion does not solely derive from their experiences with their partners. This way of interpreting communication between men and women is also significantly shaped by the widely accepted and circulated perception that men and women, as "opposite sexes," have inherently different ways of communicating that often lead to relationship conflicts. For instance, the *New York Times* best seller *He's Just Not That into You: The No-Excuses Truth to Understanding Guys* (2004), written by

Greg Behrendt and Liz Tuccillo, was designed to help women, especially "single" and "smart" women, to make sense of men's "puzzling" behaviors, including interpretations of what they "really" mean when they do and do not communicate with women.[9] This theme of "decoding" men's and boys' talk and behaviors is also regularly featured in women's and girls' magazines, a form of print media I often witnessed the young women accessing during the course of my fieldwork.[10] Thus, the media often overstate gender differences to capitalize on women's and girls' insecurities about themselves and their relationships with men and boys.

The classroom is also another important site in which these ideas about men and women's communication with each other are reinforced. As an example, researchers looking into school-based sex education have documented the ways in which both abstinence-only and comprehensive sex education curricula are based on heteronormative and gendered assumptions about students.[11] Through sex education, students are also taught about how they should communicate with partners about safe sex. Implicitly and explicitly, young women are provided with the message that they have special responsibility for initiating safe-sex communication. The sociologist Jessica Fields argues that sex education lessons about sexual communication often evade opportunities to interrogate the notion that girls and women should be the ones to initiate such conversations.[12] As I discussed in chapter 3, Latina girls are assumed to be ineffective at such sexual communication because of "Latino culture," especially machismo. But, one key sex education lesson provided to the young women I spoke with was that they are the sexual gatekeepers who are expected not only to set sexual limits but also to take the lead in acquiring knowledge about safe-sex practices. Thus, Latina girls' initiation of safe-sex communication with their male partners and their acceptance of this responsibility is a gendered sexual script that is widely transmitted and reinforced in society.[13]

"It Would Be Too Weird": Not Talking about Safe Sex with Partners

Five girls, however, reported that they had been either unable to have a conversation about safe sex with their male partners or unsuccessful in their attempt to initiate one. Three of these young women said they had not engaged their partners in such conversations because they felt too uncomfortable to do so. Marta, who had insisted that she would not be like the pregnant young woman she spotted from the bus, expressed her reluctance to discuss safe sex with her boyfriend in this way: "Just to be kinda more safe and stuff I wish we could really talk about it [safe sex]. But I can't, I think it would be too weird." When I asked her why she thought this would be case, she quickly replied, "I know him, he's gonna think I don't trust him and shit or, worse, that I'm playin' him [being deceitful]!" Rita also raised her concerns about her boyfriend's reaction when asked if she raised the topic of safe sex, exclaiming, "Hell, no! He would be trippin' if I did that! He would try to say I was the one that was trippin' and didn't trust him." The high school sophomore, who habitually twirled her dark hair around her index finger, continued, "Anyways, it ain't like I ain't being safe! I'm on the pill." According to Rita and the other four girls, although they had not managed to have safe-sex conversations with their partners, they were still handling their business because they were protecting themselves from unwanted pregnancies through the use of hormonal contraceptives.[14]

When asked whether they had any concerns about possible exposure to STDS, these girls seemed taken aback by the question and emphatically replied that they trusted their boyfriend not to place them at risk. Jeanne, the youngest of the girls I spoke with, matter-of-factly stated, "I wouldn't be doing that [sexual intercourse] if I didn't love him, which means I trust him. He wouldn't do that [transmit an STD] to me and I already told him, if he ever did, I wouldn't be with him no more." Thus, this group of young women warned their boyfriends not to stray, but such admonitions never evolved into discussions about safe sex. In other words, they were able to express their views on cheating to their boyfriends, but this was centered on an attention to betrayal, rather than sexual health. According to Marta, Jeanne, and Rita, the extent of their safe-sex communication with their partners was to make them aware that the young women were utilizing birth control. For instance, Jeanne told me, "He knows I'm taking care of myself. I mean, he ain't gonna be the one to get pregnant, so I gotta watch out for myself. . . . I guess he thinks we're already being safe and don't gotta talk about it."

However, the two other girls in this group, Iris and Inés, shared with me that their boyfriends were not aware of their use of hormonal contraceptives. Unlike Marta, Jeanne, and Rita, they had tried to broach the topic of safe sex with their partners but encountered negative responses that discouraged them from attempting it again. Inés, whose mother had slapped her when she asserted that she had not been fooled into sexual relations by her partner, animatedly described her boyfriend's response to her suggestion that he use a condom: "Girl, he looked at me like I was crazy and just got mad, saying that I was on some bullshit and that I was probably fucking around him, this and that! He just said that 'cause he just doesn't want to have to wear a condom, so he acted like I got something to hide."

Additionally, Inés and Iris also told me that they encountered steady pressure from their boyfriends to have a baby. Iris, whose mother, Luz, had asked a niece to invite Iris to visit her in college, described with evident frustration her boyfriend's insistence: "He's always like, we should have one [baby], like it's all easy to take care of one! Ain't no way I'm about to have one just 'cause he wants . . . 'cause you know who'll have to do everything? Me!" Although they insisted that they communicated to their boyfriends that they were not ready for parenthood, Inés and Iris took the extra precaution of seeking a hormonal contraceptive (both used the Depo-Provera injection). Wagging her index finger sideways to emphasize her point, Iris rolled her brown eyes and asserted, "Uh uh . . . I was like nope, ain't gonna happen. I ain't about to be a baby momma and I went and got the shot [Depo-Provera] real quick! He don't know that, though, but I know he's wondering why I haven't gotten pregnant, yet. Oh well . . . ain't gonna happen anytime right now." Like Iris, Inés choose not to reveal to her boyfriend that she was using the shot, explaining, "He doesn't think I should use anything like that, I think he thinks like I don't love him if I try not to have a baby with him." While I have no way of knowing why Inés and Iris's boyfriends wanted a baby, one reason may be related to their sense of masculinity. As I discuss later in this chapter, poor and working-class young men of color also construct their masculinity under particular constraints. It may be that, as young Latino men, Inés and Iris's boyfriends sought to establish their masculinity and adult status through fatherhood (a desire for affirmation as adults has sometimes been used to explain the behavior of Latina girls who become young mothers, as well), but, again, this is a very tentative and cautious interpretation, since I did not interview their boyfriends or other young Latinos.[15]

As demonstrated by their descriptions of their interactions with their boyfriends, this group of young women was concerned about offending their boyfriends and putting to question the love and trust they believed defined their relationship. These girls saw it as risky to request condom use and/or discuss safe sex because doing so could be interpreted as signaling their mistrust of their boyfriends, which in turn could put into question the sincerity of the girls' love for them. Furthermore, the boyfriends could interpret such requests as an indication that their girlfriends were possibly cheating on them. If it is perceived by a boyfriend and peers that the relationship is not characterized by love and/or that that the young woman is being unfaithful, she risks losing a key way in which she is able to "justify" her sexual behavior to others. [16] This group of heterosexual-identified girls did self-identify as practicing safe sex and did so on the grounds that they were preventing pregnancy, but this left them also relying on love and trust as protection against STDs. Thus, these girls were left to handle the responsibility of safe sex on their own; in a sense, it remained "their problem" to figure out.

Other heterosexual-identified girls also pointed to their relationships with their boyfriends in discussing their approaches to communicating with them about safe sex. But, as I explore in the next section, rather than focus on the importance of the respectability of the relationship itself, some of them drew on their status as girlfriends to assert a relationship between their respectability and that of their boyfriends' respectability, permitting them some control in negotiating safe-sex communication with their partners. In other words, they linked women's sexual respectability to men's sexual respectability as a safe-sex strategy.

Femininity, Masculinity, and Respectability

The enticing smells of various *frituras* (fritters)[17] wafted through the air, greeting us as we approached Paseo Boricua, the nearly mile-long residential and commercial stretch on Division Street between Western Avenue and California Avenue. Fiesta Boricua, a popular community-driven festival celebrating Puerto Rican history and culture and featuring music, art, and food, was already well under way, as evidenced by the crowds and by the salsa and reggaeton beats emanating from various booths. Our group, consisting of a couple of the youth program staff and eleven young people, had set out from Hogar del Pueblo on public transportation for the short trip to the tenth annual Puerto Rican festival in the Humboldt Park neighborhood on the city's northwest side. On that warm afternoon in early September, the program youth were relishing their last free summer days before the start of a new school year. Walking underneath the massive steel Puerto Rican flag near Western Avenue, we decided to split up into two smaller groups and meet an hour later on California Avenue near the other flag.

The group I was with slowly meandered around the crowds that congregated near various booths, pausing every so often to check out jewelry or music CDs or to purchase a snack. At one point, we came upon a small clustering of booths dedicated to health information and quick checkups, such as free blood pressure and diabetes screenings. The six young people in our group slowly walked past these booths, stopping near a table with a couple bowls of condoms and pamphlets, brochures, and flyers that was organized by Vida/SIDA.[18] A tall and cheerful Latino man at the booth, in his middle to late forties, excitedly greeted us, encouraging our group to take a closer look at the materials on the table. The youth glanced at one another and tentatively approached the booth together. As they looked over the materials on the table, the man animatedly explained the services Vida/SIDA offered, particularly highlighting its youth peer educator component. Noticing that some of the young men were repeatedly glancing at the bowl of condoms, the man pushed the bowl toward them, insisting, "Go ahead, take a couple if you want! Don't be shy!" Two of the three boys helped themselves to some condoms, making a show of it by loudly commenting that they needed them because they "get some" (have sex) all the time. The three young women in the group snickered and rolled their eyes. Clearly annoyed by her male peers' behavior, Minerva, whose eighth-grade teacher had questioned why she wanted to know about the morning-after pill, reached over and grabbed some condoms as she declared, "This [condoms] ain't only for guys!" The boys who had already taken some condoms just smirked, mumbling, "Whatever," to which the man at the booth responded, "She's right, fellas! Everyone needs to be on it about protecting themselves!" After a couple more minutes, we moved on get some *piraguas* (shaved iced with fruit-flavored syrup).

We were hanging around enjoying our different-flavored *piraguas* when we noticed that Minerva and her boyfriend, Eddie (the only young man in our group who did not take any condoms at the booth) had slightly moved away from the group. While we were unable to hear them over the music, their facial expressions and hand movements suggested that they were in the middle of an argument. Shortly thereafter, Minerva angrily walked away from Eddie to join us. Ruby, the youth program staff member with our group, asked Minerva if everything was okay. The high school junior angrily crossed her arms across her chest and exclaimed, "Yeah, he's just mad 'cause I took those condoms!" When Ruby asked her why Eddie would be mad about that, Minerva angrily replied, "'Cause he's just being stupid! So I'm just gonna ignore him right now!" Sensing that she did not want to discuss it any more, we did not probe any further, although the adults in the group did keep an eye on both of them in case we needed to intervene in their interactions with each other. But nothing further ensued between Minerva and Eddie, as they both purposefully kept their distance from each other the rest of the afternoon, every so often exchanging angry glances. When I spotted them together a few days later, it was apparent that they had reconciled, since they were walking down the street holding hands.

During our interview a couple of weeks after that incident at Fiesta Boricua, I asked Minerva about it. Slightly blushing, she explained that Eddie had been upset because he did not like that she grabbed the condoms in "the way" that she did that day: "He thinks I shouldn't have done that in front of everyone like that 'cause it was like disrespectin' him." When I inquired about how Minerva's actions could be disrespectful to Eddie, she let out a long sigh: "To Eddie, he felt that by me doing that, guys might start talking shit about me and maybe think I wasn't just with Eddie. He told me that he didn't want no one to disrespect me 'cause then he would feel disrespected, too. You know how guys are, all worried about how they look in front of other guys." Minerva's observations regarding young men's concerns about their peers' perception of them was echoed by the majority of young women, but it was particularly so with heterosexual-identified girls. Alongside such commentary, notions about respectable femininity and masculinity emerged as an important theme in this group of girls' narratives about their safe-sex communication with partners.

As already discussed in chapter 4, the young women I spoke with were invested in creating and maintaining their sexual respectability. But they were also attuned to the importance of respectability for young men, especially among their peers. Respect, particularly the ability to command it, is a critical component of masculinity. Masculinity, like femininity, is socially constructed and takes on various forms and meanings depending on how it intersects with other aspects of a person's identity, such as race/ethnicity. However, different femininities and masculinities do not carry the same amount of power in a given society. In the case of masculinity, for instance, the sociologist R. W. Connell asserts that there is a specific masculinity that is most valued, what she terms "hegemonic masculinity."[19] This form of masculinity is considered to be the ideal masculinity that men should seek to achieve and in most Western contexts is reflected through characteristics such as aggressiveness, normative heterosexuality, strength, competitiveness, and wealth. Positioned in opposition to femininity and what are perceived to be lesser forms of masculinity (i.e., gay men), hegemonic masculinity holds a dominant place within the gender hierarchy. This cultural ideal of masculinity is not necessarily the most prevalent one in a society, but, because of the value that it is assigned, especially through the mass media, men encounter pressure to pursue it even though few men are actually able to achieve it. Urban studies scholars, documenting educational and employment inequalities, have argued that young men of color living in distressed and/or marginalized communities have circumscribed access to normatively acceptable pathways to achieving status.[20] Such disparities may place the ideal of hegemonic masculinity out of reach for these groups of young men, but they can attain a meaningful respectable masculinity within their local communities through means such as the physical use of one's body to intimidate others, fighting, gang affiliations, economic self-sufficiency achieved through "slangin" or "hustlin," and being a "player." Almost all of the girls

I spoke with were cognizant of the value that their male peers placed on respectable masculinity and the centrality of sexuality to their crafting of masculine identities.

Without prompting, they had plenty to say about young men's performance of their sexual desire, particularly how they expressed their sexual competency and interest in girls and women. For instance, Olivia shared with me that her fifteen-year-old brother "got in trouble" when her mother arrived home from work early one day and walked in on him and his friends watching a pornographic film in the living room. She first laughingly recounted the incident but then became somewhat serious, telling me the following:

> I feel sorry for guys sometimes 'cause they probably feel like they gotta front like they're all into sex or whatever. They get all nervous that their boys are gonna think they're weak or something if they ain't hookin' up with girls. I see my brother doing that all the time! And I'm like, "Please, you need to quit acting like that!" But it's gotta be hard for him.

Lourdes also expressed a similar assessment of young men's performances for one another around the topic of sexuality. We were sitting on bleachers in a local park watching her friend practice with his soccer team when we turned our attention toward a group of young Latino men in their early to late teens who were hanging around a white four-door Chevy Malibu with matching rims and dark-tinted windows. It was difficult not to notice them since occasionally they blasted hip-hop and reggaeton music from the car speakers. Every so often, they would amuse themselves by checking out young women walking by; these young women were obviously made uncomfortable by the comments the young men made to them and to one another.

I suspect that most of the young women would have attempted to avoid crossing paths with this group of young men had they known that they were behaving in this manner, as I started doing around the age of eleven. At that young age, I began to dread walking past certain corners in and around my neighborhood where I knew that young and older men congregated, since they often harassed girls and young women in the same way these young men were doing in the park that day. I either went around "the long way" to avoid them altogether or tried to pretend I did not hear their comments. And, even if I wanted to stop to talk with those boys I did know who were hanging out with a group of young men, I could not, as my parents had warned me that they had better not "catch me" talking to any of them. And, in my neighborhood, there was always the possibility that some adult family member or neighbor would spot you "misbehaving" and dutifully inform your parents.

At one point, one of the young men in the group began to walk alongside two young Latinas and attempted to engage them in a conversation, but the girls nervously ignored him and did not even look his way. The young man's friends laughed loudly at his failed attempt, pointing at him and high-fiving each other. Embarrassed, the young man tried to save face in front of his peers by cupping his hands and yelling out to the girls, "Stuck-up ass bitches! I know you hear me!" Satisfied with himself, he adjusted his Chicago White Sox baseball hat and coolly walked back to his friends, who were still laughing but fist-bumped him in approval. Lourdes rolled her eyes at the young men's behavior and commented, "Those dumb-asses, they obviously ain't got nothing better to do than to bother girls! I never get that, how guys think that's how they gonna get with girls. They act like that 'cause they gotta have their boys think they can get girls anytime they want . . . which we know ain't true!" Shortly thereafter, Lourdes needed to go home. As we carefully walked down the bleachers, we decided to go "the long way" and avoid this group of young men.

The public harassment of women that we witnessed that day is certainly not confined to Latina/o communities. Gender-based public harassment is found everywhere and is perpetrated by all groups of men.[21] Asserting that such harassment reinforces gender inequality, the sociologist Carol B. Gardner writes, "In women's lives, public harassment abuses are frequent reminders of the ever-present relevance of their gender."[22] Often reacted to as a nuisance, gender-specific public harassment is generally not perceived as a serious threat to women. When compared to other forms of gender-based violence, such as rape and battery, the public harassment of women seems rather harmless to many people.[23] But the examination of public harassment through a gendered lens reveals that it functions as a mechanism through which men, including young men, assert their masculinity and attempt to maintain their dominant status in society. Men's participation in sexualized touching, sex talk, and public harassment is an example of gender practices associated with what the sociologist C. J. Pascoe calls "compulsive heterosexuality." Pascoe writes, "Taken together, these ritualized interactions continually affirm masculinity as mastery and dominance."[24] Again, not all men are able to possess a hegemonic masculinity, but, as men, they are still able to benefit from the subordination of women. In other words, while on the surface it may seem that the young men's behavior at the park that afternoon was just a harmless expression of men's sexual desire or part of their efforts to "just be one of the guys," such sexualized practices, discourses, and inter-actions serve to sustain gender inequality.

Young women told of their boyfriends' concern for how other young men treated their girlfriends. Carla, for instance, shared with me that her boyfriend had advised her not disclose to others, including me, that she was sexually intimate with him: "He even told me that if we ever broke up, not to tell my next boyfriend that I wasn't a virgin 'cause then he might use that against me and say I was just a ho or just treat me like shit." Her boyfriend's warning to her suggests that he was concerned about her *capital femenino*, a term introduced by the sociologist Gloria González-López to underscore the uses women make of the value assigned to their virginity. In her research on Mexican immigrant women and men's sexual lives, González-López found that women utilized their premarital virginity as a form of social capital not only to try to obtain economic security through marriage but to also prevent mistreatment from their future husbands.[25] Carla was the only girl to report that her boyfriend introduced a discussion about the negative social implications of virginity loss for young women.

Generally, heterosexual girls' accounts of how their boyfriends communicated with them about their sexual respectability as young women reflected the young men's preoccupation with asserting their masculinity in front of peers. For example, as Yvette discussed her relationship with her boyfriend, she commented that he was always "protective" of her, telling me, "Like he don't want guys checking me out, especially in front of him! He gets crazy jealous sometimes, but it's 'cause he doesn't want any guy thinking he can just up and disrespect me, either." The aspiring teacher with glitter daisy decals on her manicured hands went on to tell me that her boyfriend disapproved when she hung out with some of her male friends at Hogar del Pueblo, explaining, "He thinks they might try hookin' up with me or something. But, I've known these guys since like we were all like eight! They're just my boys, nothing is gonna happen! But he don't trust them." Like Yvette, five other girls described similar exchanges with their boyfriends. For example, Miriam shared with me that she had a couple of arguments with her boyfriend over his disapproval of pictures she posted of herself on her MySpace page: "He's always telling me I'm on MySpace with my friends too much. . . . He's tripped about some of my pictures on MySpace, saying that some of them make me look like I'm skanky. That ain't even true! They're just pictures with my girls and we're dressed up, you know?"

Almost all of the young women who described such interactions with their boyfriends expressed frustration at what they interpreted to be their boyfriends' overprotective behavior. A conversation I had with Fabiola illustrates this annoyance: "He [her boyfriend] be getting on my nerves when he's like that! He thinks I'm a *pendeja* [idiot] and don't know how to take care of myself around guys." And Yvette complained that she was unable to fully relax when hanging out with her friends: "I always feel like he's [her boyfriend] gonna show up when I'm doing something he ain't gonna like. Like when I am saying 'Hi' to a guy who's a friend and just giving him a hug to say 'Hi.' He straight up acts like's my dad or something!" Yvette's likening of her boyfriend's behavior to that of a parent indicates that, even though girls were able to temporarily evade their parents' surveillance, some of them still had sometimes to contend with monitoring from their boyfriends. And that Fabiola felt her boyfriend treated her like an idiot suggests that sometimes girls were regarded as being sexually naïve by their boyfriends and in need of protection, a treatment they also received from their parents. The "protective" stance of boyfriends that girls described was likely informed by the young men's intimate knowledge of how girls are utilized as gender resources by boys to establish masculine identities. But their boyfriends were most likely also concerned about the implications of this process for their own social status among their peers.

Most girls interpreted their boyfriends' behavior to be an extension of their masculinity presentations. Like Minerva, who got into an argument with her boyfriend because she grabbed condoms in front of their peers at Fiesta Boricua, other young women talked about their boyfriends' own sense of respectability. As Minerva pointed out, her boyfriend had been upset not only because she could potentially be "disrespected" because of her actions (i.e., sending out the wrong message that she was sexually available outside her relationship with her boyfriend) but also because her boyfriend would feel disrespected if she were actually mistreated by other young men. Carla, who told me that her boyfriend had warned her not to disclose her sexual history to anyone, also connected her respectability to her boyfriend's respectability as she explained his advice to me: "In front of their boys, guys wanna make themselves look like a pimp with the ladies, but nobody better come at their girl like that! If someone does, then they gonna feel like they gotta do something about it or look like a bitch. It's so stupid!" As suggested by the tone of Carla's observations about young men's reactions to how other young men approached their girlfriends, most girls seem to initially scoff at what they saw as performances on the part of their boyfriends.

But, as the interviews progressed, it became evident that young women were not completely dismissive of the significance of such "manhood acts" for boys.[26] For instance, sixteen-year-old Rosalba told me that her cousin had sustained a broken nose when he fought with another young man who had groped his girlfriend's buttocks at a party. Though she first expressed disapproval of her cousin's "temper," the bubbly young woman with braces told me that the confrontation was unavoidable: "He didn't really have a choice though. I mean, 'cause if he didn't do something about it, his boys would be calling him a pussy." This perception of young men's fighting behavior also emerged among a group of four girls at Hogar del Pueblo one afternoon. One of their friends had received a three-day school suspension for initiating a fight with another boy. As the group listened intently to a young man's animated eye-witness description of the fight, one of the young women dismissively commented that their friend was "ignorant" for fighting "just because a guy called his girlfriend a ho." Another girl quickly interjected, "Girl, what was he supposed to do!? He couldn't just let it go! If he did that, he'd look all weak and shit." The group briefly considered her observation and slowly nodded in agreement, turning back to the boy to hear the rest of the fight details. Thus, the girls may have criticized young men for caring too much about what other boys thought of them, but they were also sensitive to how young men's assertions of their masculinity mattered for their ability to claim respect.

This knowledge about boys' sense of masculinity became useful to heterosexual-identified girls in dealing with their boyfriends' resistance regarding the obtaining and use of condoms, a major task that Latina girls grappled with in their efforts to sexually handle their business. Condom use, according to these young women, was the most challenging practice to integrate into their sexual encounters because it necessitated the cooperation of their sexual partner. Girls' stories of negotiating condom use, explored next, illustrate how the girls utilized gender-sexual scripts to get their boyfriends to take responsibility for obtaining condoms and to to cooperate with condom use.

Obtaining and Using Condoms

The majority of heterosexual-identified girls believed that condoms were the most effective way to practice safe sex.[27] Nevertheless, this did not necessarily mean that they were comfortable with actually obtaining condoms, whether it was buying them at the store or acquiring them free at local health centers. As Inés put it, "Guys can just walk in and get condoms and whatever, no one thinks anything bad about them 'cause it is seen as a normal thing for them. But it ain't the same for girls, we can't just walk up in there [store] and be like, 'Give me a twelve-pack of Trojans.'" Momentarily pausing as she considered the scenario, the pensive sophomore continued in a resentful tone,

"You know they ain't thinking, 'Good for her, she's gonna protect herself.' They're mostly thinking, 'What a ho, she probably sleeps with a whole bunch of guys!' I know it shouldn't matter what people think as long as I'm doing what I gotta do, but I just can't be the one to go get them [condoms], it is too embarrassing!" Like Inés, most of these young women were understandably concerned about losing their sexual respectability, a social risk they faced if they secured condoms on their own. Young men can obtain a "reputation" for being several things, such as for being "bad," "a player," "a fighter," "a hustler," or a combination of these types of identities, but girls generally are assigned a reputation that rests almost exclusively on their sexuality, specifically sexual behavior considered inappropriate for girls. Whereas a reputation typically affirms a boy's masculine respectability among his peers, for a girl, "having a reputation" more often than not serves to negate her respectability.[28]

These young women, therefore, walked a fine line; they needed to be prepared enough to take on safe sex practices but still had to be careful not to seem to be "too prepared" to have sex, such as by obtaining and carrying condoms. In crafting an identity as a sexually respectable girl, they were mindful about how they negotiated gendered sexual scripts under the constraints of double standards. Reluctant to secure condoms on their own, they relied on their boyfriends to provide condoms. And it required some finessing on their part to encourage their partners to take on this responsibility. Consider how Yvette described being able to convince her boyfriend to acquire and use condoms:

> It was getting pretty annoying, having to tell him all the time to put on a condom before we had sex. Sometimes, he would try to play it off like he forgot to bring condoms with him. I was talking to Gina [a friend] about this and she told me to do what she did—her man used to act like that—so she told him that if he didn't put on a condom or remember to bring the condoms with him, she was going to start buying them and bringing them herself. And she also told him that she didn't care if people they both knew saw her buying condoms at the store and thought she was a ho or something. I told my boyfriend the same thing and, of course, he got all pissed off about it. I told him if I had to be the one to buy condoms, he was gonna look all weak and stupid if people found out . . . he don't play his lil' games like he used to 'cause he doesn't wanna look like a fool.

Likewise, Graciela, whom I had run into at the laundromat, said that her boyfriend had picked up free condoms at a local teen health center after she explained to him why she could not do it herself: "I told him some people are gonna talk shit about both of us if they see me in there, or even just going in or coming out. . . . So he's gonna look like he's gettin' played. No one will really say anything if he goes up in there." She added that she also pointed out to her boyfriend that if her parents found the condoms on her, they would make it difficult for them to see each other. As evidenced by Yvette's and Graciela's narratives, girls explicitly connected their sexual reputation to their boyfriends' respectability in their communication with them about condoms. They emphasized that if they were perceived to be deviating from appropriate sexual scripts for women, that this would also put into question the integrity of their boyfriends' masculinity. In other words, girls sought safe-sex cooperation from their partners by playing on their insecurities about what others thought of their masculinity, strategically bringing together notions about the good-girl/bad-girl dichotomy and masculinity.

As discussed earlier, previous research on young women's sexual identity formation has documented the relevance of meaningful relationships for girls' acceptance and meanings of their sexual experiences.[29] But girls and women do not naturally develop such relationship-centered sexual scripts on their own. They receive and negotiate ongoing lessons about what constitutes appropriate sexual behavior—when, where, how, with whom and by whom, and why—through culture, interactions with others, and their individual understandings and expectations regarding sexuality.[30] The girls I spoke with drew on their ongoing relationships with their boyfriends to get them to share responsibility for obtaining condoms by framing their respectabilities as interconnected. As sixteen-year-old Eva, whose mother, Lilia, had asked Eva's aunt to speak with her after learning of her sexual relations with her boyfriend, explained:

> Guys think they own you . . . so they don't want no one talking shit about their lady, you know, being a skank or something just because she was out buying condoms or something, because then they feel like people might be thinking he's a dumbass for being with a ho. It's not right, but that is how it is.

Put another way, girls conveyed to their boyfriends that their sexual reputations as young women had consequences for the boys' reputations as young men because of their ongoing relationship. Thus, in this way, a young woman's ability to maintain her sexual respectability became a concern for both her and her boyfriend; it was no longer just her problem.[31]

Girls also drew on notions of masculinity to address their partners' resistance to condom use. They reported that their partners expressed their resistance to condom use in two key ways; (1) complaining that they did not like the way condoms felt, and (2) meeting requests for condom use with accusations that girlfriends had been unfaithful and contracted an STD. Most girls told me that they did not need to insist on condom use every time. But it was a negotiation they still faced sometimes, even when they and their boyfriends had already discussed and agreed upon the importance of condom use. Their strategy in these interactions was to compare their partners' attitudes to those of a "real man." Describing a fight she had with her boyfriend, sixteen-year-old Nanette said, "Sometimes, we're cool, you know, we don't even got to go there and just automatically use it [condom], but sometimes, he tries to act stupid, asking why we gotta use a condom. It gets on my nerves and we end up fighting. . . . I tell him he must not be a real man, 'cause a real man ain't gotta ask why he needs to wear a condom." Other girls also shared with me that they referenced what a "real man" would do when they encountered their boyfriends' resistance to condoms. For instance, Minerva said, "I know he [her boyfriend] always wants to act like he knows what he's doing, sexually, you know? So when he's trying to get it on without a condom, I tell him, 'A real man would wear a condom 'cause a real man knows what he's doing and not playing stupid games.'" Girls, therefore, were aware that young men's performance of sexual prowess also required that they demonstrate sexual knowledge or at least the appearance of possessing such knowledge. They used this masculine sexual script as a gender strategy to negotiate condom use with their partners.[32] They did so by specifically questioning their boyfriends' safe-sex knowledge.[33]

Girls' interactions with their partners in which they explicitly linked women's sexual respectability to men's sexual respectability to secure their boyfriends' cooperation with condoms reflect what the sociologist Mimi Schippers calls "gender maneuvering." According to Schippers, gender maneuvering is the process of negotiation in which "one or more people manipulate the meaning of their own or others' gender performances in order to establish, disrupt, or change the relationship between and among masculinities and femininities."[34] As Schippers underscores, people do not only "do" femininity and masculinity; they also "do" the relationship between them.[35] In the case of the young women I spoke with, it can be argued that, by constructing their sexual respectability as significant to the integrity of their boyfriends' masculinity, they, in effect, maintain and reproduce the very gender hierarchy that limits their sexual agency in the first place. But we need to be careful to not be too quick to interpret and dismiss these interactions as indicators of gender inequality. If we keep in the mind the conditions under which this group of girls must negotiate safe sex, we can appreciate that these Latina girls' activation of culturally accepted definitions of masculinity and femininity,[36] though not transforming the unequal relationship between masculinity and femininity, did allow them to utilize gender expectations to shift some power their way in their sexual relationships.

Sexual Histories and Pleasure

Heterosexual-identified girls, however, approached their partners on the topics of sexual histories and pleasure in a more limited manner. Most of them told me that they had had only one sexual partner. At time of interview, these young women were still in an exclusive relationship with the individual they identified as their first sexual partner, whether they characterized the relationship as a "love" or a "caring" relationship.[37] Those heterosexual-identified girls whose partners had previous sexual experiences stated that they knew the age at which their partners had "lost their virginity" and the number of sexual partners they had been with in the past because they had inquired about these matters. But they did not think it was appropriate to ask for details about their previous sexual relationships. Lisa, who sought an HIV test after her boyfriend cheated on her, conveyed this when I asked if she knew whether her partner had practiced safe sex in his prior relationship(s). The aspiring elementary school teacher tilted her head sideways as she thought about her answer and replied, "I guess, I mean, I told him, 'I hope you've always been careful about that [safe sex].' And he told me that he was and not to worry about it." When I inquired as to whether she had asked him about what he had specifically done to be careful, her eyes widened, "Uh uh . . . I don't want him thinking I'm all jealous or all up in his business about who he's been with and what's he done. As long as he told me he's been safe when he was with his ex. And as long as I'm taking care of myself now." Furthermore, some girls did not think it would be useful to ask about their male partners' previous safe-sex practices because they did not think the boys would be forthcoming. Such was Jocelyn's sentiment, as she commented, "Guys are just gonna do and say what they gotta say to get some [sex] from a girl, so they might just lie anyways and tell you that they've always used a condom or they're gonna sit there and tell you that they hooked up with less girls than they really did."

This group of young women also was uncomfortable with talking about pleasure with their boyfriends. Only seven of them were able to do so. Fabiola described how she "hinted" to her boyfriend that she was curious about oral sex: "He had never gone down on me and I really wanted him to 'cause I kept hearing that it feels good. So one day, while we were messing around, I was like, 'Hey, I heard that when a guy goes down on a girl that it's supposed to feel real good.' And then he was like, 'Let's see. . . . '" Like Fabiola, these young women introduced the topic of pleasure by referring to what they had read or been told about pleasure-enhancing sexual activities, rather than framing it as their own desire or pleasure interests. And three girls shared with me that they had touched on the subject in conversations with boyfriends, but only after their partners had asked them if they enjoyed their sexual activities. Consider Patricia's interaction with her boyfriend: "He sometimes asks me if I liked what he did and I'm like 'Yeah,' I'm not like, 'Oh, this part felt good' or 'You should do this.' That would be weird." Those young women who did not discuss their pleasure or desire with male partners at all seemed somewhat uncomfortable and/or embarrassed when I asked about this topic. When I inquired as to why they did not, the girls were at a loss for words, often sheepishly replying that they did not know why this was this case.

One thing that almost all of these young women made clear to me was their agency in entering into sexual relationships, often stating that they "wanted to" or "chose to" when explaining why and how they entered into sexual relationships. They indicated that they enjoyed engaging in sexual activities. But, when asked what about their sexual activities they liked, they again initially responded, "I don't know." Searching for words to articulate why they enjoyed engaging in sexual activities, they pointed not to bodily sensations or to their sexual desire but rather to their relationships with their boyfriends. Jeanne, for instance, shared with me the following: "I like doing it with him 'cause it makes us closer." Lourdes also made a similar point: "To me, I feel good because it's how we show that we care about each other and that we trust one another." Thus, some of these girls, although unable to articulate their own sense of sexual pleasure, seemed to take pleasure in feeling connected with their boyfriends through their sexual activities. Heterosexual-identified girls' investment in crafting their sexual respectability necessitated that they carefully consider the place of sexual pleasure in cultivating that identity, which, as their stories suggest, was kept at a distance so as not undermine the identity that they were attempting to claim for themselves.

Lesbian-identified girls, however, did describe talking more directly about sexual pleasure with their partners. Unlike heterosexual-identified girls, they did not seem abashed when asked about this during their interviews. The contrast between the two groups regarding this topic was readily apparent, even in their body language. Whereas some of the heterosexual-identified girls immediately avoided eye contact and/or crossed their arms in front of them when asked about sexual pleasure, lesbian-identified girls seemed much more animated, often moving their hands to emphasize a point. For example, Arely, who had ripped a virginity pledge during a sex education class, laughed and clapped her hands when she shared with me her sexual pleasure communication with her girlfriend:

> Girl, you're probably gonna think we are crazy and shit, but we sometimes will go on the Internet to check out sex toys! We would go to a sex toy shop, like on the North Side, but I don't think we can go in 'cause we're under eighteen or whatever. We ordered one [sex toy] but had it delivered to her [partner's friend's] place, 'cause she has her own apartment. At first, I was like, "Is this weird or what?!" But now, I'm just like, "I don't care, all I know is that we like it."

Like Arely, the other lesbian-identified girls seemed to take enjoyment in considering the possibilities for sexual pleasure with their partners. This group of girls also reported exchanging details about their sexual histories with their partners, particularly their experiences in exploring their sexual attraction to girls. Nevertheless, as I describe in the next section, they still grappled with heteronormativity in their safe-sex communication with their partners.

"Get Your Learn On!": Talking Safe Sex in Lesbian Relationships

I found eighteen-year-old Barbara sitting on the front stairs of her brick three-flat and talking to two other young Latinas. Slowly getting up and dusting off the back of her jeans, she introduced me to the group. The girls nonchalantly said hi to me as I walked past them to follow her up two flights of stairs. Beginning our climb up the second flight of stairs, Barbara warned me, "My mom is probably going to try to be all up in your business, just so you know." I reassuringly smiled at her, telling her not to "worry about it." The high school senior sighed, "I'm just saying. She's like that." Arriving on the third floor, she pulled out her keys from the front pocket of her blue Cubs sweatshirt to open the door to the humble two-bedroom apartment she shared with her mother and her twenty-year-old sister. Hearing the door creak open, her mother, Roberta, met us at the door and invited me to have a seat in their living room. I had already interviewed Roberta once, and now I was there to interview Barbara for the first time. Roberta immediately instructed her daughter in Spanish to get me a glass of soda, and, even though I insisted that it was not necessary, Barbara went into their kitchen/dining room to get me a drink. A few seconds later, she returned empty-handed, complaining to her mom that her older sister, who was at work, had finished all the "pop." I again insisted that I did not need anything to drink, but Roberta shoved a few dollars in her daughter's hand and ordered her to go buy a two-liter of Squirt at the small corner store a block away.

While we waited for Barbara to return, Roberta sat down with me and asked me if I had been able to interview other mothers and daughters. Before I could reply, she told me that she hoped I had because she was unsure that my interviews with her and her daughter would be useful to me: "*Tal vez esta situación con Barbara no es algo que les pasa a otras madres e hijas* [Perhaps this situation with Barbara is not something other mothers and daughters go through]." The "situation" was that Barbara was a lesbian. I assured her that their interviews were important and helped me to learn more how Latina mothers and daughters understand and talk about sexuality and safe sex. With a polite smile, Barbara slightly shrugged her shoulders and stated, "At least I don't have to worry about her getting pregnant or a disease, since she's not interested in boys." When Barbara and I were finally ready to begin her interview, her mother went back to the enclosed back porch at the other end of the apartment to resume sewing on her machine. As my mother had done for a few years when I was growing up, Roberta was sewing piece work at home. The steady hum of the sewing machine and the Spanish radio station that Roberta was listening to as she worked provided us with privacy for our interview.

Roberta's perception that her daughter faced few to no sexual health risks as a young lesbian woman was the dominant theme that emerged in lesbian-identified girls' stories about their safe-sex communication with their partners. Like heterosexual-identified girls, these young women attempted to engage partners in these types of conversations by discussing the sexual misfortunes of someone they personally knew. Isela, for instance, narrated how a discussion about safe sex unfolded when a close friend of her partner was newly diagnosed with HIV:

> It sucks 'cause he is only thirty. When she [partner] told me about him, she was real sad but also kinda freaked out about it. And I told her, "That's why people gotta be on it about protecting themselves 'cause you just never know." And that was one of those times when we talked about taking care of ourselves, maybe 'cause we were scared.

But some of these young women also encountered partner resistance to their safe-sex efforts.

As I briefly mentioned at the beginning of this chapter, this group of girls often found that their partners argued against safe-sex practices by insisting that women who have sex with women (WSW) are at little to no risk of getting STDs, particularly HIV. Margarita, whose mother saw her kissing her partner in public, explained, "She [her partner] tells me that we're all good with safe sex 'cause she has never slept with guys and neither have I. But I tell her, 'How about the other girls you have been with? How do you know who've they've been with?'" Similarly, Imelda told me, "My girlfriend makes it seems like it's just automatically safe for us because we're lesbians. She just doesn't feel like it's a big a deal." These girls' description of their partners' low sense of vulnerability in terms of sexual-health risks is consistent with findings from previous studies on lesbians' knowledge and attitudes on safe sex.[38] I asked Imelda why she thought her partner approached safe sex in the way that she did:

> IMELDA: I think one thing may be like her doctor not doing her job and tak-
> ing her seriously.
> LORENA: Because Jessica [her partner] is lesbian? Like her doctor maybe
> thinks it is just a phase she is going through being with girls?
> IMELDA: Maybe. But not bothering to check her for STDs, too. Jessica told
> me that her doctor did a pap exam on her, but told her that she didn't
> need to get tested for STDs 'cause she ain't having sex with guys.

Gloria, who commented, "It was a crazy-ass doctor who told her this! So, of course, to her [partner], it must be legit info 'cause a doctor knows what they are talking about and I'm just being all paranoid!," also echoed Imelda's identification of the role of health care providers in contributing to her partners' stance on safe sex. Imelda's and Gloria's critique of the misinformation communicated to their partners also resonates with the health experiences of other lesbian and bisexual women.[39] Such interactions with health care practitioners may be shaped by several factors, including the practitioners' own heteronormative assumptions about lesbian sexual practices, prejudices, and ignorance about the applicability of STD prevention lessons to lesbian and bisexual women.[40] As the sociologist Teresa Scherzer notes, "Many health and social service providers reflect cultural values—often through the language of biomedicine—by continuing to regard same-sex sex, nonheterosexual identity, and nonconformist gender presentation as confusion or pathology, especially for youth."[41] The intersection of their sexual identities, age, race/ethnic identities, and access to quality health care also serves to contribute to Latina lesbian-identified girls' negative interactions with practitioners.

Furthermore, a couple of these young women reported that they and their partners also had conflicting definitions of what counted as sex, which also posed a challenge for their ability to communicate with their partners about safe sex. I had this conversation with Margarita:

> MARGARITA: She doesn't see what we do as "sex sex" [makes quotation marks with fingers]. Like kissing and touching each other . . . she says that doesn't count, though, because we ain't putting nothing in.
> LORENA: Do you think the sexual activities you and your partner do together count as sex?
> MARGARITA: I do, but, like I said, she don't. I tell her that if there are body fluids involved and if we have an orgasm, then it's gotta be sex . . . but she's like, um, "I don't think so."

Margarita's exchange with her partner on the meaning of their sexual practices underscores the social construction of sexuality—in this case, Margarita was at odds with her partner's reliance on penetration as the primary criterion by which to define sex, while Margarita interpreted an exchange of fluids and an orgasm (rather than just penetration) as indicators of sex. Additionally, their differing definitions of sex also illustrate that, generally, sex is defined by heteronormative standards. In this case, according to Margarita and her partner, their sexual practices qualify as sex only when there is penetrative sex and/or orgasm. Margarita's experience illustrates the implications of heteronormativity for the ability of young lesbian-identified women to negotiate safe sex. Margarita, for example, could not take it for granted that she and her partner were even on the same page about the meanings of their sexual practices.[42]

Given some of these challenges, lesbian-identified girls, like heterosexual-identified girls, also found that they had sometimes to convince their partners to practice safe sex. Five of the girls in this group demonstrated to their partner the importance of safe sex for women who have sex with women (WSW) by showing them a sexual health website,[43] picking up a related brochure from a health center, or printing out fact sheets. Isela, who walked off the dance floor when a young man was pushing her to kiss another young woman, described how she e-mailed her partner a link to a safe-sex fact sheet for WSW that she found on a youth-friendly website promoting sexual health: "I sent it to her, but when she didn't say anything about it to me, I was like, 'Did you get it?' and she was like, 'Get what?' I rolled my eyes and then she was like, 'I'm playing, I did!' She even showed me that she printed it out." When I asked Isela if her partner read the fact sheet, she laughingly replied, "Yep, 'cause even though she ain't want to, I made her go through it with me right there as we ate our food [they were at the food court of a mall]. I'm not sure if people heard us, but if they did, it must've sounded like some crazy shit to hear two girls talking about vibrators and condoms!" Gloria also told me that she sent her partner a link to a website to a blog by a queer black woman that had a link to other websites with sexual health information relevant to lesbian and bisexual girls. She pushed back her green and brown plastic frame glasses on the bridge of her nose and chewed her gum as she explained this: "She told me, 'Why you sending me this?' I told her, 'Look on that website, right there it tells you about how we need to take care of ourselves! Get your learn on, girl!" The instructions to learn safe-sex information that Barbara and Gloria communicated to their partners suggest that lesbian-identified girls' safe-sex communication strategies were focused on educating their partners.

That the partners of this group of girls did not think they were truly at risk may be related to the limitations of the school-based sex education they encountered. For instance, research has shown that, even with comprehensive sex education, protection messages tend to be targeted to heterosexual youth, whereas the needs or concerns of LGBTQ youth are marginalized or ignored altogether in sex education curricula. Whereas heterosexual girls drew on notions of appropriate femininity and masculinity to engage their partners in safe-sex communication and responsibility, lesbian-identified girls' strategies focused on educating their partners about safe sex. Heterosexual-identified girls may not have concentrated on educating their partners about safe sex, as lesbian-identified girls did, because such as a strategy could be too risky, potentially implying not only that their boyfriends were not sexually knowledgeable but also that they were "too" knowledgeable about sex and thus discrediting their gendered sexual respectabilities.

Conclusion

Lessons about sexual communication are an important component of school-based sex education, whether abstinence-only or comprehensive. Instruction on how to talk about sexuality provides students with the necessary skills to care for their sexual health.[44] But it is not enough to just instruct young people to ask their partners about their sexual histories or to wear a condom. Teaching students how to talk about sexuality with their partners, particularly safe sex, also requires attention to the challenges that make this difficult for them to carry out. In her classroom observation of a sex education lesson on safe-sex communication, the sociologist Jessica Fields found

that students expressed their doubts about the idea of engaging their partners in open sexual communication, pointing out that boys may get upset or
even perpetrate violence against young women for asking about their sexual
history or HIV status.[45] However, rather than address such risks and open
up a larger discussion about gender violence and norms, the teacher evaded
these issues by insisting that students "demand" safe-sex talk. Given some of
the limitations in school-based sex education, how do young people, particularly young women, address some of the obstacles they face in their efforts
at safe-sex communication with partners? This is a process we should seek
to understand before we direct young people, especially girls, to take on this
task in their sexual lives.

The narratives of the young Latinas I spoke with reveal that they developed particular strategies to carry out safe-sex communication and negotiation with their partners in the face of gender inequality and heteronormativity. Ideas about normative femininity and masculinity were both an obstacle
and a resource for heterosexual-identified girls, who knew that they did not
want to be like "one of those girls" but who also had some knowledge about
what "kind of guy" their boyfriends did not want to be, which also centered
on respectability. And, by linking their sexual respectability to that of their
boyfriends' respectability, this group of young women attempted to encourage their partners to share some responsibility for safe sex, particularly in
terms of obtaining condoms. Lesbian-identified young women also encountered inequality, but at the intersection of gender and heteronormativity.
Finding that their partners drew on assumptions and discourses that women
who have sex with women are not "at risk" for negative sexual outcomes like
those that face gay men or heterosexual and bisexual women, this group of
young women articulated strategies around education. As a way to address
their partners' gaps in knowledge as a result of misinformation provided by
health care providers or by the exclusion of same-sex sexuality in school-
based sex education, they specifically focused their efforts on helping their
partners become educated about the relevance of safe-sex communication
for women who have sex with women.

Girls' approaches to the exploration of desire and pleasure in their communication with their partners were also shaped by gender inequality and
heteronormativity. The differences in how heterosexual-identified and lesbian-identified girls handled this subject underscore how heterosexual-identified girls' boundary formation around women's sexual respectability also
limited their ability to allow themselves to fully develop their sexual subjectivity. In her research on girls' perspectives on and experiences of sexual
desire, the developmental psychologist Deborah L. Tolman has consistently

found that some girls often resist their sexual feelings as a strategy to avoid the dangers associated with sexual desire. Thus, for a significant number of girls that Tolman interviewed, desire was something that they felt that they needed to keep in check because they feared they risked the possibility of "losing control" and getting themselves in trouble if they allowed themselves to act on their desires. As Tolman observes, "Working within the institution of heterosexuality, they do not hold boys or social conventions accountable for making sexuality dangerous; rather, it is their own sexual feelings that constitute both the problem and the answer."[46] Given this, it is also possible that some of the heterosexual-identified girls I spoke with were also uncomfortable with safe-sex communication and instead shifted all of the "blame" for their limited sex communication onto their male partners.

It is also possible that some of the lesbian-identified girls were also uncomfortable with engaging their partners in safe-sex communication and instead explained the limitations that they perceived in these interactions as related to their partners' misinformation. As with heterosexuality, gender also shapes lesbian identities, practices, and desires. But as the sociologist Stevi Jackson points out, becoming and being lesbian does "require negotiating different ways of investing gender with erotic significance and different forms of gendered self-understanding."[47] Thus, we should not make the assumption that relationships between lesbians are going to be less gendered or more egalitarian just because they involve only women. On this point, the sociologist Mignon Moore writes, "Individuals with same-sex desire are not exempt from the social demand for the construction of gendered selves."[48] I interviewed only eight girls who self-identified as lesbian; three young women's gender presentation was *femme aggressive*, which is a combination of feminine gender display and masculine gender display; the gender display of the rest of the girls in this group was *femme*, or feminine woman.[49] I also did not interview their partners, nor was I able to meet them to determine their gender presentation. It is important, therefore, that we consider that the resistance that this group of young women encountered from their partners regarding safe-sex communication may also be related to how their gendered identities and power dynamics operated within these relationships. Certainly, further research on this is required.

Taken together, the safe-sex communication experiences of the young women I spoke with highlight the sexual and gender landscapes in which they are expected to "demand" sexual communication with their partners. Their observations of how gendered sexuality works and their own experiences with inequality contribute to their awareness that they cannot "just talk" to their partners about sexual safety. And, instead of "just not talking" to their partners because it is challenging to do so, as it is even for adults, these young Latinas' narratives reveal that they build on some of these very obstacles, such as heterosexual-identified girls' use of gendered social scripts and lesbian-identified girls' use of educational materials. Such strategies may not challenge gender and sexual inequality as a whole, but they do provide these young women with some power to attempt to interrupt the potential negative impact of inequality on their sexual and reproductive health.

6

Conclusion

As winter gave way to spring in April 2004, the energy level among the young people at Hogar del Pueblo picked up in anticipation of not only warmer days but also the upcoming graduation, prom, and other end-of-the-school year celebrations. During a two-week period that month, Stephanie, who had tracked down emergency contraception with the help of her friend, did not stop by the community center. The talkative seventeen-year-old typically frequented the afterschool program at least three afternoons every week. When she returned in early May, it was as if she had never been absent at all, focusing on her homework during tutoring time and chatting away with friends during free times. However, a noticeable difference now was that her mother picked her up every evening to escort Stephanie to their home, just two blocks away. Stephanie used to be able to walk home with friends. Rumor among the youth at the community center was that Stephanie was "on lockdown" because she had "got herself in trouble." But no one knew the exact details of what had happened except that it was related to sex in some way.

Weeks later, Stephanie voluntarily revealed her "trouble" to me as we discussed her plans for the summer. She shared with me that her mother had discovered that she "was not a virgin" when Stephanie's aunt found birth control pills and some condoms in Stephanie's fifteen-year-old cousin's closet. Upon confronting her cousin, Stephanie's aunt learned that Stephanie had accompanied her cousin to a health center to obtain birth control. Her aunt promptly notified Stephanie's mother about her involvement in this matter. Stephanie's mother then asked Stephanie about her own sexual behavior. After "confessing" that she "had already had sex" and that she had told her cousin where to get birth control pills and condoms, Stephanie's mother punished her by allowing her to leave the house only to attend school. After repeated requests from Stephanie, her mother finally agreed to allow her to attend the afterschool youth program under the condition that she would escort Stephanie home every day. On occasion, her mother showed up unannounced to ensure that Stephanie was indeed at the community center. Frustrated by this new heightened level of supervision, Stephanie remarked to me, "All this for trying to take care of myself. I know it ain't easy to know that your little girl isn't so innocent anymore, but she [her mom] should at least see that I'm trying to be responsible about things 'cause it ain't like it's that easy, either." Stephanie, like most of the young women, acknowledged that it was painful and difficult for their mothers and other adults in their lives to learn of their sexual behavior. But Stephanie's comment, along with the voices and experiences of the other Latina girls I came to know, underscores that, for these young women, the decision to enter into partnered sexual activities and attempt to practice safe sex involves a complex set of negotiations and challenges—and, for them, so much more is at stake than the prevention of pregnancy and STDs.

Asking Different Questions about Latina Girls' Sexual Experiences

One consistent response to the findings of this study, from a variety of individuals, is unease. These folks have included scholars, people who work directly with youth, such as social workers and teachers, and even some friends and family members. Many people are uncomfortable with the idea that young people engage in partnered sexual activities. In general, these are persons who are well intentioned and who care tremendously about young people and their healthy sexual development and their futures. We often hear and read that the practice of safe sex is challenging even for adults and that, therefore, youth, particularly girls, should delay engaging in partnered sexual activities until they are more mature or able to take on all that comes with sexual behavior, including but not limited to its health, emotional, and educational repercussions. I have found that when I discuss my work with some individuals, they cannot get past the idea that Latina girls, who are already facing so many obstacles that threaten their futures, think about and engage in sexual activities. But no matter what our perspectives are on what young people should or should not be doing sexually, they are engaging in sexual activities. For instance, according to a 2009 Pew Hispanic Center survey of young Latinas/os, 45 percent of Latina/o high school students reported having had sexual intercourse.[1] As noted by the Pew Hispanic Center, this is similar to the pattern for a nationally representative sample of high school students who participated in the Center for Disease Control's 2007 National Youth Risk Behavior Survey, in which 48 percent of all high school students reported having had sexual intercourse. Though we might not like this pattern, we simply cannot ignore this reality.

This book has delved into what this reality is like for second-generation Mexican and Puerto Rican girls. Though teen pregnancy, early motherhood, and STDs are negative sexual and reproductive health outcomes that have been documented as disproportionately impacting Latina youth, these girls' experiences with such outcomes were not the focus of this book. Instead, I have presented some of the rich insights we can gain about their sexual experiences when we ask different questions. I took as my starting point the assumption that Latina girls do have sexual agency and from there set out to explore their meanings and decision making around safe sex, paying special attention to how this was related to their negotiation of their emerging sexuality. These are young women who are coming of age in conditions similar to those of the Latina girls often described in the negative sexual-outcome statistics but whom we really do not account for in our examination of Latina girls' sexual experiences. As I have previously stated, I do not regard the girls I spoke with as exceptional. Rather, I focused on their experiences as a way to complicate and enrich our current understandings of the lives of Latina girls growing up in the United States and, specifically, our comprehension of their sexual subjectivity.

As I discussed in chapter 1, work by feminist scholars that has focused on the sexual subjectivity and agency of young people, especially young women, has opened up a critically different way to think about and discuss their sexuality that moves us away from the dominant and anxious account of their sexuality as dangerous. This line of research, as the sociologist Amy Schalet points out, contributes to the development of what she terms an "empowerment paradigm" of adolescent sexuality. But, as she well notes, although some of this scholarship incorporates the perspectives of girls and boys of color to varying degrees, none of it exclusively focuses on them. She writes that qualitative work must also "follow an explicit logic of inquiry designed to hone [*sic*] in on the specifics . . . of their conditions and experiences."[2] This book is about sexual subjectivity and agency among Latina youth. Specifically, this book complicates and broadens our understanding of Latina girls' sexual subjectivity and agency by uncovering the processes at work in how they construct sexual subjectivity and agency and the form that sexual subjectivity and agency take in the lives of this group of girls.

Young women are afforded very little space to explore and experience their sexuality in ways that are empowering to them and, especially, that privilege their sense of desire and pleasure. They encounter what the philosopher and feminist theorist Marilyn Frye calls a double bind.[3] In her essay on oppression, Frye asserts that one way in which oppression operates is by subjecting women and other oppressed groups to a double bind, which she defines as "situations in which options are reduced to a very few and all of them expose one to penalty, censure or deprivation."[4] Elaborating on this double bind, she adds, "The experience of oppressed people is that living one's life is confined and shaped by forces and barriers which are not accidental or occasional and hence avoidable, but are systematically related to each other in such a way as to catch one between and among them and restrict or penalize motion in any direction."[5] Though there may be some overlap in how various groups experience oppression, as Frye and other feminist scholars assert, groups also experience the shape, power, and interlocking of those forces and barriers, such as racism, sexism, classism, and heteronormativity, differently. Most scholars working with and on the "empowerment paradigm" of adolescent sexuality agree that inequality, in its various manifestations, work against girls' ability to develop themselves as sexual subjects. I have shown that by asking different questions about the sexual lives of Latina girls, particularly centering on their meanings and approaches to safe sex, we are able to discern more clearly how gender, sexuality, race/ethnicity, class, and generational status shape the contours of their sexual experiences.

Within larger public discussions of the perils of teenage sexuality that monopolize how we frame and address this dimension of young people's lives, Latina youth are made both invisible and visible. They are rendered invisible by the assumption that the experiences of middle- and upper-class white young women are the norm, the yardstick by which we measure all other girls, and yet, they are made quite visible to us by the constant association of teen pregnancy with young Latinas by which teen pregnancy among Latina youth is regularly described as a "normal" and "cultural" phenomenon. In this overriding narrative, Latina girls are consistently portrayed as "wanting to get pregnant," as fulfilling some sort of family and/or cultural tradition, and/or as seeking a sense of purpose and respect through motherhood. This account of Latina girls' sexual experiences and outcomes, which is often the starting point of our discussions of these girls' sexuality, is further legitimated by gendered racialized representations of them in the media. This is the larger sociocultural backdrop in which Latina girls find themselves having to carve out their identities. The Latina girls I spoke with were aware and critical of how they are depicted and talked about in larger society, and their stories demonstrate that their development of their sexual subjectivity and agency was also a strategy by which they resisted these portrayals of them. Their constant assertions about the girls they were not like or going to become reveal that their negotiation of their emerging sexual identities was also bound up with their formation of their gendered racial/ethnic identities. In others words, these were interrelated processes that shaped how they constituted and enacted their sexual subjectivity and agency.

At the Intersection of Various Forces and Barriers

As U.S.-born daughters of Mexican and Puerto Rican immigrants and/or migrants, young Latinas grapple with making sense of who they are and what is "normal" or "allowable" in terms of their experiences as teenage girls growing up in the United States. They do this within the location they find themselves in U.S. racial/ethnic hierarchies. Though Latinas/os are classified as an ethnic group, racial processes have significantly defined their experiences in the United States.[6] Shaped by a history of U.S. conquest and colonization in their homelands and in their communities in the United States, Mexicans and Puerto Ricans (along with other Latina/o groups) have been subjected to racialization processes.[7] Racial formations in the United States and elsewhere, however, have also drawn upon gender and sexual processes and ideologies to sustain themselves. Thus, Latina girls' sexual subjectivity unfolds in a larger sociocultural and political context in which the worth of women rests heavily on their sexuality, particularly their desirability and their availability to men, which is also constructed along racial/ethnic lines. This contributes to the production of a gendered sexual hierarchy in which middle- and upper-class heterosexual white women are regarded as the norm, their sexual worthiness validated by the characterization of the sexualities of other women as deviant.

As young women of color who engaged in partnered sexual activities and sought to practice safe sex, the Latina girls I spoke with negotiated their sexual subjectivity by cautiously crafting it around particular notions about what constitutes women's sexual respectability. Although sexual respectability, as a discourse and a practice, has been identified as significant to marginalized communities' strategies for challenging racial stereotypes and discrimination, to my knowledge, we do not really understand how young people living in these communities, such as second-generation Latina girls, take up sexual respectability as discourse and practice. Fully aware that respectability could be denied to them because of their sexual behavior, the girls I spoke with sought to claim it for themselves by employing specific strategies to reduce this possibility. The ways that they assembled and utilized strategies to do so demonstrate that Latina girls' engagement with ideas and decisions about sexual self-protective efforts are also intimately connected to their sense of their positioning in this society and what they want for their futures. In other words, though the prevention of unplanned pregnancy and/or sexually transmitted diseases was certainly important to these girls' sense of their sexual respectability as young women, they were aware that the stakes also required them to respond to the overlapping inequalities they encountered in their daily lives.

One key way in which they did this was by establishing a symbolic boundary of sexuality that was grounded in sexual respectability. As I outlined in chapters 2 and 4, sexual respectability for my informants operated as a gendered sexual and racial/ethnic boundary formation by which they set themselves apart from other sexually active Latina girls, particularly those stigmatized as "baby mommas" and "hos/skanks" and white young women. Appropriate femininity for them also incorporated a woman's ability to "handle her business," that is, to assume sexual responsibility for the prevention of unplanned pregnancies and STDs. Through this process, they attempted to defy their stigmatization and their homogenization, but, in distancing themselves from the young women in their communities labeled as "sexually deviant," they inadvertently reinforced the justification for the gendered sexual and racialized stigmatization of Latina girls. They also distinguished themselves from white young women, but not on the basis of their ability to sexually "handle their business." Instead, they did so on the basis of their perceptions of white young women's performance of gendered sexuality, which they interpreted as lacking in sexual integrity and morality. They primarily formed this notion of white young women from media images of them rather than from interactions with them. This "oppositional gaze" is another way in which Latina girls push back against negative images of themselves. The feminist author bell hooks articulates the concept of "oppositional gaze" to explain how black communities challenge the ways they are constructed as the "other." She writes, "In resistance struggle, the power of the dominated to assert agency by claiming and cultivating 'awareness' politicizes 'looking' relations—one learns to look a certain way in order to resist."[8] Latina girls utilized a narrative about the shameless sexuality of young white women to fashion a gendered sexual subjectivity that was specifically grounded in their identities as Latinas and that affirmed their sexual respectability.

However, their mothers could contest their claim to this identity, as we saw in chapter 2. Families are one of the significant social spaces in which we define our gender identities. Since mothers, in general, are often expected to assume most, if not all of the parenting responsibilities, particularly in relation to daughters, the mothers of the young women in this study were the individuals with whom the young women most often negotiated their gendered racial/ethnic identity in their families. When mothers were confronted with knowledge about their daughters' sexual behavior, they not only had to make sense of and respond to it but also had to grapple with what it meant for their identities as Mexican and Puerto Rican mothers of U.S.-born daughters. As their narratives reveal, this entailed their negotiation of the needs of their daughters, particularly their efforts to offer their daughters sexual guidance while simultaneously maintaining their own claim to a status as a good mother. In other words, their daughters' sexual respectability was connected to their own respectability. This indicates that Latina mothers' approaches to the sex education of their daughters can be understood as a relational gendered dynamic.

Often, the study of gender relations within families focuses on interactions between men and women, but women also work to establish their gender identities through their relationships with each other. Social forces outside the family, such racial/ethnic processes, shape interactions between family members. In my study, Latina mothers' sexual ascription of white girls was a response to their racialization that allowed them to situate themselves in a superior position in relation to white woman and to discipline their daughters as gendered racial/subjects. As the sociologist Yen Le Espiritu explains, "because womanhood is idealized as the repository of tradition, the norms that regulate women's behaviors become a means of determining and defining group status boundaries."[9] Latina mothers' ability to validate daughters' gendered racial/ethnicity identities was a form of power that they utilized against their daughters.

Heteronormativity and homophobia also informed the mothers' responses to lesbian-identified girls. Refusing to acknowledge their daughters' sexual agency in choosing to enter into partnered sexual activities with other young women, these mothers identified their daughters' partners as the source of their daughters' violation of heteronormative expectations. This was layered with racial meanings when their daughters' partners were white young women, of whom they already made sexual ascriptions as immoral and promiscuous. But these mothers' reactions to their lesbian-identified daughters were also put together with an eye toward their families, since they were especially concerned about how extended family members would treat their daughters. However, as their narratives indicate, this did not reflect a belief that Latinas/os were more homophobic than the larger society but arose from the fact that they saw homophobia play out in and outside their communities. Furthermore, they were aware that their mothering would be called into question because of their daughters' defiance of heteronormative rules and this behavior would not be as "excusable" as that of heterosexual-identified girls, who had more "room for mistakes" because their errors occurred in the context of heterosexual relationships. These mothers, therefore, focused much of their energy on attempting to present their daughters as heterosexual to family members, rather than on providing sexual guidance to their daughters or seeking information to make available to their daughters. In doing so, they demanded their daughters' cooperation in these efforts, especially insisting that their daughters perform a heterosexual femininity through their dress and behavior. This was how mothers sought to conceal their daughters' same-sex behaviors, but it could also be related to their interpretation of their daughters' same-sex relationship as only a "temporary" thing—a phase that daughters would outgrow when they matured and claimed their "true" gendered sexual identities. Thus, heteronormativity and homophobia operated to restrict Latina mothers' communication with their lesbian-identified daughters and to also alienate them from other mothers because they tended to see their experiences with their daughters as not "normal" or as not part of the range of challenges that Latina mothers encounter in raising daughters in a U.S. context.

Latina girls and their mothers rework their meanings and practices of gender and sexuality under particular constraints. I see them doing this within what the late Chicana cultural theorist Gloria Anzaldúa called the *intersticios*. She asserted that women of color are caught between "los intersticios, the spaces between the different worlds she inhabits."[10] The stories of the Mexican and Puerto Rican women I spoke with provide us with a glimpse of what it means to live in these *intersticios* and, importantly, how they move between and across these spaces and challenge the constraints they encounter on a daily basis.

Practical Considerations

Schools are a significant social sphere in which formal sexual-related information is made available to young people. The quality of school-based sex education has important implications for their understandings of themselves as sexual beings and their ability to make informed choices that allow them to have control of their sexual experiences. This requires that adults acknowledge young people as sexual subjects.

Under the Bush administration, however, young people were not perceived in this manner. Instead, they were generally directed, through abstinence-only-until-marriage sex education, to compartmentalize that aspect of themselves until they could be safe—that is, until they were married. As I discussed in chapter 3, until recently, the federal government provided much monetary support for abstinence-only education, governed by an eight-point definition of abstinence that left no political or social ambiguity as to what constituted "effective" sex education. However, beginning in 2010, the federal government made funding available for sex education programs that do not exclusively focus on abstinence. Instead, the Obama administration has centered its attention on teen pregnancy prevention, rather than promoting an abstinence-only agenda. This funding is in the form of a five-year grant of $375 million to be shared by twenty-eight sex education programs that have been determined to lower the pregnancy rates among their participants, regardless of their focus.[11] Though it focuses primarily on the prevention of pregnancy, the important aspect of this funding strategy is that it does not privilege abstinence-only sex education. Furthermore, it is also significant that, at the local level, the Chicago Public School Board of Education unanimously voted, on April 26, 2006, to approve the Family Life and Comprehensive Sexual Health Education policy. A celebrated decision by individuals and organizations invested in improving CPS sex education policy, this policy requires Chicago public schools to teach comprehensive, age-appropriate sexuality education to students in grades six through twelve. The policy is noteworthy given that neither the state nor the federal government offers guidelines on how to teach sex education in public schools. Such shifts in the way we approach the sex education of young people creates space for the consideration and implementation of alternative approaches.

These changes are significant given that the production and dissemination of school-based sex education occurs in a larger educational context characterized by inequalities. The sex education narratives of the Latina girls I came to know supports the assessment of other feminist scholars that school-based sex education may reproduce disadvantages already present in young women's lives, even when the intention is to empower them. Feminist scholars have especially named the ways that school-based sex education incorporates gender and heteronormative assumptions, as I noted in chapter 2. My findings expand our understanding of how these inequalities enter into sex education by specifically looking at how sex education is experienced by Latina youth, offering insight into how race/ethnicity interacts with these inequities. Quite often, when we deliberate on educational policies and curriculum in general, there is some recognition of the need to more inclusive of students' diverse cultural backgrounds to engage them in the learning process. The sociologist Angela Valenzuela's research, for instance, makes evident the negative impact on students when school administrators and teachers disregard their backgrounds. She highlights the detrimental impact of what she terms "subtractive schooling" on students of Mexican descent, which, as she describes it, is an educational approach that takes away rather than incorporates students' cultural resources and identities, such as language.[12] The sex education experiences of the young Latinas in this study suggest that there was some attempt by teachers and/or sex educators to address them as Latina students. However, their approaches seemed to be heavily guided by gendered sexual and racial/ethnic stereotypes about Latinas and Latinos. And Latina girls were not blind to this—their response to this practice was evident in the resentment they expressed as they shared their stories with me. Their experiences reveal how important it is to take into account students' identities, experiences, and perspectives in developing sex education and to proceed in an informed manner, rather than operate from assumptions. Thus, the determination of what is most important to convey to students in sex education should not be made solely by school administrators, teachers, and sex educators. The process should include other local players who also have an investment in the well-being of community youth, such as neighborhood organizations that work with young people, parents, and, most important, students. As I listened to the girls' stories about their sex education, I could not help wondering what their sex education experiences would have been like had they had been given an opportunity to share with the adults making sex education decisions for them what they felt they needed to learn. If we want students to take their sex education seriously and to benefit from it, then we need to take the students seriously as sexual subjects.

As I outlined in chapter 3, abstinence-only-until-marriage and comprehensive sex education are currently the two main approaches to school-based sex education in the United States. For those individuals and groups that acknowledge young people as sexual subjects, comprehensive sex education is favored because it is designed to provide young people with the knowledge and skills that enable them to make informed and positive choices. I agree that comprehensive sex education is more responsive to the sexual realities and challenges faced by young people. But I also agree with the sociologist Jessica Fields that we should move away from our dichotomous thinking about sex education—comprehensive sex education or abstinence-only sex education—and think about the subject more broadly, in terms of its potential for helping young people address the inequities they face. Given what I have learned from speaking to young Latinas, this means that we need to consider the possibility that a "one size fits all" approach to comprehensive sex education may not be the most productive model. Much effort has been put into establishing comprehensive sex education as the "better" of the two forms of school-based sex education, and we certainly need to be able to demonstrate the positive outcomes associated with this approach, but we should also dedicate energy to improving it. One way this can be done is to begin with the acknowledgment that, while there is overlap in young people's experiences, there are also ways in which their experiences differ depending on their various identities and their positioning in the larger society. Thus, for example, while the lesson that utilization of condoms and/or other barrier methods minimizes one's sexual risks is applicable to all young people, we also need to take into account the meanings that various groups assign to such practices and how these meanings, in turn, shape the safe-sex practices that young people accept and reject in relation to safe sex. For the young Latinas I spoke with, this decison was shaped by a complex interplay of gender, sexuality, race/ethnicity, class, and age. An appreciation of how this translates into young people's experience of their sexual lives, especially the development of their sexual subjectivity and agency, would allow us to move away from sex education informed by stereotypes about Latinas and Latinos and toward sex education that is relevant and accessible to them. This is a significant way we should work to develop the "comprehensive" in comprehensive sex education.

Comprehensive sex education can also be improved if we make a concentrated effort to address the context of gender inequality in which young people are directed to "take charge of their lives" and to practice safe sex. As I previously pointed out, research, including this study, has consistently demonstrated that school-based sex education is often uncritically taught and is based on assumptions about gendered sexual differences. As I demonstrated in chapter 3, for the Latina girls in my study, this was tailored around notions of Latina femininity and Latino masculinity that communicated to them not only that their male peers were always thinking only about sex and how to "get it" from them but also that they were doing so in a manner that would put young women at risk for negative sexual outcomes. Such approaches reinforce not only the message that girls are sexual objects but the idea that sexual behavioral differences between men and women are natural. The heterosexual-identified Latina girls I spoke with drew on strategic constructions of masculinity and femininity to attempt to discuss and obtain safe sex cooperation from their male partners—these were the tools that they had to work with.

Comprehensive sex education can also be expanded to offer students the opportunity to develop other sexual health-enhancing skills. For example, it can teach students how to unpack assumptions about gendered sexuality and how to consider what gives rise to the gender-sexual inequalities they observe and, importantly, how to address them. This is important for several reasons. First, it serves to provide a space for students to learn about the power of heteronormativity and for educators to be mindful of how it enters into the lessons they provide students. This will ensure that queer-identified students are included as students of sex education, rather than being marginalized in yet another way in their schools. Second, it may especially allow young women to become more comfortable in acknowledging and owning their right to sexual pleasure and desire. Finally, it can facilitate more egalitarian relationships among young women and men. As Schalet asserts, "if we are going to ask how teenagers can develop sexual subjectivity—no small feat for those twice their age—then we should also ask what conditions and capacities allow them to form good relationships with each other."[13] Thus, comprehensive sexuality education should do more than just affirm gender inequality. It should integrate an approach to gender that acknowledges it as a social relation that is indeed powerful in shaping our sexual experiences but that can also be challenged and reworked.

Involving Families and Communities

It is generally assumed that the families of young Latinas do not provide them with the sexual guidance they need to avoid negative sexual outcomes. More often than not, when we look to their families, we are scrutinizing their mothers, given that parenting in families is organized by gender. It is not uncommon for some observers who advocate for Latina girls' need for school-based sex education to point to their families' problematic "cultural attitudes" as the reason that school-based sex education should be made available to Latina youth. The patterns that we see with Latina girls' negative sexual outcomes are presumed to stem primarily from the socialization they receive in their families. Yet, as we have seen in chapter 2, Mexican and Puerto Rican mothers attempted to be responsive to the emerging sexualities of their daughters but did so under particular constraints. Their experiences, along with those of their daughters, indicate that, rather than think of formal sex education as something best handled by schools or by parents, it would productive to extend school-based sex education to incorporate students' families and communities. There may be ways for public schools to partner with local community organizations to design sex education workshops for parents or for parents and their children. The mothers that I spoke with who had participated in mother-daughter workshops at Casa de la Mujer felt that they had benefited from them, and those who did not participate in such workshops expressed a genuine interest in learning more about how to offer sexual guidance to their children. Teaching young people how to protect and have control of their sexual health should be seen not as the responsibility of just schools or just parents but, rather, as a collaborative community effort. Schools, families, and community organizations can support one another in this, effectively offering young people the consistent support they need to make informed sexual choices.

If we are committed to offering young people guidance on how to navigate the adolescent sexual landscape they find themselves in, then we need to better understand how they currently experience it, paying attention to their decision making and the meanings they assign to their sexuality and sexual practices. The young Latina women I came to know sought to assert some control over their sexual experiences and bodies, as well as their futures. And this, for them, did not mean that they deserved to be denied a place of respect in their social worlds, including the larger society in which they are disadvantageously positioned in a number of ways. They sought this place of respect through their approaches to safe sex. Their narratives make it evident that we need to be willing to ask different types of questions about young people's sexuality, questions that may not be appealing to us because they require us to acknowledge young people, particularly young women, as sexual subjects. We may be uncomfortable perceiving of girls in this way, and we may not like the answers they provide us with about this aspect of their lives, but such an approach can shed light on how to develop effective sex education strategies that are responsive to these young women's sexual realities.

APPENDIX A

Profile of Research Participants

Race-Ethnicity Codes		Sexual Identity Codes		Household Type Codes	
MX	Mexican	h	heterosexual	TP	Two-Parent Household
PR	Puerto Rican	l	bisexual	FH	Female-Headed Household

Name	Age	Race/ Ethnicity	Sexual Identity	Household Type	Mother's Name/Age
Daughter-Mother Dyads					
Arely	17	PR	l	TP	Elsa; 35
Asucena	16	MX	h	TP	Dolores; 40
Barbara	18	MX	l	FH	Roberta; 42
Carla	17	MX	h	FH	Conchita; 41
Elvia	17	PR	h	FH	Jasmine; 39
Eva	16	MX	h	FH	Lilia; 46
Imelda	17	PR	l	TP	Gina; 38
Inés	16	MX	h	FH	Julia; 38
Irene	16	PR	h	TP	Teresa; 38*
Iris	15	PR	h	TP	Luz; 35
Jeanne	13	PR	h	TP	Teresa; 38
Jocelyn	17	PR	h	TP	Sara; 40
Margarita	18	MX	l	TP	Martina; 49

Name	Age	Race/ Ethnicity	Sexual Identity	Household Type	Mother's Name/Age
Minerva	17	MX	h	TP	Carmen; 35
Miriam	16	MX	h	TP	Emma; 39
Patricia	15	PR	h	TP	Maria; 33
Rita	15	MX	h	FH	Betina; 40
Samantha	17	PR	h	FH	Francisca; 40
Soledad	16	MX	h	TP	Aracelia; 38

Young women whose mothers were not interviewed

Name	Age	Race/ Ethnicity	Sexual Identity	Household Type	Mother's Name/Age
Alicia	18	MX	h	TP	
Annabelle	18	MX	h	TP	
Camila	18	PR	h	FH	
Celia	17	PR	h	FH	
Cristina	18	PR	l	TP	
Fabiola	18	PR	h	FH	
Graciela	17	MX	h	TP	
Gloria	16	MX	l	FH	
Isela	17	MX	l	TP	
Juanita	16	PR	h	TP	
Linda	17	MX	l	TP	
Lisa	15	MX	h	FH	
Lourdes	17	MX	h	TP	

Name	Age	Race/ Ethnicity	Sexual Identity	Household Type	Mother's Name/Age
Maritza	16	PR	h	TP	
Marta	15	PR	h	TP	
Nanette	16	PR	h	TP	
Norma	16	PR	h	FH	
Olivia	17	PR	h	TP	
Rosalba	16	MX	h	TP	
Stephanie	17	MX	h	TP	
Yvette	16	PR	h	FH	

*Teresa and her two daughters, Irene and Jeanne, participated in this study.

Methodological Notes

Three of the organizations—Chi-Town Health Teen Center, Hogar del Pueblo, and Centro Adelante—were located in the West Town area of Chicago at the time of my data collection. The Chi-Town Health Teen Center, a nonprofit organization, has been offering services to young people who are between the ages of twelve and twenty-one since 1984. Most of the young women who access the health center are Latina and report living below the federal poverty line. Operating as a one-stop shop, the health center offers services that include family planning, health education, prenatal care, mental health care, advocacy, and case management. A nonprofit social service agency, Centro Adelante has been serving the West Town community since the turn of the twentieth century. Services offered there during my fieldwork included child-care programs such as Head Start, services for seniors, a teen program, and a community computer resource center. I recruited participants from the center's youth program, which provided resources for community youth to build academic and leadership skills.

Also a nonprofit organization, Hogar del Pueblo has been in the West Town community since the late 1800s, providing comprehensive services to Chicago's low-income families, primarily immigrants. Currently, Latinas/os are the primary population that use the resources offered by Hogar del Pueblo. Throughout my field research, I worked with the youth program, specifically the mentoring program, which connects Hogar del Pueblo youth with Chicago professionals for weekly one-on-one sessions centered on academics, college preparation, and life skills. Since 1998, all students who have participated in the mentoring component of the program have graduated from high school, and the majority of them have gone on to attend college. Hogar del Pueblo is located in the community in which I grew up, and my family has utilized and benefited from the services offered there. As a child, for instance, I participated in some summer programs, and different family members have accessed the center for a range of resources throughout the years, such as assistance with "*los papeles para la ciudadanía* [with citizenship paperwork]," health services, and ESL classes.

Initially, I was going to limit my research sites to the West Town area, but I decided to include Casa de la Mujer after consistently being referred there by the directors and program coordinators of the other organizations, who thought it would facilitate identification of potential Latina mother-daughter dyads. Casa de la Mujer, a nonprofit organization in the Pilsen community, has been providing comprehensive services aimed at Latinas for more than thirty years. Some of the programs and services offered include resources for victims of domestic violence, a leadership development program, and a mother-daughter program. I recruited study participants from the mother-daughter program, Entre Nosotras, which has been offered since 2000. The program provides Latina mothers and their daughters an opportunity to develop leadership skills as they learn to effectively communicate with each other and explore larger social issues that impact them, their families, and their communities.

Collecting and Analyzing Data

I was allowed to introduce myself to potential study participants at all of the agencies, except at the teen health center. At that field site, I was permitted only to post flyers that described my research project throughout the center. I was allowed to volunteer in different capacities, determined by program coordinators, at all of the organizations except at Casa de La Mujer.[1] For instance, I was able to consistently volunteer as a tutor for a weekly mentor program offered at Hogar del Pueblo, in addition to assisting with summer enrichment activities there. This allowed me to establish a more consistent relationship with some of the girls in my study, while also increasing the reliability of the findings. Moreover, this was one strategy that I purposively undertook in my reciprocation efforts as a researcher.

All of the young women and mothers in this sample initiated contact with me if they were interested in participating in the project. Prior to our first scheduled interview, I provided the girls with a consent form, in the language of their choice, for them and their parents and/or guardians to read and sign. I collected the signed form on the day of our first interview. In the case of the young women whose mothers participated in this project, the mothers would typically read and sign the consent form on the day of the interview. For both the young women and their mothers, I invited them to ask questions or share concerns that they wanted me to address before formally beginning our interviews. While I sought parental consent whenever possible, this was not an option for all of the girls because of the sensitive nature of the research topic, particularly because in some cases girls' parents were not aware of their daughters' sexual experiences. In these cases, obtaining parental consent would not have been feasible and would have posed a risk for these young women. Instead, an advocate was identified at each site who agreed to act in the best interests of young women who were minors throughout the duration of their participation in the research.

All interviews were audio-recorded with the permission of the girls and the mothers, but I often took handwritten notes. Each day that I went into the field, I immediately recorded my observation notes when I arrived home and, occasionally, at the research sites, usually in an unused space, such as an office or room. Although I had apprised people at the research sites of my presence there as a researcher, I chose to record my field notes as unobtrusively as possible so as not to distract youth and adults from their activities at the organizations. I also wanted to avoid making the young women uncomfortable in these settings. This method also permitted me to be reflexive throughout the research process because I kept a daily record of the challenges, setbacks, and decision making that shaped my fieldwork experiences.

I transcribed all interviews verbatim. After identifying dominant and recurrent themes and patterns, I performed detailed coding of the data, drawing from the Listening Guide method.[2] This method involves several readings of each narrative, listening for one particular dimension each time. I read each interview at least four times to cross-check recurrent themes, layers within themes, and contradictions expressed by study participants with regard to certain themes. Thus, the ideas I present in this book were derived from the methods of grounded theory, meaning that, while my research was informed by my knowledge of the literature on this topic, I concentrated on exploring the themes that emerged inductively from the interviews and field notes.[3]

Negotiating Representations and Knowledge

I encountered one methodological challenge related to my recruitment of mother-daughter dyads. As explained in chapter 1, I gained access to mothers through their daughters, who were asked to offer my contact information to their mothers if they thought that their mothers would be interested in participating in the project. However, this was also dependent on whether they felt comfortable with having their mothers speak with me. For example, there were girls who thought that their mothers might be interested in being study participants but who preferred that I not interview them. Although I did not probe any further, most of these young women conveyed concern about how their mothers would depict them in an interview, speculating that their mothers would say negative things about them. One young woman, for instance, remarked, "Don't even waste your time with my mom 'cause she's just gonna talk her shit . . . she's gonna sit there and tell you that I'm *'muy rebelde y grosera'* [too rebellious and vulgar]." I also suspect that some young women were concerned that sensitive information about them would be revealed to their mothers, despite my reassurances of strict confidentiality before, during, and after the interview process.

And mothers, like their daughters, also expressed concern about their daughters' portrayal of them. As we discussed basic background information at the beginning of the interviews, such as age and place of origin, mothers often interjected occasional statements about their performances as mothers. For example, while discussing her employment history, one mother remarked, "I worked out of necessity, and I think I set a good example by showing my daughters that you have to make an effort for the things you want in life. But maybe if I would've been able to be home more, maybe I could've guided them better." Feminist analyses of mothering have revealed the unfair ways in which women are held accountable for "society's ills" when they fail to conform to "good mothering" standards set by the dominant society.[4] As the education and psychology scholar Jill McLean Taylor and her colleagues observe, "The tragedy is that this view, according to which women have so much influence and yet so little power, is believed and internalized by many women, who then see themselves as 'bad' mothers if their lives and the lives of their children do not measure up to an image of perfection that is in fact impossible to achieve."[5] Sensitive to this issue, I was careful that my questions did not contribute to this problematic framing of mothers. I did not want the mothers I interviewed to interpret my questions as implying that they had failed in parenting their daughters. And, usually, at some point in the interview, they asked me about my own mother, specifically about how my mother socialized my siblings and me around issues of gender and sexuality. This line of inquiry typically surfaced as they verbalized some of the challenges they had encountered with their daughters around these issues. As stated earlier, I understood this line of questioning by my informants as a critical way in which they made sense of my identity. And, although it is well noted that the unequal power between the researcher and study participants can never fully be eliminated from the research process,[6] my decision to address such questions was informed by my commitment to attending to some of the inequality of power between us.

The questions from girls and their mothers that I did not answer were those that would have compromised the confidentiality of study participants. Issues of confidentiality surfaced most often in my interviews with mothers, which I anticipated as a feature of this project. Even though the consent form and accompanying information sheet clearly stated that I would not and could not disclose any details about their daughters' interview, I made certain to reiterate this specific point to mothers at the beginning of our interviews. Nonetheless, some mothers attempted to obtain information, directly or indirectly, about their daughters' sexual behavior and attitudes. Thus, I had to be especially alert to this issue in my dialogues with mothers to avoid inadvertently disclosing any information.

Ethical and Political Responsibilities in Knowledge Production

When people casually inquired about the subject of my research, I generally replied that it was on "Latina youth and sexuality." Without fail, people always had something to say about the topic. Their comments frequently equated the sexuality of Latina girls with unplanned pregnancy and almost always led to the question I encountered routinely in these informal conversations: "*So why are so many Latina teens getting pregnant and becoming teen mothers?*" And, inevitably, people offered answers to their own question, which commonly reduced Latina sexuality to just a reflection of "Latino culture," including but not limited to what they perceived to be negative attitudes toward birth control (influenced by Catholic teachings), machismo (including the sexual repression and silencing of Latinas' sexuality), and the desire for big families. I was not surprised by these remarks and the question that preceded them because they reflect the prevailing negative perceptions of Latina youth. Nonetheless, this type of commentary did tend to unsettle me because it evoked the unease that continually loomed over my research, and still does, which is my apprehension about the implications of my representation of the young Latinas and mothers who shared so much with me about their intimate lives. In my quest to challenge and complicate stereotypical and one-dimensional understandings of Latinas' lives, I have always found myself asking, "Who will read about their experiences, and how will this information be utilized and for what purpose?" While I have outlined the intended multilayered contributions of this project in the introduction and conclusion chapters of this book, I also recognize that the findings can be misused to justify the anxieties about the sexuality of Latinas and reinforce efforts to control the bodies of women of color, especially within the current anti-immigration climate in the United States. The feminist Chicana historian Emma Pérez writes, "If discourse reveals the history of sexuality, then women of color face an obstacle. . . . We have been spoken about, written about, spoken at but never spoken with or listened to."[7] It is my hope that, in centering the voices of Latina women and girls in this book, we can recognize the tremendous value in speaking with and listening to them.

NOTES

CHAPTER 1

1. The term Latino/Latina is generally understood to refer to persons of Mexican, Puerto Rican, Cuban, Dominican, Central, or South American descent. Latinas/os in the United States utilize various terms to identify their specific ethnicity. For example, some second-and third-generation Mexicans and Puerto Ricans in the United States may refer to themselves as Chicana/o or Nuyorican, respectively. Self designated labels, such as Chicana/o or Nuyorican, serve to affirm ethnic cultural pride and are political, highlighting the U.S. experiences of these groups. They also sometimes reflect the labeling practices of Latina/o groups concentrated in particular U.S. regions, such as in California or New York. I highlight the generational status of my study participants, but I use the terms Latinas/os, Mexican, and Puerto Rican when referring to them since these are the terms they used to identify their ethnicity, a practice that is common among these groups in Chicago.
2. "Safer sex" is the preferred term among comprehensive sex and sexual health educators because it underscores that sexual activities are not 100 percent risk-free and that efforts should be focused on teaching individuals how to minimize their risks for negative sexual-related outcomes. However, most people are more familiar with the language of "safe sex," which is why I decided to use this term, rather than "safer sex," in my interviews with girls.
3. For critiques of this "crisis" approach to female adolescent sexuality, see Fine, 1998; Irvine, 1994; Murry, 1996; Tolman, 1996.
4. Luker, 1996; Nathanson, 1991; Patton, 1996; Tolman, 1994.
5. Fine, 1988; Murry, 1996; Nathanson, 1991.
6. Irvine, 1994; Petchesky, 1984.
7. Irvine, 1994.
8. Collins, 2004; Espiritu, 2001; Higginbotham, 1993; Hine, 1994; Moore, 2011; Schalet, Hunt, and Laidler, 2003; White, 2001; Wolcott, 2001.
9. Some previous studies that have provided rich information about young women's sexual subjectivity include Carpenter, 2005; Dunn, 1988; Fine, 1988; Martin, 1996; Schalet, 2010; Schalet, Hunt, and Laidler, 2003; Sheff, 2005; Tolman, 2002; Thompson, 1995.

10. Tolman, 2002, p. 6.
11. Brooks-Gunn and Paikoff, 1997; Martin 1996.
12. See, for instance, Carpenter, 2005; Martin, 1996; Taylor, Gilligan, and Sullivan, 1995; Thompson, 1995; Tolman, 1994; Tolman 2002.
13. West and Zimmerman, 1987.
14. See, for instance, Chafetz, 1990; Deutsch, 2007; Lorber, 2005; Ridgeway, 2011; Risman, 1998.
15. See, for instance, D'Emilio, 1983; Nagel, 2003; Rubin, 1984; Somerville, 2000; Trujillo, 1991; Weeks, 2003.
16. See, for instance, Butler, 1990; González-López, 2005; Ingraham, 1994; Jackson, 2006; Rich, 1980; Rubin, 1984.
17. Butler, 1990.
18. Rubin, 1984.
19. Crenshaw, 1989; Collins, 1990; Hurtado, 1996.
20. Collins, 1990.
21. See, for instance, Ayala, 2006; González-López, 2005; Hurtado 2003; Toro-Morn and Alicea, 2003.
22. See, for instance, Cantú, 2000; Cantú, 2009; Carrillo, 2002; González-López and Vidal-Ortiz, 2008; Gutiérrez, 2008; Peña, 2005.
23. Lamont, 2002; Swidler, 1986; Young, 2004.
24. Swidler, 1986, pp. 275–277. Swidler defines strategies of action as "general solutions to the problem of how to organize action over time, rather than specific ways of attaining particular ends" (Swidler, 2001, p. 82).
25. The study was reviewed and approved by the Human Subjects Committee at the University of California at Santa Barbara.
26. U.S. Census Bureau, 2004. ACS (American Community Survey), www.census.gov/acs/www/index.html (accessed March 4, 2009).
27. De Genova and Ramos-Zaya, 2003; Garcia and Rúa, 2007; Padilla, 1985; Rúa, 2001.
28. This young woman was third generation (meaning that her parents were born in the United States).
29. Chicago Fact Finder: Your Census Information Resource for Chicagoland Communities, 2005. Institute for Latino Studies, University of Notre Dame, http://www.nd.edu/~chifacts/chicago.html.
30. Chicago Fact Finder: Your Census Information Resource for Chicagoland Communities. 2005. Institute for Latino Studies, University of Notre Dame, http://www.nd.edu/~chifacts/chicago.html.
31. Zentella, 1987, pp. 176–177.
32. See, for instance, Baca Zinn, 1979; Collins, 1991; Naples, 2003; Souza, 1995; Zavella, 1996; Zavella, 1997.
33. Naples, 2003, p. 49.
34. Bolak, 1996, p. 114.
35. Islam, 2000, p. 43.

36. Mies, 1983; Oakley, 1981; Reinharz, 1979.
37. See for instance, Baca Zinn, 1979; Collins, 1990; Pattillo-McCoy, 1999; Pérez, 2003; Zavella, 1997.
38. Pew Hispanic Center, 2009.
39. Martin, Hamilton, Sutton, Ventura, Menacker, and Kirmeyer, 2006.
40. Chase-Lansdale and Brooks-Gunn, 1995; Denner and Guzmán, 2006; Furstenberg Jr., Cook, Eccles, Elder, and Sameroff, 1999; South and Crowder, 1997.
41. In their book *Managing to Make It: Urban Families and Adolescent Success*, Furstenberg Jr., Cook, Eccles, Elder, and Sameroff (1999) interrupt the widely disseminated and accepted explanation that the poverty that follows economically disadvantaged youth into their adult lives is the fault of their parents, who are generally depicted as lacking appropriate parenting skills and/or as not caring enough to parent their children in a manner that facilitates their ability to improve their life circumstances. Through interviews and case studies of poor families living in five inner-city Philadelphia communities, Furstenberg Jr. and his colleagues identify some of the beliefs and practices that families, particularly parents, develop and draw on to help their children succeed.
42. See for instance Carter, 2005; Gandara, 1995; Lopez, 2003.
43. In her book *Keepin' it Real: School Success beyond Black and White* (2005), Carter complicates explanations for the achievement gap experienced by African American and Latino students by challenging the often cited explanation that socioeconomically disadvantaged youth of color do not fare well in terms of educational outcomes because they equate educational achievement with "acting white." Carter reveals that students' rejection of "acting white" does not translate into a rejection of educational success but rather reflects their concerns about being able to retain their cultural identities and ways of being in school settings that often devalue their backgrounds. She found that students who were academically successful, those she calls the "cultural straddlers," were able to skillfully navigate across various cultural worlds in ways that allowed them to maintain their racial or ethnic identity.
44. Reinharz, 1992, p. 167.
45. Leadbeater and Way, 1996; Murry, 1996.

CHAPTER 2

1. Cohen, 1997, p. 440.
2. Hutchinson, 2001; O'Sullivan, Meyer-Bahlberg, Heino, and Watkins, 2001; Meneses, 2004; Nadeem, Romo, and Sigman, 2006; Taylor, Gilligan, and Sullivan, 1995.
3. Hochschild, 1994, p. 4.
4. Ibid.

5. Magnified moments can be rich sites from which to explain the social construction of gender and sexuality. For example, by focusing on the experiences of four- and five-year-old children at a youth soccer opening ceremony as a magnified moment, the sociologist Michael Messner (2000) demonstrates how magnified moments can provide insight into how gender is socially constructed, in this case, through various interactional, structural, and cultural processes that reinforce each other.

6. Only one mother reported that she looked through her daughter's e-mail messages, with the help of another daughter who was knowledgeable about computers and the Internet.

7. Also known as "love bites," these are marks or bruises on the skin caused by kissing, sucking, or biting the skin.

8. Alarcon, 1981; Hurtado, 1996; Trujillo, 1991.

9. This is not to deny that a culture of love and romance is marketed to young women, which may shape their interactions with sexual partners and how they make sense of those relationships. Feminist scholars have critiqued the culture of love and romance marketed to young women through films, reality shows, magazines, and novels. They point out that, given the limitations placed on young women's expression of sexuality, it is not surprising that girls refer to love as a justification for their sexual behavior. See, for instance, Asencio, 2002; McRobbie, 1991; Souza, 1995.

10. Almost all of the girls who identified as heterosexual reported the race/ethnicity of their sexual partners as Latino (only one indicated that her sexual partner was African American). Three of the eight lesbian-identified girls in this study reported the race/ethnicity of their sexual partner as white; I interviewed the mothers of these three young women.

11. See, for instance, Chan, 1989; Rust, 1996; Trujillo, 1991; Zavella, 1997.

12. In my use of the phrase "Talkin' Safe Sex," I am drawing on Patricia Zavella's term "talkin' sex." Zavella decided on this phrase to "convey the sense of awkwardness" that the Chicanas and Mexicanas she interviewed "often felt in describing feelings, experiences, sensations they rarely articulated except in occasional safe spaces" (Zavella, 2003, p. 230). Zavella argues that these women's talk of sex is contradictory in that it reflects both acquiescence and contestation.

13. Elliott, 2010; Jaccard, Dittus, and Gordon, 2000; Kirkman, Rosenthal, and Feldman, 2002; Rosenthal and Feldman, 1999.

14. See Elliott, 2010; González-López, 2005; Romo, Bravo, Cruz, Rios, and Kouyoumdjian, 2010. Note: The mothers in Elliott's study did emphasize abstinence-only to their daughters and sons, but they expressed their doubts about whether their children would wait until marriage.

15. González-López, 2003, p. 235.

16. Bonilla, 2005; González-López, 2005.

17. See, for instance, Briggs, 2002; Carrillo, 2002; González-López, 2005; Hirsch, 2003; Lopez, 2008; Suárez Findlay, 1999.
18. Hirsch, 2003.
19. See Alicea, 1997; Cantú, 2009; Espiritu, 2001; González-López, 2005; Hirsch, 2003; Hondagneu-Sotelo, 1994; Peña, 2005; Pérez, 2004; Toro-Morn and Alicea, 2003.
20. Patricia R. Pessar (2003), in her assessment of how gender has been accounted for in migration studies, notes that early work on this topic, though important, was limited in it binary treatment of women's experiences of migration as either emancipatory or subjugating.
21. González-López, 2005.
22. Other scholars have also found that immigrant mothers educate their daughters on gender and sexuality through the things they say about other women rather than by conveying messages on these issues in organized lessons to their daughters. See, for instance, Espín, 1991; Trujillo, 1991.
23. Latina Feminist Group, 2001.
24. Collins, 1990, p. 208.
25. Alicea, 1997; Collins, 1990; Segura and Pierce, 1994; Taylor, Gilligan, and Sullivan, 1995; White, 1999.
26. Douglas and Michaels, 2004; Hays, 1996; Stone, 2007; Willard, 1988.
27. Martin, 2003, p. 57
28. A total of four mothers reported that they were not employed outside the home. These mothers were all in two-parent households.
29. Addressing the limitations in the research on women of Mexican origin, Segura was interested in exploring differences and similarities among women born in the United States (Chicanas) and those who immigrated to the United States. Segura found that immigrant status informed differences in how these two groups of mothers understood motherhood and employment.
30. Segura, 1994.
31. Seven mothers (out of eleven mothers who reported being in two-parent households) stated that they also made known their daughters' sexual behavior to their daughters' fathers.
32. There is a need for further research on fathers' communication about sexuality with their children. However, one study that accounted for fathers', mothers', and adolescents' perspectives on fathers' communication with their children about sexuality found that one challenge that fathers encountered was the idea that same-gender communication was more effective. It also found that mothers communicated better than fathers and that mothers have more intimate relationships with their children (Kirkman, Rosenthal, and Feldman, 2002).
33. Garcia, 2001.

34. See, for instance, Hillier, 2002; Raymond, 1994.

35. Rich, 1980; Trujillo, 1991.

36. As in the anthropologist Patricia Zavella's (2003) interviews with Chicana and Mexicana women about sexuality, the mothers and daughters who spoke with me recounted that, while conversations about gay men did occur among family members, these were usually intended to be humorous and centered on jokes or name calling, rather than serious discussions of same-sex identities, behaviors, and desires. There was even less conversation about women's same-sex experiences.

37. Nagel, 2001, p. 124.

38. Only four mothers briefly commented on interracial dating during our interviews. They expressed greater concern about their daughters taking on behaviors and attitudes that they associated with young white women. This is not to imply that interracial dating and marriage are not discussed among Latinas/os, however.

39. Frankenberg, 1993, p. 16.

40. As Espiritu argues, the sexuality of women "is one of the few sites where economically and politically dominated groups can construct the dominant group as other and themselves as superior" (Espiritu, 2001, p. 421).

41. As I discuss in chapter 3, the young women I interviewed perceived themselves to be different not only from white young women but also from other Latina girls in their communities, such as immigrant and migrant girls and young women, whom they thought of as sexually irresponsible.

42. In chapter 3, I discuss how Latina girls construct their identities in response to racialized gender stereotypes about them that are found within the larger society.

43. It is very possible that my position not only as a researcher but as a Mexican woman (born and raised in Chicago) affected how the Mexican and Puerto Rican women in this study discussed their perceptions of each other. For instance, I wonder to what degree the distinctions they spoke of were informed by their understandings of me as a Latina.

44. In her ethnographic study of Puerto Rican transnational communities in Chicago, Gina Pérez (2003) also found that Puerto Rican women perceived differences between themselves and Mexican women in relation to marriage. Pérez noted that Puerto Rican women described Mexican women as "*sufridas*" (long suffering), while Mexican women depicted Puerto Rican women as "*rencorosas*" (spiteful, resentful).

45. See Collins, 1991; hooks, 1984; Pardo, 1998.

46. Ayala, 2006.

47. Deniz Kandiyoti defines patriarchal bargain as those rules and scripts that regulate gender relations "to which both genders accommodate and acquiesce, yet which may nonetheless be contested, redefined, and renegotiated" (Kandiyoti, 1988, p. 286).

48. As Nagel points out, ethnic boundaries fall along several dimensions, such as social, spatial, cultural, and political, but they are also sexual. According to Nagel, how sexuality and ethnicity come together, particularly "how they give power to one another" to give shape to racial/ethnic boundaries, remains underexplored (Nagel, 2003, p. 5).

49. Collins, 1991; Espiritu, 2001; Lopez and Hasso, 1998; Sandoval, 1991.

CHAPTER 3

1. Portions of this chapter have appeared in different form in the following journal article: "'Now, Why Do You Want to Know about That?': Heteronormativity, Sexism, and Racism in the Sexual (Mis)Education of Latina Youth," *Gender & Society* 23(4): 520–541.

2. Samantha was one of two young women in my sample who engaged in such activism pertaining to youth sexuality education.

3. See, for instance, Fields, 2008; Irvine, 2002; Luker, 2006; Moran, 2000.

4. Ericksen and Steffan, 1999; Fields, 2008; Patton, 1996.

5. Patton, 1996, p. 43.

6. See Connell and Elliott, 2009; Barton, 2007; Fields, 2008; Fine, 1988; Fine and McClelland, 2006; Tolman, 1994.

7. Fields, 2008.

8. Black and Latina/o students constitute 87 percent of CPS students; Latinas/os make up 41 percent of CPS students; http://www.cps.edu/About_CPS/At-a-glance/Pages/stats_and_facts.aspx(accessed March 5, 2011).

9. Sexuality Information and Education Council of the United States (SIECUS), n.d., "Fact Sheet: Abstinence-Only-Until-Marriage Q and A," http://www.siecus.org/ (accessed June 24, 2008). See also Boonstra, 2007; Irvine, 2002; Luker, 2006.

10. This may be attributed to the fact that all the Latina youth I interviewed reported more exposure to sex education in elementary school than high school (where it occurred less frequently, often only as part of health lesson in Physical Education classes or as part of special lecture in the school auditorium). It was in middle school that they first had the opportunity to engage the topic in a structured and sanctioned setting.

11. All respondents who reported access to abstinence-only sex education (AOE) indicated that the instructors were women, and all but two of the girls who reported receiving comprehensive sex education (CSE) indicated that the CSE educators were women. Girls reported more variation in the race/ethnicity of sex educators. AOE and CSE educators were described as white, African American, Latina, or other, with the majority of instructors identified as white by the girls.

12. With the exception of three respondents, the rest of the sample reported interactions only with middle school female teachers when discussing their

sex education experiences. The race/ethnicity of middle school teachers were reported as white (23); African American (8); Latina/o (5); and other (4).

13. I borrow the term "knowing girls" from Jessica Fields (2007). But even outside the context of sex education, students of color are often perceived to be "too" sexually aware. See, for instance, Bettie, 2003; Ferguson, 2000; Kaplan, 1997.

14. Fine, Weis, and Roberts, 2000.

15. Chavez, 2004; Gutiérrez, 2008; Inda, 2002.

16. Gutiérrez, 2008.

17. See, for instance, Roberts, 1997; Smith, 2005.

18. Ferguson, 2000.

19. Khayatt, 1995; Pascoe, 2007; Petrovic and Ballard, 2005; Trudell, 1993; Walton, 2005.

20. For example, Horn, Meiners, North, Quinn, and Sullivan (2009) conducted a web-based assessment of fifty-seven preprofessional teacher education program in Illinois (January 2007–January 2008) and assigned 72 percent of the evaluated programs a failing grade. They argue that the absence of terms such as "sexual orientation" and "gender identity" in the programs' conceptual frameworks suggest that teachers are not being adequately trained within their teacher preparation programs to be inclusive of LGBTQ youth.

21. Guzmán, 2006; Kumashiro, 2001; Rodríguez, 2003.

22. The weekly tutoring program is offered through a partnership with a business. It has been offered since 1984. The program focuses on academics, and each student is provided a mentor who will work closely with her or him during the academic year. Students who successfully complete the program receive some scholarship funds to help offset their college expenses. The program boasts a 100 percent high school graduate rate, and over 90 percent of program participants going on to college.

23. These young women did not see motherhood as a pathway to adulthood, contradicting findings from other studies on Latina girls from similar backgrounds. Education was perceived to be the key route to their accomplishment of womanhood. Some of the heterosexual-identified girls discussed planning to get married after obtaining their college education and before having children, and two of the lesbian-identified girls described planning to "settle down" in the same order. But, for most of the young women, marriage was something they seemed ambivalent about at this point in their lives, as reflected in Lourdes's and Annabelle's ideas about their futures.

24. Jones-Corrrea, 2002; Kasinitz, Waters, Mollenkopf, and Anil, 2002; Louie, 2006; Rumbaut, 2002.

25. Lopez, 2003; Louie, 2006; Suárez-Orozco, 1987; Suárez-Orozco and Suárez-Orozco, 1995.

26. Suárez-Orozco, 1987.

27. Some educational research has focused on comparing the school achievement of Latina/o immigrant students and their U.S.-born co-ethnics. Some of this research indicates that immigrant students fare better in terms of academic achievement than later generations of Latina/o students, with for instance, higher graduation rates (see, for instance, Portes and Zhou, 1993; Portes and Rumbaut, 1990; Ogbu, 1991; Valenzuela, 1999). Other studies, however, suggest that later generations of Latina/o students have higher academic achievement (see, for instance, Chapa, 1988; Hurtado, Hayes-Bautista, Valdez, and Hernandez, 1992). These different findings reveal a need for further research on the impact of generational status on Latina/o students' academic achievement, which must also incorporate a consideration of various other factors, including but not limited to language fluency, context of reception, gender, and socioeconomic status (see Rumbaut, 1995). Much of this research has particularly focused on Mexican-origin students (immigrant vs. U.S. born).

28. Ayala, 2006; Hubbard, 2005; Hurtado, 2003; Jarrett, 1994; Lopez, 2003.

29. See, for instance, Carter, 2007; Flores-Gonzalez, 1999; Fordham, 1993; Hubbard, 2005; Lopez, 2003.These scholars have complicated the explanation offered by Ogbu (1987) that the low educational achievement of black and Latina/o students (groups Ogbu describes as "involuntary minorities") is a result of processes of incorporation and their racialization. According to Ogbu, experiences with these processes contribute to students' development of an "oppositional" identity through which they position themselves against academic achievement because it is interpreted as an effort to assimilate to the dominant white society. However, scholars in this area have asserted that we need to account for variations in academic achievement within and across groups. Thus, we need to consider how gender intersects with race/ethnicity and class to produce different outcomes. Hubbard, for example, found that gender mattered for how African American boys and girls perceived opportunity and reacted to discrimination, impacting their orientations to college (Hubbard, 2005, p. 612).

30. Ogbu, 1987.

31. Lopez , 2003, p. 38.

32. Corsaro, 2005; Harris, 2004; Wyn and White, 1997.

33. Baker, 2010; Harris, 2004; McRobbie, 2007; Ringrose, 2007.

34. Ringrose, 2007, p. 485. Ringrose, along with other feminist scholars, has observed that this "successful girls" discourse intersects with what they describe as a postfeminist discourse. For instance, McRobbie (2007) argues that girls and young women have been provided with a new social/sexual contract by which they are provided with certain "powers" in exchange for no longer utilizing a feminist critique. McRobbie and others point out that this "postfeminist" discourse indicates that feminism, especially a feminist

critique, is now interpreted by younger generations of women as outdated or no longer necessary or applicable.

35. An Illinois State Board of Education standardized test, the ITBS was formerly administered to students in the elementary schools, grades 1–8. This test was used to compare Chicago students' achievements to those of a representative national sample of students. After thirty-three years, the ITBS was replaced in 2005 by the Stanford Learning First test.

36. An Illinois State Board of Education standardized test, the ISAT covers the following subjects: reading, math, and writing in grades 3, 5, and 8, in addition to science and social science in grades 4 and 7. This test measures individual student achievement against the Illinois Learning Standards. The ISAT replaced the Illinois Goal Assessment Program (IGAP) in the 1998–1999 academic year.

37. As has been documented, some teachers in low-performing schools are critical of and do attempt to counteract the damaging impact of high-stakes testing and accountability upon school culture, student learning, and the control they have in classroom lessons (Lipman, 2004).

38. Research that has considered the experiences and attitudes of teachers in relation to sexuality education suggests that, in general, teachers do not feel comfortable teaching sexuality education or are ill prepared to teach the material (Levenson-Gingiss and Hamilton, 1989; Rodriguez, Young, Renfro, Asencio, and Haffner, 1997). For example, a study of preservice teachers found that they are not adequately provided with sex education training as part of the undergraduate curriculum designed to prepare them to become teachers (Rodriguez, Young, Renfro, Asencio, and Haffner, 1997). Key findings from this study (based on a sample survey of 169 colleges and universities) revealed that only 14 percent of the institutions required a health education course for all preservice teachers and no institutions required a sexuality education course for all preservice teachers. In addition to accounting for the sexuality education training of teachers, it is also important to consider teachers' perceptions of sexuality education itself. Comparing a 1999 national survey of seventh-through twelfth-grade public school teachers with a survey conducted in 1988, Darroch, Landry, and Singh (2000) found that 41 percent of teachers surveyed in 1999 were cited abstinence as the central lesson they wanted to communicate to students, whereas only 25 percent of the teachers surveyed in 1988 did so.

39. In chapter 4, I explore in detail Latina girls' use of a "handlin' your business" discourse to explain their meanings and practices of safe sex.

40. Bettie (2003) also found such expressions of cynicism about boys among the girls she interviewed.

41. Tolman, 1994, p. 327.

42. Hyams, 2006; Burns and Torre, 2004.\

43. Burns and Torre, 2004, p. 133.

44. Ayala, 2006; Bettie, 2003; Burns and Torre, 2004; Fordham, 1993; Hubbard, 1999; Hyams, 2006.

45. Fields and Tolman, 2006.

46. Fields, 2008.

47. Fine and McClelland, 2006.

48. McRobbie, 2007, p. 727.

CHAPTER 4

1. Lamont and Molnár, 2002, p. 168.
2. Heterosexual-identified girls' assumption that sex was defined primarily as penile-vaginal intercourse underscores the persistence and the power of compulsory heterosexuality in shaping interpretations of sexual behaviors (Rich, 1980; Rubin, 1984).
3. Only two girls also discussed "no sex" as "safe sex." These young women understood "no sex" to mean the absence of penal-vaginal intercourse. They included in their description of "safe sex" behaviors such as kissing, hugging, masturbation, and oral sex (because to them, oral sex did not qualify as "sex").
4. Asencio, 2002; Ericksen and Steffan, 1999; Patton, 1996.
5. Until the Surgeon General's 1988 AIDS prevention campaign, there were no official nationwide efforts to promote risk reduction or even to explain clearly the mechanics of HIV transmission. Youth began to be addressed as an audience for such campaigns in 1990, when the incidence of HIV among youth became too large to ignore (Patton, 1996).
6. Research, as well Latina fiction, has indicated that young Latinas experience limited mobility outside their home as a way for their families to safeguard their emerging sexualities. See, for instance, Castillo, 1994; Cisneros, 1992; Fregoso, 1999; Horowitz, 1983: Hurtado, 2003; Santiago, 1998; Souza, 1995; Zavella, 1997.
7. Fifteen girls believed that their parents would force them or pressure them to marry their sexual partner as a way to address an unplanned pregnancy.
8. Reproductive justice activists and scholars, particularly women of color, have criticized mainstream understandings of reproductive rights that focus on only "choice" and abortion. As they have well noted, the language of "choice" disregards how women's different experiences, such as those related to gender, race/ethnicity, sexuality, immigration, and poverty, shape the power that women have over their reproductive lives. Additionally, they point out that, while the ability to have a "choice" about abortion is important to all women, it is necessary to also incorporate such issues as access to reproductive health services, sexual and reproductive education, and health insurance into our conceptualization of

reproductive rights. See, for instance, Gutiérrez, 2008; Roberts, 1997; Ross, 2004; Silliman, Gerber Fried, Ross, and Gutiérrez, 2004; Smith, 2005.

9. Pew Hispanic Center and Pew Forum on Religion and Public Life, 2007.

10. Additionally, a 2009 survey by the Public Policy Institute of California found differences in attitudes on abortion between immigrant and U.S.-born Latinas/os; 62 percent of Latina/o immigrants supported greater restrictions on abortion, whereas 65 percent of U.S.-born Latinas/os indicated that they believed the government should not interfere with a woman's access to abortion (Baldassare, Paluch, and Petek, 2009).

11. Gutiérrez, 2008; Roberts, 1997; Ross, 2004; Silliman, Gerber Fried, Ross, and Gutiérrez, 2004; Smith, 2005.

12. For some of the young women, the terms HIV and AIDS were interchangeable, and they were unable to make a distinction between the two terms.

13. MacLeod, 1987; Sennett and Cobb, 1972.

14. Levy, 2005; Phillips, 2000; Schaffner, 2006; Tanenbaum, 2000; Tolman, 1994, Tolman, 2002.

15. Connell, 1987.

16. Collins, 2004. There may be group-specific ways to produce a femininity that is rewarded, such as one based on body weight, skin color, hair length and texture, and/or use of makeup. However, it is important to bear in mind that, depending on the context, only some women may be able to produce a femininity that is considered to be desirable, so not all women may have access to privilege through their expressions of femininity. See, for instance, Banks, 2000; Candelario, 2007; Hamilton, 2007.

17. Hochschild, 1989; Hamilton, 2007; Levy, 2005.

18. Gibbs, 1985; Fine, Weiss, and Roberts, 2000; Tolman, 2002.

19. Luker, 1996; Murry, 1996; Nathanson, 1991.

20. Love also surfaced in some girls' narratives of their first sexual experiences. For further discussion of this point, see Garcia, 2009a.

21. Asencio, 2002; Souga 1995; Fine, 1988; Martin, 1996; Thompson, 1995; Tolman, 2002.

22. In her ethnographic study on Puerto Rican youth, Marysol Asencio also found that youth commonly perceived females as the source of disease. While men typically responded that they had to watch whom they slept with "'cause the girl might have something," women typically responded that they worried about their partners having been exposed to infection because "guys go out with sluts and get things from them" (Asencio, 2002, p. 85).

23. In her study of black young mothers, Kaplan (1997) found that teen mothers gossiped about other teen mothers to paint themselves in a better light on the basis of the "moral structure" they constructed for teen mothers in the community. According to Kaplan, young mothers would gossip about

other teen mothers' length of time on welfare or the age at which they became mothers.

24. Horowitz, 1983, p. 135.

25. Latina girls in this study did not seem to acknowledge early motherhood as a pathway to adulthood, but they did see it as a pathway to respectability for young women who had lapsed in terms of their sexual responsibility.

26. West and Zimmerman, 1987.

27. Horowitz, 1983, p. 131–132.

28. West and Zimmerman, 1987.

29. Laura Carpenter's (2005) work on young Americans' interpretations and experiences of virginity loss demonstrates the importance of understanding how sexual, gender, and racial-ethnic identities matter for the meanings that young people assign to virginity and virginity loss.

30. Pew Hispanic Center, 2009.

31. It is also worth noting that this survey also found that teen motherhood increased between the second and third generation, from 16 percent to 21 percent of the sample. Most research that accounts for the sexual outcomes of Latina/o youth compares their outcomes to those of other racial/ethnic groups, such as African American and white youth. Little research has focused on patterns among Latina/o youth themselves, such as outcomes for first- and second- generation Latina/o youth. It is necessary to explore whether recent immigration is a protective factor or not for Latina girls, since they are assumed to be more closely tied to the gendered sexual practices of their communities of origin, which may or may not impose more restrictions on young women than are found in U.S. Latina/o communities.

32. This finding supports the results of a survey conducted by Tolman and her colleagues on girls' sexual agency and sexual health. Tolman and colleagues found that "conventional femininity ideology may function as a barrier-and, conversely, that critique of femininity ideology may offer a booster-to adolescent girls' sexual health" (Tolman, 1999, p. 137).

33. Brown, 2003; Levy, 2005; Tanenbaum, 2000; Tolman, 1996; Wilkins, 2004.

34. It was not uncommon during the course of my fieldwork for me to hear some Latina/o youth tease someone for "acting white" for different reasons, whether dancing skills, style of dress, or way of speaking. Other researchers have also documented this type of interaction among youth of color; see, for instance, Bettie, 2003; Fordham and Ogbu, 1986; Pascoe, 2007.

35. Diamond, 2005.

36. See Brown, 2003; Bettie, 2003; Jones, 2010; Lees, 1993; Schaffner, 2006; Tanenbaum, 2000; Tolman, 1996; Wilkins, 2004.

37. Brown, 2003, p. 32.

38. In the quote I use, the sociologist Amy Wilkins is specifically discussing how girls of color (Puerto Rican and black young women) participate in

their own sexual subordination. Wilkins is referring to the "reversal of the racial hierarchy," in which the boys of color in her study "use" white women who are seen as "Puerto Rican Wannabes" for sex to protect the virtue of girls of color (as white men have done to women of color to safeguard the sexual virtue of white women). Wilkins asserts that when girls of color also construct white women as "whores" who are disposable and position themselves as morally superior, they reproduce a sexual double standard for women and "buy into their own sexual subordination" (Wilkins, 2004, p. 115). Other scholars have also offered analyses of women's judgment of women, particularly their evaluation of sexual expressions, as reflecting internalized oppression that serves to strengthen men's domination over women in society because women are pitted against one another. See for instance, Brown, 2003; Lees, 1993; Tolman, 1996.

39. Moore and Rosenthal, 1993, p. 68.

40. As Aapola, Gonick, and Harris note, study of the friendships among young women have focused on problems or conflicts in these friendships, disregarding how young women can be resources for one another (Aapola, Gonick, and Harris, 2005, p. 119).

41. Many of the young women reported that they were not allowed to date and/ or have boyfriends yet.

42. Rich, 1980; Rubin, 1975; Zavella, 2003.

43. Hillier, 2002; Raymond, 1994.

44. See, for instance, Deutsch, 2007; Lorber, 1994; Lorber, 2005; Lucal, 1999; Martin, 2003; Risman, 1998; West and Zimmerman, 1987.

45. I am building on Amy Wilkins's observation that, while research has provided some insight into how racial, gender, and class categories are contested and may fluctuate, we also need to focus our attention on how "fluctuations on one boundary construct and deconstruct other boundaries" (Wilkins, 2004, p. 120).

CHAPTER 5

1. Amaro, 1994; Amaro and Raj, 2000; Angulo-Ortiz, 2009; Bowleg, Belgrave, and Reisen, 2000; Gomez and Marín, 1996; Muehlenhard and Rodgers, 1988; O'Sullivan and Allgeier, 1998.

2. Amaro, 1994; Amaro, 1995.

3. Richardson, 2000.

4. At time of interview, thirty-two girls identified their sexual partner as their boyfriend or girlfriend. The remaining eight young women did not characterize their relationship with their sexual partner as a boyfriend/girlfriend relationship but rather described it as a "friend/someone you care about" relationship.

5. While only six young woman (out of forty) reported this type of experience and conversation with partners, it is possible that other young women

also had had their own brushes with "scares" or had had negative outcomes but decided not share this information with me for various reasons. For example, given the stigma associated with having an STD, it is possible that young women chose not to disclose such personal information to me, especially since they self-identified as practicing safe sex and had self-selected to participate in a study about girls' meanings and practices of safe sex. However, this does not mean that young people are less credible than adults in their accounts of their sexual experiences and histories. The possibility that some of the girls chose not to report or even underreported negative sexual-health outcomes reminds us of the challenges in conducting sexuality research.

6. Arnett, 1995; Christensen and Roberts, 1998; Durham, 2004; Milkie, 1994.

7. Durham, 2004, p. 143.

8. Brown and Newcomer, 1991; Durham, 1998; Durham, 2004; Nayak and Kehily, 2008; Vargas, 2009.

9. The self-improvement book was featured on *The Oprah Winfrey Show*, and a film based on the book was released in 2009.

10. Studies focused on girls' consumption of magazines have documented the focus on sex and sexuality in this media form. See, for instance, Duffy and Gotcher, 1995; Durham, 1998.

11. See, for instance, Fine, 1998; Fields, 2008; Connell and Elliott, 2009.

12. Fields, 2008, p. 86.

13. Three heterosexual-identified young women and one-lesbian identified woman did report that their partners initiated and/or willingly participated in safe-sex conversations.

14. In general, girls who used hormonal contraceptives used either the birth control pill or the Depo-Provera injection.

15. See, for instance, Kimmel, Hearn, and Connell, 2005; Majors and Billson, 1992.

16. Asencio, 2002; Martin, 1996; Souza, 1995; Thompson, 1995; Tolman, 2002.

17. Deep-fried snacks filled with vegetables, meat, and seafood.

18. In 1988, the Puerto Rican Cultural Center (PRCC) founded Vida Health Clinic in the Humboldt Park community to respond to Chicago Latina/os' experiences with HIV/AIDS. This initiative is now commonly known as Vida/SIDA and is an HIV/AIDS service organization offering free, anonymous, and confidential HIV and STI testing and counseling, as well as peer education; http://prcc-chgo.org/vidasida/ (accessed July 26, 2010).

19. Connell, 1987.

20. See Anderson, 1990; Bourgois, 1996; Horowitz, 1983; MacLeod, 1987; Vigil, 1988; Young, 2004.

21. Some women also participate in gender-specific public harassment. But, as Carole B. Gardner notes, "Few women have practiced gender-specific public harassment toward strange men with anything like the same sense

of freedom, entitlement, and righteousness that men exhibit, aside from the breach that teen or young adult women sometimes accomplish in groups" (Gardner, 1995, p. 9).

22. Gardner, 1995, p.9.

23. Recently, some observers have attempted to draw attention to public harassment. Hollaback, founded in New York in 2005, provides women with an opportunity to respond to harassment by "outing" their harassers with cell-phone photos and blog posts on Hollaback websites in more than thirty cities. There are antiharassment campaigns—and efforts to draw awareness to the issue (Little, 2010). For instance, Hollaback NYC was also able to partner with New Yorkers for Safe Transit to get the New York Metropolitan Transportation Authority to hang antiharassment ads in subway trains.

24. Pascoe, 2007, pp. 86–87. Pascoe is building on the concept of compulsory heterosexuality, introduced by Adrienne Rich (1980). Rich theorizes heterosexuality as an institution and argues that heterosexuality is not innate but rather an institution that has perpetuated male privilege. Heterosexuality, understood as an institution, organizes women's and men's relationships, including the expectation that women and men will be sexually oriented toward each other. And men and women adopt heterosexual identities and express these identities in a society that rewards those who take up heterosexuality and punishes those who do not, so such mechanisms induce and even compel heterosexual identification and behavior.

25. González-López, 2005, pp. 41-42.

26. Schrock, and Schwalbe, 2009.

27. Twenty of the thirty-two heterosexual-identified girls in this study reported using condoms (although not exclusively condoms in all cases; for instance, some utilized the birth control pill in conjunction with condoms).

28. I do not argue that the girls are focused solely on protecting their sexual reputations. In particular contexts, other reputations may also be available to young women that allow them to navigate their particular circumstances. For instance, Nikki Jones's (2010) research on inner-city African American girls reveals that some girls craft reputations as fighters in their communities as part of their survival strategies in contexts that are characterized by violence. Jones found that some girls may intentionally violate gender expectations to take on a "fighter" identity as a way to address their vulnerability to violence (interpersonal and random), gain respect, and gain more freedom and movement on the street in spaces that usually are more accessible to men. Jones, however, points out that this also may make such young women vulnerable to sanctions for their "gender inappropriate behavior."

29. Asencio, 2002; Dietrich, 1998; Faulker and Mansfield, 2002; Garcia, 2009a; Schalet, 2010; Tolman, 2002.

30. Gagnon and Simon, 1973; Simon and Gagnon, 1987; Taris and Semin, 1997; Weeks, 2003.

31. However, this is not to suggest that boys and girls both stand to gain and lose sexual respectability in the same ways or to the same extent.
32. As introduced by Arlie Hochschild, the concept of a "gender strategy" refers to "a plan of action through which a person tries to solve problems at hand, given the cultural notions of gender at play" (Hoschchild, 1989, p.15).
33. It is important to underscore here that girls' strategies around condoms were elaborated upon at the intersection of gender, sexuality, and age. Most of these girls had male partners who were close to them in age. If their partners were older, the age difference did not exceed three years. Generally, girls with partners who were more than two years older than them reported feeling less power to demand to condoms; this may be because gender inequality and age differences intersected to produce additional disadvantages for these particular young women.
34. Schippers, 2002, p. xiii.
35. Schippers builds on Butler's theorization of gender as a performance.
36. The anthropologist Claudia Fonseca also found that working-class Brazilian women utilized ideas about masculinity and femininity in strategic ways. She explored these women's uses of rumors about unfaithful women and their cuckolded husbands, pointing out that attention to the uses of gossip, particularly about sexual transgression, also provide insight into power relations between women and men (Fonseca, 2003, p. 71).
37. In their narratives, the girls identified two types of relationships as appropriate for virginity loss: those defined by love and those characterized by a mutual sentiment of caring. For further discussion of this point, see Garcia, 2009a.
38. See, for instance, Aaron, Markovic, Danielson, Honnald, Jonasky, and Schmidt, 2001; Power, McNair, and Carr, 2009; Scherzer, 2000.
39. Scherzer, 2000; Stevens, 1998; White and Dull, 1998.
40. The limited research and funding in the area of lesbian sexual health may contribute to the inadequate knowledge that some health care practitioners have with regard to lesbians' risk for STDs (Bauer and Welles, 2001; McNair, 2005).
41. Scherzer, 2000, p. 94.
42. And, yet, it is possible that discussions about conflicting definitions of sex may open up opportunities for sexual communication and alternative constructions of sex among queer-identified youth, given that they are often made invisible in the safe-sex discourses found in school-based sex education.
43. Only two of the lesbian-identified girls' families owned a computer. The rest of these young women relied on public computers available in library and Internet cafes.
44. Lam, Mak, Lindsay, and Russel, 2004.
45. Fields, 2008, pp. 85–87.

46. Tolman, 2002, p. 115.
47. Jackson, 2006, p. 116.
48. Moore, 2008, p. 339.
49. I draw my description of the gender presentations of this group of girls from the categories that the sociologist Mignon Moore lays out in her study of gender presentation among black lesbians (Moore, 2006).

CHAPTER 6

1. Pew Hispanic Center, *Between Two Worlds: How Young Latinos Come of Age in America*, Washington, DC (December 11, 2009).
2. Schalet, 2009, p. 157.
3. Frye, 2003.
4. Frye, 2003, p. 2.
5. Frye, 2003, p. 4.
6. For further discussion on the racialization of Latinas/os, see Almaguer, 2003; Darder and Torres, 1998; Gracia and De Grieff, 2000, Rodríguez Domínguez, 2005.
7. Omi and Winant, 1994; Bonilla-Silva, 1997.
8. hooks, 1992, p. 116.
9. Espiritu, 2001, p. 421
10. Anzaldúa, 1987, p. 42.
11. Abstinence programs will still receive a $50 million annual federal grant; states can apply for these grants, which require them to provide $3 for every $4 of federal aid.
12. Valenzuela, 1999.
13. Schalet, 2010, p. 158.

APPENDIX B

1. In the interest of preserving group cohesion and trust in the Entre Nosotras program, the program coordinator rightfully restricted my access to this group, even as a volunteer. In this space, I was allowed only to introduce myself and my project and to provide my contact information.
2. Tolman, 2001; Way, 1996.
3. Glaser and Strauss, 1967.
4. See, for instance, Collins, 1994; Espiritu, 2001; Segura and Pierce, 1994.
5. Taylor, Gilligan, and Sullivan, 1995, p. 74.
6. See Acker, Berry, and Esseveld, 1991; Oakley, 1981; Reinharz, 1992.
7. Pérez, 1991, p. 175.

Aapola, Sinikka, Marnina Gonick, and Anita Harris. 2005. *Young Femininity: Girl-hood, Power, and Social Change.* New York: Palgrave Macmillan.

Aaron, Deborah J., Nina Markovic, Michelle E. Danielson, Julie A. Honnold, Janine E. Janosky, and Nancy J. Schmidt. 2001. "Behavioral Risk Factors for Disease and Preventative Health Practices among Lesbians." *American Journal of Public Health* 91(6): 972–975.

Acker, Joan, Kate Barry, and Johanna Esseveld. 1991. "Objectivity and Truth: Prob-lems in Doing Feminist Research." In *Beyond Methodology: Feminist Scholar-ship as Lived Research*, edited by Mary M. Fonow and Judith A. Cook, 133–153. Bloomington: Indiana University Press.

Alarcón, Norma. 1981. "Chicana's Feminist Literature: A Re-vision through Malintzin/or Malintzin: Putting Flesh Back on the Object." In *This Bridge Called My Back: Writings by Radical Women of Color*, edited by Cherríe Moraga and Gloria Anzaldúa, 182 90. Watertown, MA: Persephone Press.

Alicea, Marixsa. 1997. "A Chambered Nautilus: The Contradictory Nature of Puerto Rican Women's Role in the Social Construction of a Transnational Community." *Gender & Society* 11(5): 597–626.

Almaguer, Tomás. 1994. *Racial Fault Lines: The Historical Origins of White Supremacy in California.* Berkeley: University of California Press.

Almaguer, Tomás. 2003. "At the Crossroads of Race: Latino/a Studies and Race Making in the United States." In *Critical Latin American and Latino Studies*, edited by Juan Poblete, 206–222. Minneapolis: University of Minnesota Press.

Amaro, Hortensia. 1994. "Gender and Sexual Risk Reduction: Issues to Consider." Proceedings from the National HIV/AIDS Research Conference, Defining the Path for Future Research, April 23–24, 1994. http://latino.sscnet.ucla.edu/research/aids/conf/genderse.htm (accessed January 25, 2006).

Amaro, Hortensia. 1995. "Love, Sex, and Power: Considering Women's Realities in HIV *Prevention.*" *American Psychologist* 50(6): 437–447.

Amaro, Hortensia, and Anita Raj. 2000. "On the Margin: Power and Women's HIV Risk and Reduction Strategies." *Sex Roles* 42(7/8): 723–749.

Anderson, Elijah. 1990. *Race, Class, and Change in an Urban Community.* Chi-cago: University of Chicago Press.

Angulo-Ortiz, Francisca. 2009. "The Role of Pap Smears in Negotiating Risk: Lati-nas' Perceptions of Trust and Love in Sexual Relationships with Men." *National Women's Studies Association Journal* 21(3): 166–190.

Anzaldúa, Gloria. 1987. *Borderlands/La Frontera: The New Mestiza*. San Francisco: Aunt Lute.

Arnett, J. 1995. "Adolescents' Uses of Media for Self-Socialization." *Journal of Youth and Adolescence* 24: 519–530.

Asencio, Marysol. 2002. *Sex and Sexuality among New York's Puerto Rican Youth*. Boulder, CO: Lynne Rienner.

Ayala, Jennifer. 2006. "Confianza, Consejos, and Contradictions: Gender and Sexuality Lessons between Latina Adolescent Daughters and Mothers." In *Latina Girls: Voices of Adolescent Strength in the United States*, edited by Jill Denner and Bianca L. Guzmán, 29–43. New York: New York University Press.

Baca Zinn, Maxine. 1979. "Field Research in Minority Communities: Ethical, Methodological and Political Observations by an Insider." *Social Problems* 27: 209–219.

Baker, Joanne. 2010. "Great Expectations and Post-Feminist Accountability: Young Women Living Up to the 'Successful Girls' Discourse." *Gender and Education* 22(1): 1–15.

Baldassare, Mark, Dean Bonner, Jennifer Paluch, and Sonja Petek. 2009. "PPIC Statewide Survey: Californians and Population Issues." Public Policy Institute of California.

Banks, Ingrid. 2000. *Hair Matters: Beauty, Power, and Black Women's Consciousness*. New York: New York University Press.

Barton, Colleen. 2007. "Whispers in the Walls: Unspoken Words in the Public School Fortress." *American Journal of Sexuality Education* 2(1): 21–37.

Bauer, G., and S. Welles. 2001. "Beyond Assumptions of Negligible Risk: Sexually Transmitted Diseases and Women Who Have Sex with Women." *American Journal of Public Health* 91(8): 1282–1286.

Behrendt, Greg, and Liz Tuccillo. 2004. *He's Just Not That into You: The No-Excuses Truth to Understanding Guys*. New York: Simon Spotlight Entertainment.

Bettie, Julie. 2003. *Women without Class: Girls, Race, and Identity*. Berkeley: University of California Press.

Bolak, Hale. 1996. "Studying One's Own in the Middle East: Negotiating Gender and Self-Other Dynamics in the Field." *Qualitative Sociology* 19: 107–130.

Bonilla, Dulce Reyes. 2005. "Let's Talk about Sexo." Color Lines: News for Action. http://www.colorlines.com/article.php?ID=35 (accessed April 16, 2010).

Bonilla-Silva, Eduardo. 1997. "Rethinking Racism: Toward a Structural Interpretation." *American Sociological Review* 62: 465–480.

Boonstra, Heather D. 2007. "The Case for a New Approach to Sex Education Mounts: Will Policymakers Heed the Message?" *Guttmacher Policy Review* 10 (2): 2–7.

Bourgois, Philippe. 1996. *In Search of Respect: Selling Crack in El Barrio*. Cambridge: Cambridge University Press.

Bowleg, Lisa, Faye Z. Belgrave, and Carol A. Reisen. 2000. "Gender Roles, Power Strategies, and Precautionary Sexual Self-Efficacy: Implications for Black and Latina Women's HIV/AIDS Protective Behaviors." *Sex Roles* 42 (7/8): 613–635.

Briggs, Laura. 2002. *Reproducing Empire: Race, Sex, Science, and U.S. Imperialism in Puerto Rico*. Berkeley: University of California Press.

Brooks-Gunn, Jeanne, and Paikoff, Roberta. 1997. "Sexuality and Developmental Transitions during Adolescence." In *Health Risks and Developmental Transitions during Adolescence*, edited by John Schulenberg, Jennifer L. Maggs, and Klaus Hurrelman, Laurie Chassin, 190–219. Cambridge: Cambridge University Press.

Brown, Jane D., and Susan F. Newcomer. 1991. "Television Viewing and Adolescents' Sexual Behavior." *Journal of Homosexuality* 21: 77–92.

Brown, Lyn Mikel. 2003. *Girlfighting: Betrayal and Rejection among Girls*. New York: New York University Press.

Burns, April, and Maria Elena Torre. 2004. "Shifting Desires: Discourses of Accountability in Abstinence Only Education in the United States." In *All about the Girl: Culture, Power, and Identity*, edited by Anita Harris, 127–137. New York: Routledge.

Butler, Judith. 1990. *Gender Trouble: Feminism and the Subversion of Identity*. New York: Routledge.

Candelario, Ginetta E. B. 2007. *Black behind the Ears: Dominican Racial Identity from Museums to Beauty Shops*. Durham, NC: Duke University Press.

Cantú, Lionel. 2000. "Entre Hombres/Between Men: Latino Masculinities and Homosexualities." In *Gay Masculinities*, edited by Peter Nardi, 224–246. Thousand Oaks, CA: Sage.

Cantú, Lionel. 2009. *The Sexuality of Migration: Border Crossings and Mexican Immigrant Men*. New York: New York University Press.

Carpenter, Laura M. 2005. *Virginity Lost: An Intimate Portrait of First Sexual Experiences*. New York: New York University Press.

Carrillo, Héctor. 2002. *The Night Is Young: Sexuality in Mexico in the Time of AIDS*. Chicago: University of Chicago Press.

Carroll, Rebecca. 1997. *Sugar in the Raw: Voices of Young Black Girls in America*. New York: Crown Trade Paperbacks.

Carter, Prudence L. 2007. *Keepin' It Real: School Success beyond Black and White*. New York: Oxford University Press.

Castillo, Ana. 1994. *Massacre of the Dreamers: Essays on Xicanisma*. Albuquerque: University of New Mexico Press.

Chafetz, Janet Saltzman. 1990. *Gender Equity: An Integrated Theory of Stability and Change*. Newbury Park, CA: Sage.

Chan, Connie S. 1989. "Issues of Identity Development among Asian American Lesbians and Gay Men." *Journal of Counseling and Development* 68(1): 16–21.

Chapa, Jorge. 1988. "The Question of Mexican American Assimilation: Socioeconomic Parity of Underclass Formation?" *Public Affairs Comment* 35(1): 1–14.

Chase-Lansdale, P. Lindsay, and Jeanne Brooks-Gunn. 1995. *Escaping from Poverty: What Makes a Difference for Children*. New York: Cambridge University Press.

Chavez, Leo. 2004. "A Glass Half Empty: Latina Reproduction and Public Discourse." *Human Organization* 4(2): 173–188.

Christensen, Peter G., and Donald F. Roberts. 1998: *It's Not Only Rock n' Roll: Popular Music in the Lives of Adolescents*. Creskill, NJ: Hampton.

Cisneros, Sandra. 1992. *Woman Hollering Creek*. Houston: Arte Público Press.

Cohen, Cathy. 1997. "Punks, Bulldaggers, and Welfare Queens: The Radical Potential of Queer Politics." *GLQ: A Journal of Lesbian and Gay Studies* 3: 437–465.

Collins, Patricia Hill. 1990. *Black Feminist Thought: Knowledge, Consciousness, and the Politics of Empowerment*. New York: Routledge.

Collins, Patricia Hill. 1991. "Learning from the Outsider Within: The Sociological Significance of Black Feminist Thought." In *Beyond Methodology: Feminist Scholarship as Lived Research*, edited by Mary Margaret Fonow and Judith A. Cook, 35–59. Bloomington: Indiana University Press.

Collins, Patricia Hill. 2004. *Black Sexual Politics: African Americans, Gender, and the New Racism*. New York: Routledge.

Collins, Randall. 2004. *Interaction Ritual Chains*. Princeton, NJ: Princeton University Press.

Connell, Catherine, and Sinikka Elliott. 2009. "Beyond the Birds and the Bees: Learning Inequality through Sexuality Education." *American Journal of Sexuality Education* 4(2): 83–102.

Connell, R. W. 1987. *Gender and Power: Society, the Person, and Sexual Politics*. Stanford: Stanford University Press.

Corsaro, William. 2005. *The Sociology of Childhood*. 2nd ed. Thousand Oaks, CA: Pine Forge Press.

Crenshaw, Kimberle. 1989. "Demarginalizing the Intersection of Race and Sex: A Black Feminist Critique of Antidiscrimination Doctrine, Feminist Theory, and Antiracist Politics." *University of Chicago Legal Forum* 1989: 139–167.

Darder, Antonia, and Rodolfo D. Torres. 1998. "Latinos and Society: Culture, Politics, and Class." In *The Latino Studies Reader: Culture, Economy, and Society*, edited by Antonia Darder and Rodolfo D. Torres, 3–26. Malden, MA: Blackwell.

Darroch, Jacqueline E., David J. Landry, and Susheela Singh. 2000. "Changing Emphases in Sexuality Education in U.S. Public Secondary Schools, 1988–1999." *Family Planning Perspectives* 32(5): 204–212.

De Genova, Nicholas, and Ana Y. Ramos-Zayas. 2003. *Latino Crossings: Mexicans, Puerto Ricans, and the Politics of Race and Citizenship*. New York: Routledge.

D'Emilio, John. 1983. "Capitalism and Gay Identity." In *Powers of Desire: The Politics of Sexuality*, edited by Ann Snitow, Christine Stansell, and Sharon Thompson, 100–116. New York: Monthly Review Press.

Denner, Jill, and Bianca L. Guzmán, eds. 2006. *Latina Girls: Voices of Adolescent Strength in the United States*. New York: New York University Press.

Deutsch, Francine. 2007. "Undoing Gender." *Gender & Society* 21(1): 106–127.

Diamond, Lisa. 2005. "I'm Straight, but I Kissed a Girl": The Trouble with American Media Representations of Female-Female Sexuality. *Feminism and Psychology* 15(1): 104–110.

Dietrich, Lisa C. 1998. *Chicana Adolescents: Bitches, 'Ho's, and Schoolgirls*. Westport, CT: Praeger.

Douglas, Susan J., and Meredith W. Michaels. 2004. *The Mommy Myth: The Idealization of Motherhood and How It Has Undermined All Women*. New York: Simon and Schuster.

Duffy, Margaret, and J. Michael Gotcher. 1995. "Crucial Advice on How to Get the Guy: The Rhetorical Vision of Power and Seduction in the Teen Magazine *YM*." *Journal of Communication Inquiry* 20: 32–47.

Dunn, Jennifer L. 1998. "Defining Woman: Notes toward an Understanding of Structure and Agency in the Negotiation of Sex." *Journal of Contemporary Ethnography* 26(4): 479–510.

Durham, Meenakshi G. 1998. "Dilemmas of Desire: Representations of Adolescent Sexuality in Two Teen Magazines." *Youth and Society* 29: 369–389.

Durham, Meenakshi G. 2004. "Constructing the 'New Ethnicities': Media, Sexuality, and Diaspora Identity in the Lives of South Asian Immigrant Girls." *Critical Studies in Media Communication* 21(2): 140–161.

Elliott, Sinikka. 2010. "Talking to Teens about Sex: Mothers Negotiate Resistance, Discomfort, and Ambivalence." *Sexuality Research and Social Policy* 7(4): 310–322.

Ericksen, Julia A., with Sally A. Steffan. 1999. *Kiss and Tell: Surveying Sex in the Twentieth Century*. Cambridge, MA: Harvard University Press.

Espín, Oliva M. 1991. *Women Crossing Boundaries: A Psychology of Immigration and Transformations of Sexuality*. New York: Routledge.

Espiritu, Yen Le. 2001. "'We Don't Sleep Around Like White Girls Do': Family, Culture, and Gender in Filipina American Lives." *Signs* 26: 415–440.

Faulkner, Sandra L., and Phyllis Kernoff Mansfield. 2002. "Reconciling Messages: The Process of Sexual Talk for Latinas." *Qualitative Health Research* 12(3): 310–328.

Ferguson, Ann A. 2000. *Bad Boys: Public Schools in the Making of Black Masculinity*. Ann Arbor: University of Michigan Press.

Fields, Jessica. 2007. "Knowing Girls: Gender and Learning in School-Based Sexuality Education." In *Sexual Inequalities and Social Justice*, edited by Niels Teunis and Gilbert Herdt, 66–85. Berkeley: University of California Press.

Fields, Jessica. 2008. *Risky Lessons: Sex Education and Social Inequality*. New Brunswick, NJ: Rutgers University Press.

Fields, Jessica, and Deborah L. Tolman. 2006. "Risky Business: Sexuality Education and Research in U.S. Schools." *Sexuality Research and Social Policy* 3(4): 63–76.

Fine, Michelle. 1988. "Sexuality, Schooling, and Adolescent Females: The Missing Discourse Desire." *Harvard Educational Review* 58: 29–53.

Fine, Michelle, and Sara I. McClelland. 2006. "Sexuality Education and Desire: Still Missing Discourse of Desire." *Harvard Educational Review* 76(3): 297–337.

Fine, Michelle, Lois Weis, and Rosemary Roberts. 2000. "Refusing the Betrayal: Latinas Redefining Gender, Sexuality, Culture, and Resistance." *Education/ Pedagogy/Cultural Studies* 22: 87–119.

Flores-González, Nilda. 1999. "Puerto Rican High Achievers: An Example of Ethnic and Academic Identity Compatibility." *Anthropology and Education Quarterly* 30(3): 343–362.

Fonseca, Claudia. 2003. "Philanderers, Cuckolds, and Wily Women: Reexaming Gender Relations in a Brazilian Working-Class Neighborhood." In *Changing Men and Masculinities in Latin America*, edited by Matthew C. Gutmann, 61–83. Durham, NC: Duke University Press.

Fordham, Signithia. 1993. "'Those Loud Black Girls': (Black)Women, Silence, and Gender 'Passing' in the Academy." *Anthropology and Education Quarterly* 24(1): 3–32.

Fordham, Signithia, and John U. Ogbu. 1986. "Black Students' School Success: Coping with the Burden of 'Acting White.'" *Urban Review* 18(3): 176–206.

Frankenberg, Ruth. 1993. *White Women, Race Matters: The Social Construction of Whiteness*. Minneapolis: University of Minnesota Press.

Fregoso, Rosa Linda. 1999. "Re-Imagining Chicana Urban Identities in the Public Sphere, Cool Chuca Style." In *Between Woman and Nation: Nationalisms, Transnational Feminisms, and the State*, edited by Caren Kaplan, Norma Alarcón, and Minoo Moallem, 72–91. Durham, NC: Duke University Press.

Furstenberg Jr., Frank F., Thomas D. Cook, Jacquelynne Eccles, Glen H. Elder Jr., and Arnold Sameroff. 1999. *Managing to Make It: Urban Families and Adolescent Success*. Chicago: University of Chicago Press.

Fyre, Marilyn. 2003. "Oppression." In *Privilege: A Reader*, edited by Michael Kimmel and Abby Ferber, 13–21. Boulder, CO: Westview Press.

Gagnon, John, and William Simon. 1973. *Sexual Conduct: The Social Sources of Human Sexuality*. Chicago: Aldine.

Gagnon, John, and William Simon. 2003. "Sexual Scripts: Origins, Influences, and Changes." *Qualitative Sociology* 26(4): 491–497.

Gándara, Patricia C. 1995. *Over the Ivy Walls: The Educational Mobility of Low-Income Chicanos*. Albany: State University of New York Press.

Garcia, Lorena. 2001. "Sexuality and Responsibility: A Case Study of Sexual
    Agency among Latina Adolescents." M.A. thesis, Sociology Department, Uni-
    versity of California at Santa Barbara.
Garcia, Lorena. 2009a. "Love at First Sex: Latina Girls' Meanings of Virginity
    Loss and Relationships." *Identities: Global Studies in Culture and Power* 16(5):
    601–621.
Garcia, Lorena. 2009b. "'Now Why Do You Want to Know about That?': Het-
    eronormativity, Sexism, and Racism in the Sexual (Mis)Education of Latina
    Youth." *Gender & Society* 23(4): 520–541.
Garcia, Lorena, and Mérida Rúa. 2007. "Processing Latinidad: Mapping Latino
    Urban Landscapes through Chicago Ethnic Festivals." *Latino Studies* 5(3):
    317–339.
Gardner, Carole B. 1995. *Passing By: Gender and Public Harrassment.* Berkeley:
    University of California Press.
Gibbs, Jewelle Taylor. 1985. "City Girls: Psychosocial Adjustment of Urban
    Black Adolescent Females." *SAGE: A Scholarly Journal on Black Women* 2(2):
    28–36.
Glaser, Barney G., and Anselm Strauss. 1967. *The Discovery of Grounded Theory:
    Strategies for Qualitative Research.* Chicago: Aldine.
Gómez, Cynthia A., and Barbara VanOss Marín. 1996. "Gender, Culture, and
    Power: Barriers to HIV Prevention Strategies for Women." *Journal of Sex
    Research* 33: 355–362.
Gonzalez-López, Gloria. 2003. "De Madres a Hijas: Gendered Lessons on Virgin-
    ity across Generations of Mexican Immigrant Women." In *Gender and U.S.
    Migration: Contemporary Trends*, edited by Pierrette Hondagneu-Sotelo,
    217–240. Berkeley: University of California Press.
González-López, Gloria. 2005. *Erotic Journeys: Mexican Immigrants and Their Sex
    Lives.* Berkeley: University of California Press.
González-López, Gloria, and Salvador Vidal-Ortiz. 2008. "Latinas and Latinos,
    Sexuality, and Society: A Critical Sociological Perspective." In *Latinas/os in
    the United States: Changing the Face of America*, edited by Havidán Rodríguez,
    Rogelio Sáenz, and Cecilia Menjívar, 308–322. New York: Springer.
Gracia, Jorge J. E., and Pablo De Greiff, eds. 2000. "An Introduction." In *Hispanic/
    Latino Ethnicity, Race, and Rights*, 1–22. New York: Routledge.
Gutiérrez, Elena R. 2008. *Fertile Matters: The Politics of Mexican-Origin Women's
    Reproduction.* Austin: University of Texas Press.
Guzmán, Manolo. 2006. *Gay Hegemony/Latino Homosexualities.* New York:
    Routledge.
Hamilton, Laura. 2007. "Trading on Heterosexuality: College Women's Gender
    Strategies and Homophobia." *Gender & Society* 21(2): 145–172.
Harris, Anita. 2004. *Future Girl: Young Women in the Twenty-First Century.* New
    York: Routledge.

Hays, Sharon. 1996. *The Cultural Contradictions of Motherhood*. New Haven: Yale University Press.

Hernández, Daisy, and Bushra Rehman, eds. 2002. *Colonize This!: Young Women of Color on Today's Feminism*. New York: Seal Press.

Higginbotham, Evelyn Brooks. 1993. *Righteous Discontents: The Women's Movement in the Black Baptist Church, 1880–1920*. Cambridge, MA: Harvard University Press.

Hillier, Lynne. 2002. "It's a Catch-22": Same-Sex Attracted Young People on Coming Out to Parents." *New Directions for Child and Adolescent Development* 97: 73–91.

Hillier, Lynne, Lyn Harrison, and Deborah Warr. 1988. "'When You Carry Condoms All the Boys Think You Want It': Negotiating Competing Discourses about Safe Sex." *Journal of Adolescence* 21: 15–29.

Hine, Darlene Clark. 1994. *Hine Site: Black Women and the Re-Construction of American History*. Brooklyn, NY: Carlson.

Hirsch, Jennifer S. 2003. *A Courtship after Marriage: Sexuality and Love in Mexican Transnational Families*. Berkeley: University of California Press.

Hochschild, Arlie Russell. 1989. *The Second Shift*. New York: Avon Books.

Hochschild, Arlie R. 1994. "The Commercial Spirit of Intimate Life and the Abduction of Feminism: Signs from Women's Advice Books." *Theory, Culture and Society* 11(1): 1–24.

Hondagneu-Sotelo, Pierrette.1994. *Gendered Transitions: Mexicans Experiences of Immigration*. Berkeley: University of California Press.

hooks, bell. 1984. *Feminist Theory: From Margin to Center*. Boston: South End Press.

hooks, bell. 1992. "The Oppositional Gaze: Black Female Spectators." In *Black Looks: Race and Representation*, 115–131. Boston: South End Press.

Horn, Stacey S. 2007. "Adolescents' Acceptance of Same Sex Peers Based on Sexual Orientation and Gender Expression." *Journal of Youth and Adolescence* 36: 363–371.

Horn, Stacey, Erica Meiners, Connie North, Therese Quinn, and Shannon Sullivan. 2009. "Visibility Matters: Higher Education and Teacher Preparation in Illinois: A Web-Based Assessment of LGBTQ Presence." The Illinois Safe Schools Alliance. http://www.illinoissafeschools.org/page_attachments/0000/0116/visibility_matters_full_report_final.pdf.

Horowitz, Ruth. 1983. Honor and the American Dream: Culture and Identity in a Chicano Community. New Brunswick, NJ: Rutgers University Press.

Hubbard, Lea. 1999. "College Aspirations among Low-Income African American High School Students: Gendered Strategies for Success." *Anthropology and Educational Quarterly* 30(3): 363–383.

Hubbard, Lea. 2005. "The Role of Gender in Academic Achievement." *International Journal of Qualitative Studies in Education* 18(5): 605–623.

Hurtado, Aída. 1996. *The Color of Privilege: Three Blasphemies on Race and Feminism*. Ann Arbor: University of Michigan Press.

Hurtado, Aída. 1998. "The Politics of Sexuality in the Gender Subordination of Chicanas." In *Living Chicana Theory*, edited by Carla Trujillo, 383–428. Berkeley: Third Woman Press.

Hurtado, Aida. 2003. *Voicing Chicana Feminisms: Young Women Speak Out on Sexuality and Identity*. New York: New York University Press.

Hurtado, Aída, David E. Hayes-Bautista, R. Burciaga Valdez, and Anthony C. R. Hernandez. 1992. *Redefining California: Latino Social Engagement in a Multicultural Society*. Los Angeles: UCLA Chicano Studies Research Center.

Hutchinson, Mary K. 2001. "The Influence of Sexual Risk Communication between Parents and Daughters on Sexual Risk Behaviors." *Family Relations* 51: 238–257.

Hyams, Melissa. 2006. "La Escuela: Young Latina Women Negotiating Identities in School." In *Latina Girls: Voices of Adolescent Strength in the United States*, edited by Jillian Denner and Bianca. L. Guzmán, 93–108. New York: New York University Press.

Inda, Jonathan X. 2002. "Biopower, Reproduction and the Migrant Woman's Body." In *Decolonial Voices: Chicana and Chicano Cultural Studies in the 21st Century*, edited by Arturo J. Aldama and Naomi. Quiñonez, 98–112. Bloomington: University of Indiana Press.

Ingraham, Chrys. 1994. "The Heterosexual Imaginary: Feminist Sociology and Theories of Gender." *Sociological Theory* 12(2): 203–219.

Irvine, Janice M. 1994. "Cultural Differences and Adolescent Sexualities." In *Sexual Cultures and the Construction of Adolescent Identities*, edited by Janice M. Irvine, 3–28. Philadelphia: Temple University Press.

Irvine, Janice. 2002. *Talk about Sex: The Battles over Sex Education in the United States*. Berkeley: University of California Press.

Islam, Naheed. 2000. "Research as an Act of Betrayal: Researching Race in an Asian Community in Los Angeles." In *Racing Research Researching Race: Methodological Dilemmas in Critical Race Studies*, edited by France Winddance Twine and Jonathan W. Warren, 35–66. New York: New York University Press.

Jaccard, James, Patricia J. Dittus, and Vivian Gordon. 2000. "Parent-Teen Communication about Premarital Sex." *Journal of Adolescent Research* 15(2): 187–208.

Jackson, Stevi. 2006. "Interchanges: Gender, Sexuality, and Heterosexuality: The Complexity (and Limits) of Heteronormativity." *Feminist Theory* 7(1): 105–121.

Jacob, Iris, ed. 2002. *My Sisters' Voices: Teenage Girls of Color Speak Out*. New York: Holt.

Jarrett, Robin L. 1994. "Living Poor: Family Life among Single-Parent, African American Women." *Social Problems* 41(1): 30–49.

Jones, Nikki. 2010. *Between Good and Ghetto: African American Girls and Inner-City Violence*. New Brunswick, NJ: Rutgers University Press.

Jones-Correa, Michael. 2002. "The Study of Transnationalism among the Children of Immigrants: Where We Are and Where We Should be Headed." In *The Changing Face of Home: The Transnational Lives of the Second Generation*, edited by Peggy Levitt and Marcy C. Waters, 221–241. New York: Russell Sage Foundation.

Kandiyoti, Deniz. 1988. "Bargaining with Patriarchy." *Gender & Society* 2(3): 274–290.

Kaplan, Elaine Bell. 1997. *Not Our Kind of Girl: Unraveling the Myths of Black Teenage Motherhood*. Berkeley: University of California Press.

Kasinitz, Philip, Mary C. Waters, John H. Mollenkopf, and Merih Anil. 2002. "Transnationalism and the Children of Immigrants in Contemporary New York." In *The Changing Face of Home: The Transnational Lives of the Second Generation*, edited by Peggy Levitt and Marcy C. Waters, 96–122. New York: Russell Sage Foundation.

Khayatt, Didi. 1995. "Compulsory Heterosexuality: Schools and Lesbian Students." In *Knowledge, Experience, and Ruling Relations: Studies in the Social Organization of Knowledge*, edited by M. Campbell and Ann Manicom, 149–163. Toronto: University of Toronto Press.

Kimmel, Michael, Jeff Hearn, and R. W. Connell. 2005. *Handbook of Studies on Men andMasculinities*. Thousand Oaks, CA: Sage.

Kirkman, Maggie, Doreen A. Rosenthal, and Shirley Feldman. 2002. "Talking to a Tiger: Fathers Reveal their Difficulties in Communicating about Sexuality with Adolescents." *New Directions for Child and Adolescent Development, Special Issue, Talking Sexuality: Parent-Adolescent Communication* 97: 57–74.

Kumashiro, Kevin K. 2001. "Queer Students of Color and Antiracist, Antiheterosexist Education: Paradoxes of Identity and Activism." In *Troubling Intersections of Race and Sexuality: Queer Students of Color and Anti-Oppressive Education*, edited by Kevin K. Kumashiro, 1–26. Lanham: Rowman and Littlefield.

Lam, Amy G., Amy Mak, Patricia D. Lindsay, and Stephen T. Russell. 2004. "What Really Works?: An Exploratory Study of Condom Negotiation Strategies." *AIDS Education and Prevention* 16(2): 160–171.

Lamont, Michèle. 2002. "Culture and Identity." In *Handbook of Sociological Theory*, edited by Jonathan H. Turner, 171–185. New York: Kluwer Academic/Plenum Publishers.

Lamont, Michèle, and Virág Molnár. 2002. "The Study of Boundaries in the Social Sciences." *Annual Review of Sociology* 28: 167–195.

Latina Feminist Group. 2001. *Telling to Live: Latina Feminist Testimonios*. Durham, NC: Duke University Press.

Leadbeater, Bonnie J. Ross, and Niobe Way, eds. 1996. *Urban Girls: Resisting Stereotypes, Creating Identities*. New York: New York University Press.

Leadbeater, Bonnie J. Ross, and Niobe Way, eds. 2007. *Urban Girls Revisited: Building Strengths*. New York: New York University Press.

Lees, Sue. 1993. *Sugar and Spice: Sexuality and Adolescent Girls*. London: Penguin.

Levenson-Gingiss, Phyllis, and Richard Hamilton. 1989. "Evaluation of Training Effect on Teacher Attitudes and Concerns Prior to Implementing a Human Sexuality Education Program." *Journal of School Health* 59(4): 156–160.

Levy, Ariel. 2005. *Female Chauvinist Pigs: Women and the Rise of Raunch Culture*. New York: Free Press.

Lipman, Pauline. 2004. *High Stakes Education: Inequality, Globalization, and Urban School Reform*. New York: Routledge Falmer.

Little, Anita. 2010. "Hollaback Goes Global: Here's What to Do When a Perv Hits a Nerve." *Ms.* (Summer): 14.

Lopez, Iris. 2008. *Matters of Choice: Puerto Rican Women's Struggle for Reproductive Freedom*. New Brunswick, NJ: Rutgers University Press.

Lopez, Laura M., and Frances S. Hasso. 1998. "Frontlines and Borders: Identity Thresholds for Latinas and Arab-American Women." In *Everyday Inequalities: Critical Inquiries*, edited by Jodi O'Brien and Judith A. Howard, 253–280. Malden, MA: Blackwell.

Lopez, Nancy. 2003. *Hopeful Girls, Troubled Boys: Race and Gender Disparity in Urban*. New York: Routledge.

Lorber, Judith. 1994. *Paradoxes of Gender*. New Haven: Yale University Press.

Lorber, Judith. 2005. *Breaking the Bowls: Degendering and Feminist Change*. New York: W. W. Norton.

Louie, Vivian. 2006. "Growing Up Ethnic in Transnational Worlds: Identities among Second-Generation Chinese and Dominicans." *Identities: Global Studies in Culture and Power* 13: 363–394.

Lucal, Betsy. 1999. "What It Means to Be Gendered Me: Life on the Boundaries of a Dichotomous Gender System." *Gender & Society* 13(6): 781–797.

Luker, Kristin. 1996. *Dubious Conceptions: The Politics of Teenage Pregnancy*. Cambridge, MA: Harvard University Press.

Luker, Kristin. 2006. *When Sex Goes to School: Warring Views on Sex and Sex Education Since the Sixties*. New York: W. W. Norton.

MacLeod, Jay. 1987. *Ain't No Makin' It: Aspirations and Attainment in a Low-Income Neighbhorhood*. 2nd ed. Boulder, CO: Westview Press.

Majors, Bill, and Janet M. Billson. 1992. *Cool Pose: The Dilemmas of Black Manhood in America*. New York: Lexington Books.

Martin, Joyce A., B. E. Hamilton, P. D. Sutton, S. J. Ventura, F Menacker, and S. Kirmeyer. 2006. "Births: Final Data for 2004." *National Vital Statistics Report* 55(1).

Martin, Karin A. 1996. *Puberty, Sexuality, and the Self: Girls and Boys at Adolescence*. New York: Routledge.

Martin, Karin A. 2003. "Giving Birth Like a Girl." *Gender & Society* 17(1): 54–72.

McNair, Ruth. 2005. "Risks and Prevention of Sexually Transmissible Infections among Women Who Have Sex with Women." *Sexual Health* 2(4): 209–217.

McRobbie, Angela. 1991. *Feminism and Youth Culture: From Jackie to Just Seventeen*. London: Macmillan.

McRobbie, Angela. 2007. "Top Girls? Young Women and the Post-Feminist Sexual Contract." *Cultural Studies* 21 (4–5): 718–737.

Meneses, L. M. 2004. "Ethnic Differences in Mother-Daughter Communication about Sex." *Journal of Adolescent Health* 34(2): 154.

Messner, Michael A. 2000. "Barbie Girls Versus Seas Monsters: Children Constructing Gender." *Gender & Society* 14(6): 765–784.

Mies, Maria. 1983. "Towards a Methodology for Feminist Research." In *Theories of Women's Studies*, edited by Gloria Bowles and Renate Duelli Klein, 117–139. London: Routledge and Kegan Paul.

Milkie, Melissa. 1994. "Social World Approach to Cultural Studies: Mass Media and Gender in the Adolescent Peer Group." *Journal of Contemporary Ethnography* 23: 354–380.

Moore, Mignon R. 2006. "Lipstick or Timberlands? Meanings of Gender Presentation in Black Lesbian Communities." *Signs: Journal of Women in Culture and Society* 32(1): 113–139.

Moore, Mignon R. 2008. "Gendered Power Relations among Women: A Study of Household Decision Making in Black, Lesbian Stepfamilies." *American Sociological Review* 73(2): 335–356.

Moore, Mignon. 2011. *Invisible Families: Gay Identities, Relationships, and Motherhood among Black Woman*. Berkeley: University of California Press.

Moore, Susan, and Doreen Rosenthal. 2003. *Sexuality in Adolescence*. London: Routledge.

Moore, Susan, and Doreen Rosenthal. 2006. *Sexuality in Adolescence: Current Trends*. London: Routledge.

Moran, Jeffrey. 2000. *Teaching Sex: The Shaping of Adolescence in the 20th Century*. Cambridge, MA: Harvard University Press.

Muehlenhard, Charlene L., and Carie S. Rodgers. 1998: "Token Resistance to Sex: New Perspectives on an Old Stereotype." *Psychology of Women Quarterly* 22: 443–446.

Murry, Velma McBride. 1996. "Inner-City Girls of Color: Unmarried, Sexually Active Nonmothers." In *Urban Girls: Resisting Stereotypes, Creating Identities*, edited by Bonnie J. Ross Leadbeater and Niobe Way, 272–290. New York: New York University Press.

Nadeem, Erum, Laura F. Romo, and Marian Sigman. 2006. "Knowledge about Condoms among Low-Income Pregnant Latina Adolescents in Relation to Explicit Maternal Discussion of Contraceptives." *Journal of Adolescent Health* 39: 119.e9–119.e15.

Nagel, Joane. 2001. "Racial, Ethnic, and National Boundaries: Sexual Intersections and Symbolic Interactions." *Symbolic Interaction* 24(2): 123–139.

Nagel, Joane. 2003. *Race, Ethnicity, and Sexuality: Intimate Intersections, Forbidden Frontiers*. New York: Oxford University Press.

Naples, Nancy A. 2003. *Feminism and Method: Ethnography, Discourse Analysis, and Activist Research*. New York: Routledge.

Nathanson, Constance A. 1991. *Dangerous Passage: The Social Control of Sexuality in Women's Adolescence*. Philadelphia: Temple University Press.

Nayak, Anoop, and Mary Jane Kehily, eds. 2008. "Consuming Gender." In *Gender, Youth, and Culture: Young Masculinities and Feminities*, 126–156. New York: Palgrave Macmillan.

Oakley, Ann. 1981. "Interviewing Women: A Contradiction in Terms." In *Doing Feminist Research*, edited by Helen Roberts, 30–61. Boston: Routledge and Kegan Paul.

Ogbu, John U. 1987. "Variability in Minority School Performance: A Problem in Search of an Explanation." *Anthropology and Education Quarterly* 18(4): 312–334.

Ogbu, John U. 1991. "Immigrant and Involuntary Minorities in Comparative Perspective." In *Minority Status and Schooling: A Comparative Study of Immigrant and Involuntary Minorities*, edited by Margaret A. Gibson and John U. Ogbu, 3–33. New York: Garland.

Omi, Michael, and Howard Winant. 1994. *Racial Formations in the United States: From the 1960s to the 1990s*. New York: Routledge.

O'Sullivan, Lucia F., and Elizabeth Rice Allgeier. 1998. "Feigning Sexual Desire: Consenting to Unwanted Sexual Activity in Heterosexual Dating Relationships." *Journal of Sex Research* 35: 243–243.

O'Sullivan, Lucia, F., Meyer-Bahlberg, F. L. Heino, and Beverly Watkins. 2001. "Mother-Daughter Communication about Sex among Urban African-African and Latino Families." *Journal of Adolescent Research* 16: 269–292.

Padilla, Elena. 1947. "Puerto Rican Immigrants in New York and Chicago: A Study in Comparative Assimilation." Ph.D. dissertation, Department of Anthropology, University of Chicago, Chicago.

Padilla, Felix. 1985. *Latino Ethnic Consciousness: The Case of Mexican Americans and Puerto Ricans in Chicago*. Notre Dame, IN: University of Notre Dame Press.

Pardo, Mary S. 1998. *Mexican American Women Activists: Identity and Resistance in Two Los Angeles Communities*. Philadelphia: Temple University Press.

Pascoe, C. J. 2007. *Dude, You're a Fag: Masculinity and Sexuality in High School*. Berkeley: University of California Press.

Pattillo-McCoy, Mary. 1999. *Black Picket Fences: Privilege and Peril among the Black Middle Class*. Chicago: University of Chicago Press.

Patton, Cindy. 1996. *Fatal Advice: How Safe-Sex Education Went Wrong*. Durham, NC: Duke University Press.

Peña, Susana. 2005. "Visibility and Silence: Mariel and Cuban American Gay Male Experience and Presentation." In *Queer Migrations: Sexuality, U.S. Citizenship, and Border Crossings*, edited by Eithne Luibhéid and Lionel Cantú, 125–145. Minneapolis: University of Minnesota Press.

Pérez, Emma. 1991. "Sexuality and Discourse: Notes from a Chicana Survivor." In *Chicana Lesbians: The Girls Our Mothers Warned Us About*, edited by Carla Trujillo, 159–184. Berkeley: Third Woman Press.

Pérez, Gina M. 2003. "Puertorriqueñas Rencorosas y Mejicanas Sufridas: Gendered Ethnic Identity Formation in Chicago's Latino Communities." *Journal of Latin American Anthropology* 8(2): 96–125.

Pérez, Gina M. 2004. *The Near Northwest Side Story: Migration, Displacement, and Puerto Rican Families*. Berkeley: University of California Press.

Pessar, Patricia R. 2003. "Engendering Migration Studies: The Case of New Immigrants in the United States." In *Gender and U.S. Immigration: Contemporary Trends*, edited by Pierrete Hondagneu-Sotelo, 20–42. Berkeley: University of California Press.

Petchesky, Rosalind P. 1984. *Abortion and Woman's Choice: The State, Sexuality, and Reproductive Freedom*. New York: Longman.

Petrovic, John E., and Rebecca M. Ballard. 2005. "Unstraightening the Ideal Girl: Lesbians, High school, and Spaces to Be." In *Geographies of Girlhood: Identities in Between*, edited by Pamela J. Bettis and Natalie G. Adams, 195–210. Mahway, NJ: Lawrence Erlbaum Associates.

Pew Hispanic Center. 2009. *Between Two Worlds: How Young Latinos Come of Age in America*. Washington, DC. December 11.

Pew Hispanic Center and Forum on Religion and Public Life. 2007. Changing Faiths: Latinos and the Transformation of American Religion. Washington, DC. April 25.

Phillips, Lynn M. 2000. *Flirting with Danger: Young Women's Reflections on Sexuality and Domination*. New York: New York University Press.

Portes, Alejandro, and Min Zhou. 1993. "The New Second Generation: Segmented Assimilation and Its Variants." *Annals of the American Academy of Political and Social Science* 530: 74096.

Portes, Alejandro, and Rubén G. Rumbaut. 1990. *Immigrant America: A Portrait*. Berkeley: University of California Press.

Power, Jennifer, Ruth McNair, and Susan Carr. 2009. "Absent Sexual Scripts: Lesbian and Bisexual Women's Knowledge, Attitudes and Action Regarding Safer Sex and Sexual Health Information." *Culture, Health, and Sexuality* 11(1): 67–81.

Ramos-Zayas, Ana Y. 2003. *National Performances: The Politics of Class, Race, and Place in Puerto Rican Chicago*. Chicago: University of Chicago Press.

Raymond, Diane. 1994. "Homophobia, Identity, and the Meanings of Desire: Reflections on the Cultural Construction of Gay and Lesbian Adolescent Sexuality." In *Sexual Cultures and the Construction of Adolescent Identities*, edited by Janice Irvine, 115–150. Philadelphia: Temple University Press.

Reinharz, Schulamit. 1979. *On Becoming a Social Scientist*. San Francisco: Jossey-Bass.

Reinharz Schulamit. 1992. *Feminist Methods in Social Research*. New York: Oxford University Press.

Rich, Adrienne. 1980. "Compulsory Heterosexuality and Lesbian Existence." *Signs: Journal of Women in Culture and Society* 5(4): 631–660.

Richardson, Diane. 2000. "The Social Construction of Immunity: HIV Risk Perception and Prevention among Lesbians and Bisexual Women." *Culture, Health and Sexuality* 2(1): 33–49.

Ridgeway, Cecilia. 2011. *Framed by Gender: How Gender Inequality Persists in the Modern World*. New York: Oxford University Press.

Ringrose, Jessica. 2007. "Successful Girls? Complicating Post-Feminist, Neoliberal Discourses of Educational Achievement and Gender Equality." *Gender and Education* 19(4): 471–489.

Risman, Barbara J. 1998. *Gender Vertigo: American Families in Transition*. New Haven: Yale University Press.

Roberts, Dorothy. 1997. *Killing the Black Body: Race, Reproduction, and the Meaning of Liberty*. New York: Pantheon Books.

Rodríguez, Juana Maria. 2003. *Queer Latinidad: Identity Practices, Discursive Spaces*. New York: New York University Press.

Rodríguez, Monica, Rebecca Young, Stacie Renfro, Marysol Asencio, and Debra Haffner. 1997. "Teaching Our Teachers to Teach: A Study on Preparation for Sexuality Education and HIV/AIDS Prevention." *Journal of Psychology and Human Sexuality* 9(3–4): 121–141.

Rodríguez Domínguez, Victor M. 2005. "The Racialization of Mexican Americans and Puerto Ricans: 1890s–1930s." *CENTRO: Journal of the Center for Puerto Rican Studies* 17(1): 71–105.

Romo, Laura F., Magali Bravo, Maria Elena Cruz, Rebeca M. Rios, and Claudia Kouyoumdjian. 2010. "El Sexo no es Malo": Maternal Values Accompanying Contraceptive Use Advice to Young Latina Adolescent Daughters." *Sexuality Research and Social Policy* 7: 118–127.

Rosenthal, Doreen A., and Feldman, S. Shirley. 1999. "The Importance of Importance: Adolescents' Perceptions of Parental Communication about Sexuality." *Journal of Adolescence* 22(6): 835–852.

Ross, Loretta. 2002. "Just Choices: Women of Color, Reproductive Health, and Human Rights." In *Policing the National Body: Race, Gender, and Criminalization*, edited by Jael Silliman and Anannya Bhattacharjee, 147–174. Boston: South End Press.

Rúa, Merida. 2001. "Colao Subjectivities: PortoMex and MexiRican Perspectives on Language and Identity." *CENTRO: Journal of the Center for Puerto Rican Studies* 13(2): 117–133.

Rubin, Gayle. 1984. "Thinking Sex: Notes for a Radical Theory of the Politics of Sexuality." In *Pleasure and Danger: Exploring Female Sexuality*, edited by Carole S. Vance, 269–319. Boston: Routledge and Kegan Paul.

Rumbaut, Rubén G. 1995. "The New Californians: Comparative Research Findings on the Educational Progress of Immigrant Children." In *California's Immigrant Children: Theory, Research and Implications for Educational Policy*, edited by Rubén G. Rumbaut and Wayne A. Cornelius, 17–70. La Jolla, CA: Center for U.S.-Mexican Studies, University of California, San Diego.

Rumbaut, Rubén G. 2002. "Ties That Bind: Immigration and Immigrant Families in the United States." In *The Changing Face of Home: The Transnational Lives of the Second Generation*, edited by Peggy Levitt and Marcy C. Waters, 43–95. New York: Russell Sage Foundation.

Rust, Paula C. 1996. "Managing Multiple Identities: Diversity among Bisexual Women and Men." In *Bisexuality: The Psychology and Politics of an Invisible Minority*, edited by Beth A. Firestein, 53–83. Thousand Oaks, CA: Sage.

Sandoval, Chela. 1991. "U.S. Third World Feminism: The Theory and Method of Oppositional Consciousness in the Postmodern World." *Genders* 10 (Spring): 1–24.

Santiago, Esmeralda. 1998. *Almost a Woman*. New York: Vintage Books.

Schaffner, Laurie. 2006. *Girls in Trouble with the Law*. New Brunswick, NJ: Rutgers University Press.

Schalet, Amy. 2009. "Subjectivity, Intimacy, and the Empowerment Paradigm of Adolescent Sexuality: The Unexplored Room." *Feminist Studies* 35(1): 133–160.

Schalet, Amy. 2010. "Sexual Subjectivity Revisited: The Significance of Relationships in Dutch and American Girls' Experiences of Sexuality." *Gender & Society* 24(3): 304–329.

Schalet, Amy, Geoffrey Hunt, and Karen Joe-Laidler. 2003. "Respect and Autonomy: The Articulation and the Meaning of Sexuality among the Girls in the Gang." *Journal of Contemporary Ethnography* 32(1): 108–143.

Scherzer, Teresa. 2000. "Negotiating Health Care: The Experiences of Young Lesbian and Bisexual Women." *Culture, Health, and Sexuality* 2(1): 87–102.

Schippers, Mimi. 2002. *Rockin' out of the Box: Gender Maneuvering in Alternative Hard Rock*. New Brunswick, NJ: Rutgers University Press.

Schrock, Doug, and Michael Schwalbe. 2009. "Men, Masculinity, and Manhood Acts." *Annual Review of Sociology* 35: 277–295.

Segura, Denise A. 1994. "Working at Motherhood: Chicana and Mexican Immigrant Mothers and Employment." In *Mothering: Ideology, Experience, and Agency*, edited by Evelyn Nakana Glenn, Grace Chang, and Linda Rennie Forcey, 211–233. New York: Routledge.

Segura, Denise A., and Jennifer Pierce. 1994. "Chicana/o Family Structure and Gender Personality: Chodorow, Familism, and Psychoanalytic Sociology Revisited." *Signs: Journal of Women in Culture and Society* 12(1): 62–91.

Sennett, Richard, and Jonathan Cobb. 1972. *The Hidden Injuries of Class*. New York: Vintage Books.

Sheff, Elisabeth. 2005. "Polyamorous Women, Sexual Subjectivity and Power." *Journal of Contemporary Ethnography* 34(3): 251–283.

Silliman, Jael, Marlene Gerber Fried, Loretta Ross, and Elena R. Gutiérrez. 2004. *Undivided Rights: Women of Color Organize for Reproductive Justice*. Cambridge, MA: South End Press.

Simon, William, and John Gagnon. 1987. "A Sexual Scripts Approach." In *Theories of Human Sexuality*, edited by James H. Geer and William O'Donohue, 363–384. New York: Plenum Press.

Smith, Andrea. 2005. "Beyond Pro-Choice versus Pro-Life: Women of Color and Reproductive Justice." *National Women's Studies Association Journal* 17(1): 119–140.

Somerville, Siobhan. 2000. *Queering the Color Line: Race and the Invention of Homosexuality in American Culture*. Durham, NC: Duke University Press.

South, Scott J,. and Crowder, Kyle D. 1997. "Escaping Distressed Neighborhoods: Individual, Community, and Metropolitan Influences." *American Journal of Sociology* 102(4): 1040–1084.

Souza, Caridad. 1995. "Entre la Casa and la Calle: Adolescent Pregnancy among Puertorriqueñas in a Queens Neighborhood." Ph.D. dissertation, Ethnic Studies Department, University of California at Berkeley.

Stevens, Patricia E. 1998. "The Experiences of Lesbians of Color in Health Care Encounters: Narrative Insights for Improving Access and Quality." In *Gateways to Improving Lesbian Health and Health Care: Opening Doors*, edited by Cristy M. Ponticelli, 77–94. Binghamton, NY: Haworth Press.

Stone, Pamela. 2007. *Opting Out? Why Women Really Quit Careers and Head Home*. Berkeley: University of California Press.

Suárez-Orozco, Marcelo. 1987. "'Becoming Somebody': Central American Immigrants in U.S. Inner-City Schools." *Anthropology and Education Quarterly* 18(4): 287–299.

Suárez-Orozco, Marcelo, and Carola Suárez-Orozco. 1995. *Transformations: Immigration, Family Life, and Achievement Motivation among Latino Adolescents*. Stanford: Stanford University Press.

Suárez Findlay, Eileen J. 1999. *Imposing Decency: The Politics of Sexuality and Race in Puerto Rico, 1870–1920*. Durham, NC: Duke University Press.

Swidler, Ann. 1986. "Culture in Action: Symbols and Strategies." *American Sociological Review* 51(2): 273–286.

Swidler, Ann. 2001. *Talk of Love: How Culture Matters*. Chicago: University of Chicago Press.

Tanenbaum, Leora. 2000. *Slut! Growing up Female with a Bad Reputation*. New York: Perennial.

Taris, Toon W., and Günn R. Semin. 1997. "Gender as a Moderator of the Effect of the Love Motive and Relational Context on Sexual Experience." *Archives of Sexual Behavior* 26 (2): 159–180.

Taylor, Jill McLean, Carol Gilligan, and Amy M.Sullivan. 1995. *Between Voice and Silence: Women and Girls, Race and Relationships*. Cambridge, MA: Harvard University Press.

Thompson, Sharon. 1995. *Going All the Way: Teenage Girls' Tales of Sex, Romance, and Pregnancy*. New York: Hill and Wang.

Tolman, Deborah L. 1994. "Doing Desire: Adolescent Girls' Struggles for/with Sexuality." *Gender & Society* 8(3): 324–342.

Tolman, Deborah L. 1996. "Adolescent Girls' Sexuality: Debunking the Myth of the Urban Girl." In *Urban Girls: Resisting Stereotypes, Creating Identities*, edited by Bonnie J. Ross Leadbeater and Niobe Way, 255–271. New York: New York University Press.

Tolman, Deborah L. 1999. "Femininity as a Barrier to Positive Health for Adolescent Girls." *Journal of American Medical Women's Association* 54: 133–138.

Tolman, Deborah L. 2001. "Echoes of Sexual Objectification: Listening for One Girl's Erotic Voice." In *From Subjects to Subjectivities: A Handbook of Interpretive and Participatory Methods*, edited by Deborah L. Tolman and Mary Bryndon-Miller, 130–144. New York: New York University Press.

Tolman, Deborah L. 2002. *Dilemmas of Desire: Teenage Girls Talk about Sexuality*. Cambridge, MA: Harvard University Press.

Toro-Morn, Maura I., and Marixsa Alicea. 2003. "Gendered Geographies of Home: Mapping Second- and Third-Generation Puerto Ricans' Sense of Home." In *Gender and U.S. Immigration: Contemporary Trends*, edited by Pierrette Hondagneu-Sotelo,194–216. Berkeley: University of California Press.

Trudell, Bonnie N. 1993. *Doing Sex Education: Gender Politics and Schooling*. New York: Routledge.

Trujillo, Carla. 1991. "Chicana Lesbians: Fear and Loathing in the Chicano Community." In *The Girls Our Mothers Warned Us About*, edited by Carla Trujillo, 186–194. Berkeley: Third Woman Press.

Valenzuela, Angela. 1999. *Subtractive Schooling: U.S.-Mexican Youth and the Politics of Caring*. New York: State University of New York Press.

Vargas, Lucila. 2009. *Latina Teens, Migration, and Popular Culture*. New York: Peter Lang.

Vigil, James Diego. 1988. *Barrio Gangs: Street Life and Identity in Southern California*. Austin: University of Texas Press.

Walton, Gerald. 2005. "The Hidden Curriculum in Schools: Implications for Lesbian, Gay, Bisexual, Transgender, and Queer Youth." *Alternate Routes* 21: 18–29.

Way, Niobe. 1996. "Between Experiences of Betrayal and Desire: Close Friendships among Urban Adolescents." In *Urban Girls: Resisting Stereotypes, Creating Identities*, edited by Bonnie J. Ross Leadbeater and Niobe Way, 173–192. New York: New York University Press.

Weeks, Jeffrey. *Sexuality*. 1st ed. 2003. London: Routledge.

West, Candace, and D. H. Zimmerman. 1987. "Doing Gender." *Gender & Society* 1(2):125–151.

White, E. Frances. 2001. *Dark Continents of Our Bodies: Black Feminism and the Politics of Respectability*. Philadelphia: Temple University Press.

White, Jocelyn C., and Valeria T. Dull. 1998. "Room for Improvement: Communication between Lesbians and Primary Care Providers." In *Gateways to Improving Lesbian Health and Health Care: Opening Doors*, edited by Cristy M. Ponticelli, 95–100. Binghamton, NY: Haworth Press.

White, Renee T. 1999. *Putting Risk in Perspective: Black Teenage Lives in the Era of AIDS*. Lanham, MD: Rowman and Littlefield.

Wilkins, Amy C. 2004. "Puerto Rican Wannabes: Sexual Spectacle and the Marking of Race, Class, and Gender Boundaries." *Gender & Society* 18(1): 103–121.

Willard, Ann. 1988. "Cultural Scripts for Mothering." In *Mapping the Moral Domain: A Contribution of Women's Thinking to Psychological Theory and Education*, edited by Carol Gilligan, Janie Victoria Ward, and Jill McLean Taylor, with Betty Bardige, 225–243. Cambridge, MA: Harvard University Press.

Wolcott, Victoria W. 2001. *Remaking Respectability: African American Women in Interwar Detroit*. Chapel Hill: University of North Carolina Press.

Wyn, Johanna and Rob White. 1997. *Rethinking Youth*. London: Sage.

Young, Alford A., Jr. 2004. *The Minds of Marginalized Black Men: Making Sense of Mobility, Opportunity, and Future Life Chances*. Princeton, NJ: Princeton University Press.

Zavella, Patricia. 1996. "Feminist Insider Dilemmas: Constructing Ethnic Identity with Chicana Informants." In *Feminist Dilemmas in Fieldwork*, edited by Diane L. Wolf, 138–159. Boulder, CO: Westview.

Zavella, Patricia. 1997. "Playing with Fire: The Gendered Constructions of Chicana/Mexicana Sexuality." In *The Gender/Sexuality Reader: Culture, History, Political Economy*, edited by Roger N. Lancaster and Micaela di Leonardo, 392–408. New York: Routledge.

Zavella, Patricia. 2003. "Talking Sex: Chicanas and Mexicans Theorize about Silences and Sexual Pleasures." In *Chicana Feminisms: A Critical Reader*, edited by Gabriela F. Arredondo, Aída Hurtado, Norma Klahn, Olga N. Ramírez, and Patricia Zavella, 228–253. Durham, NC: Duke University Press.

Zentella, Ana Celia. 1987. "Language and Female Identity in the Puerto Rican Community." In *Women and Language in Transition*, edited by Joyce Penfield, 167–179. Albany: State University of New York Press.

ABOUT THE AUTHOR

Lorena Garcia is Assistant Professor of Sociology at the University of Illinois at Chicago.